# Genre and Institutions

## Social Processes in the Workplace and School

Edited by
Frances Christie and J. R. Martin

CONTINUUM
London and New York

Continuum
Wellington House, 125 Strand, London WC2R 0BB
370 Lexington Avenue, New York, NY 10017-6503

First published by Cassell in 1997. Reprinted in paperback in 2000.

ISBN 0-304-33766-8 (hardback)
    0-8264-4740-6 (paperback)

(CIP) available at the British Library

Typeset by Textype Typesetters, Cambridge
Printed and bound in Great Britain by Biddles Ltd, *www.biddles.co.uk*

# Genre and Institutions

# Open Linguistics Series

*Series Editor*
Robin F. Fawcett, Cardiff University

The *Open Linguistics Series*, to which this book makes a significant contribution, is 'open' in two senses. First, it provides an open forum for works associated with any school of linguistics or with none. Linguistics has now emerged from a period in which many (but never all) of the most lively minds in the subject seemed to assume that transformational-generative grammar – or at least something fairly closely derived from it – would provide the main theoretical framework for linguistics for the foreseeable future. In Kuhn's terms, linguistics had appeared to some to have reached the 'paradigm' stage. Reality today is very different. More and more scholars are working to improve and expand theories that were formerly scorned for not accepting as central the particular set of concerns highlighted in the Chomskyan approach – such as Halliday's systemic theory (as exemplified in this book), Lamb's stratificational model and Pike's tagmemics – while others are developing new theories. The series is open to all approaches, then – including work in the generativist-formalist tradition.

The second sense in which the series is 'open' is that it encourages works that open out 'core' linguistics in various ways: to encompass discourse and the description of natural texts; to explore the relationship between linguistics and its neighbouring disciplines such as psychology, sociology, philosophy, artificial intelligence, and cultural and literary studies; and to apply it in fields such as education and language pathology.

Relations between the fields of linguistics and artificial intelligence are covered in a sister series, Communication in Artificial Intelligence. Studies that are primarily descriptive are published in a new series, Functional Descriptions of Language.

**Recent titles in the series**

*Construing Experience Through Meaning: A Language-based Approach to Cognition*,
   M. A. K. Halliday and Christian M. I. M. Matthiessen
*Culturally Speaking: Managing Rapport through Talk across Cultures*,
   Helen Spencer-Oatey (ed.)
*Educating Eve: The 'Language Instinct' Debate*, Geoffrey Sampson
*Empirical Linguistics*, Geoffrey Sampson
*The Intonation Systems of English*, Paul Tench
*Language Policy in Britain and France: The Processes of Policy*, Dennis Ager
*Language Relations across Bering Strait: Reappraising the Archaeological and Linguistic Evidence*, Michael Fortescue
*Learning Through Language in Early Childhood*, Clare Painter
*Pedagogy and the Shaping of Consciousness: Linguistic and Social Processes*,
   Frances Christie (ed.)
*Register Analysis: Theory and Practice*, Mohsen Ghadessy (ed.)
*Researching Language in Schools and Communities: Functional Linguistic Perspectives*,
   Len Unsworth (ed.)
*Summary Justice: Judges Address Juries*, Paul Robertshaw
*Thematic Development in English Texts*, Mohsen Ghadessy (ed.)
*Ways of Saying: Ways of Meaning. Selected Papers of Ruqaiya Hasan*, Carmel Cloran,
   David Butt and Geoffrey Williams (eds)
*Words, Meaning and Vocabulary: An Introduction to Modern English Lexicology*,
   Howard Jackson and Etienne Zé Amvela

# Contents

# Contributors

**Frances Christie** is Professor of Language and Literacy Education at the University of Melbourne.

**Caroline Coffin** is a Lecturer in Language and Literacy at the Open University, Milton Keynes, UK.

**Rick Iedema** is engaged in a project on the discourses of policy planning with the School of Health Services Management at the University of New South Wales, Sydney.

**J. R. Martin** is Associate Professor of Linguistics at the University of Sydney.

**David Rose**'s interest in literacy, and its role in shaping the consciousness of peoples and the structures of their societies, arose initially from a long involvement with Australian Aboriginal communities.

**Joan Rothery** is a literacy consultant.

**Maree Stenglin** is Manager of Education Services at the Australian Museum.

**Robert Veel** is a Sydney-based independent researcher and consultant in language education.

**Peter White** is a linguist based at the University of Sydney.

# Introduction

This volume emerges from about fifteen years' research into genre in Australia, undertaken by systemic functional (SF) linguists associated with the Department of Linguistics at the University of Sydney. Michael Halliday had opened the Department of Linguistics in 1976, and two of the contributors here – Frances Christie and Joan Rothery – were among the first group of students in the new MA programme he instituted. Shortly after the opening of the department, in 1977, Jim Martin arrived to finish his doctoral thesis under Halliday's supervision, before taking up a tutoring position in 1978. As the years passed, Martin and Rothery commenced their study of writing in the primary school, leading to their first early descriptions of written genres in the early 1980s. Both Rothery and Christie commenced doctoral studies with Martin, and they were among the first of his doctoral students working on both a development of genre theory and an associated development of register theory. While Martin and Rothery continued their study of written genres, Christie, who had moved away from Sydney, worked on the genres of classroom talk, and associated descriptions of the ways written genres relate to patterns of classroom talk. Just as Martin and Rothery were to turn their attention increasingly to the genres of older writers, so too Christie in time turned her attention to the classroom talk of the upper primary school and, later, to that of the secondary school.

In more recent years, a younger generation of educational linguists and linguists (as well as Rothery) worked with Martin in the 'Write It Right' Project (1991–94), funded by the New South Wales Disadvantaged Schools Program and the New South Wales Education and Training Foundation. The latter project attempted to examine the written genres of a range of significant key learning areas of secondary education (English, history, science, mathematics and geography), and to consider their relationship to the written genres of selected work situations (the media, science industry and administration). Many, but not all the participants in this project have contributed chapters in this book. Christie, at least, is not of that group, having continued to work in professional contexts well away from Sydney, and in the pursuit of what, following many of the ideas of Bernstein, she would call the pedagogic discourse of schooling.

Given the great quantity of work on genre theory that has been developed over the years, one volume of this kind can do no more than introduce a little of what has actually been achieved. Still, what is presented here constitutes a representative discussion. As such, it serves to offer readers both an account of some current SF thinking about genre, and an illustration of how it is that Halliday's functional grammar remains a critical tool in the enterprise of genre analysis and research.

While the reader might well choose to read the chapters here in any order, a sequence is nonetheless intended. Martin offers an overview of some critical theoretical perspectives that shape much of the discussion in later chapters. Rose, Iedema and White each take one significant site in which the genres of the workplace or community are examined. Thus, Rose considers the genres of science and technology, Iedema those of administration in a sampling of worksites, and White considers the narratives of 'hard news' reporting in the daily press. Christie's chapter then introduces a sequence of chapters that explore the genres of schooling. Hers is primarily devoted to oral genres, and to the manner in which particular pedagogic subject positions are constructed in pedagogic talk. The chapters of Veel, Coffin, and Rothery and Stenglin then go on to examine written genres in a range of significant secondary school subjects: science, history and English.

This book is not about pedagogy, though several of its chapters address questions of pedagogy, and it will, hopefully, interest many educators and teacher educators. Rather, it presents a theory about the role of genre in the social construction of experience, and its thesis includes the view that educational processes are critical in the building of various social positionings of relevance in the wider world beyond school, the world of work and community participation. We hope the book will be of interest, then, to linguists and social theorists of many kinds, all engaged in the scholarly pursuit of genres and their role in the building of social reality.

*Frances Christie*                                          *J. R. Martin*
*University of Melbourne*                          *University of Sydney*

# 1  Analysing genre: functional parameters

*J. R. Martin*

## Resources

In this chapter we will outline in general terms the linguistic framework deployed throughout the volume, and consider in a little more detail some recent developments that bear critically on the analyses undertaken. Essentially, these analyses are informed by the model of language known as systemic functional linguistics (hereafter SFL), especially the variety of that model which has evolved in Australia since 1975. The most accessible introduction to this variety of SFL is Eggins (1994).

The functional grammar of English assumed here is that outlined in Halliday (1985a/1994), and elaborated by Matthiessen (1995). Beyond this, the discourse analyses undertaken draw on Halliday and Hasan (1976) and Martin (1992a). The model of context in focus here has evolved out of earlier work by Martin (1985b/1989) and Ventola (1987) and will be considered in more detail below.

We should also clarify here that a substantial portion of the research impelling the development of the model since the early 1980s has been carried out in the field of educational linguistics. The chapters by Coffin, Iedema, Rose, Rothery and Stenglin, Veel, and White in fact draw on research into secondary school and workplace literacy based in the Metropolitan East Region of the New South Wales Department of Education's Disadvantaged Schools Program in the early 1990s. This research and the materials deriving from it represented the second phase of literacy initiatives informed by SFL in the region (the first being the late 1980s primary school focused Language and Social Power Project). For a critical introduction to the issues contextualizing this work, see Cope and Kalantzis (1993). Martin was the chief academic consultant for both phases of this research, and was in addition supervisor of doctoral research by Christie, Iedema, Rose, Rothery and White. As a result it would be fair to say that the variety of SFL deployed here has been strongly influenced by University of Sydney SFL and its involvement in the development of 'genre-based' literacy pedagogy and curriculum (for mid-term reviews, see Christie 1992 and Martin 1993a).

## Modelling language in context

Functional linguistics is centrally concerned with showing how the organization of language is related to its use. In SFL this concern is pursued by
modelling both language and social context as semiotic systems in a relationship of **realization** with one another. In such a model social context
and language metaredound (Lemke 1995) – which is to say that social
context comprises patterns of language patterns. Realization also entails
that language construes, is construed by and (over time) reconstrues
social context. One of the images commonly used to outline this relationship is presented in Figure 1.1, with language and social context as co-
tangential circles.

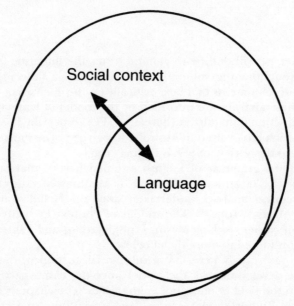

**Figure 1.1** Language as the realization of social context

Adding to this model, SFL treats the organization of language and of
social context as functionally diversified along similar lines. With language,
functional diversification is modelled through **metafunctions** – ideational,
interpersonal and textual. Ideational linguistic resources are concerned
with representation, interpersonal resources with interaction, and textual
resources with information flow. In SFL this intrinsic functional organization is projected on to context, redounding with the variables of field,
tenor and mode – where field focuses on institutional practices, tenor on
social relations and mode on channel. Useful discussions of linguistic
metafunctions in relation to register variables are found in Halliday
(1978), Halliday and Hasan (1980/1985/1989) and Martin (1991). The
functional diversification reviewed here is laid over the language/social

context relation in Figure 1.2; note the proportionality[1] of the intrinsic and extrinsic functionality – field is to ideational resources as tenor is to interpersonal resources as mode is to textual resources.

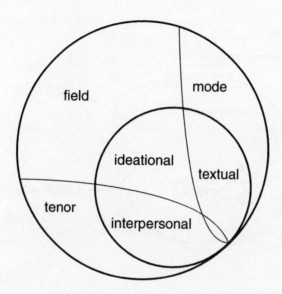

**Figure 1.2** Functional diversification of language and social context

To begin, we looked at the issue of realization in relation to the relationship between language and social context. At this point we return to realization, by way of unpacking the 'internal' organization of language and of social context. As far as language is concerned, SFL follows Hjelmslev in assuming a fundamental separation of content and expression planes. The content plane is concerned with the construal of meaning; the expression plane with the organization of segmental and prosodic realizations of meaning in spoken or written language (phonology/graphology), or sign. Developing Hjelmslev, SFL takes the step of stratifying his content plane – as lexicogrammar and discourse semantics. Lexicogrammar focuses on resources for incorporating ideational, interpersonal and textual meaning as clauses and smaller units (groups/phrases, words and morphemes), as in Halliday (1985a/1994) and Matthiessen (1995), with lexis integrated as a more delicate perspective on grammar (Hasan 1987). Discourse semantics focuses on resources for integrating clauses with one another as cohesive text, as in Halliday and Hasan (1976) and Martin (1992a). If we unpack the inner circle of language in Figures 1.1 and 1.2, we arrive at the stratified model outlined in Figure 1.3 – as discourse semantics metaredounding with lexicogrammar, metaredounding in its turn with phonology/graphology.

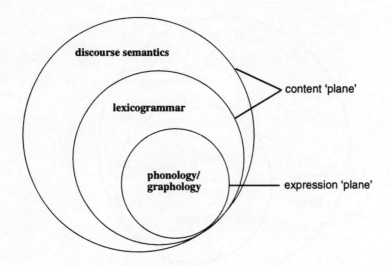

**Figure 1.3** Stratification within language – as metaredundancy

Social context, in the model assumed here, is also treated as a stratified system[2] – comprising the levels of register and genre (as in Eggins and Martin 1996). Register is used as a general composite term for the field, mode and tenor variables introduced earlier.[3] Set up as a level in this way, register is designed to interface the analysis of social context naturally with the metafunctionally diversified organization of language resources. Genre on the other hand is set up above and beyond metafunctions (at a higher level of abstraction) to account for relations among social processes in more holistic terms, with a special focus on the stages through which most texts unfold. The relation of genre to register as complementary perspectives on the social 'content' of language (i.e. context) is thus comparable in some respects to the relation of discourse semantics to lexicogrammar as complementary perspectives on language's own content plane. Genre and register constitute a stratified perspective on what Hjelmslev referred to as connotative semiotics – semiotic systems that make use of another semiotic system as their expression plane (as opposed to denotative semiotics that have an expression plane of their own). The relation of connotative to denotative semiosis in the model is outlined in Hjelmslev's terms in Figure 1.4 (for further discussion, see Martin 1992a).

In earlier models of context (e.g. Martin 1992a), an additional layer of

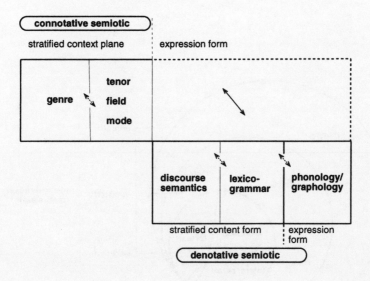

**Figure 1.4** Language's stratified content form in relation to a stratified model of social context

context was set up, referred to as ideology, to focus attention on the distribution of discursive resources in a culture, and the divergent ways in which social subjects construe social occasions. This modelling strategy does not appear to have fostered the dialogue among functional linguists and critical theorists that was intended (cf. Threadgold 1991, 1993, 1994). An alternative strategy for enhancing this dialogue will be suggested below. For purposes of this volume, then, the metaredundancy[4] model outlined in Figure 1.5 will suffice. In such a model, register (encompassing field, tenor and mode) contextualizes language and is in turn contextualized by genre.

## Genesis (and subjectivity)

Throughout the period of research canvassed by chapters in this volume, Halliday and Matthiessen were drawing increasing attention to language change (e.g. Halliday 1993b, Matthiessen and Halliday in press). The central issue here has to do with **instantiation** – the manifestation of system in process, and the way in which manifestations rebound on and ultimately reconstrue the system from which they derive. Halliday (e.g. 1991, 1992a, b, c, 1993a) suggests a model in which language is conceived as a set of probabilistic systems, each instantiation of which in some way re-inflects

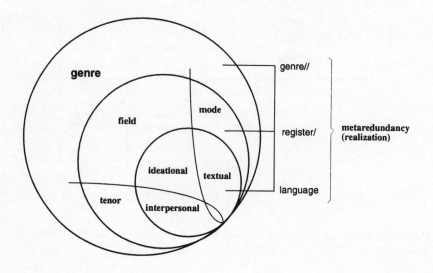

**Figure 1.5** Language metaredounding with register, metaredounding with genre

probability – just as a cricketer's batting average fluctuates slightly with every run scored. What we call 'change' has to do with a drift of reverberations over time that in some way perturbs the system, making way for new resources. Nesbitt and Plum (1988) provide the classic insight into this process of semantic evolution in the context of clause complex relations. Note that a probabilistic model of this kind highlights the way in which connotative semiotics like register and genre are realized through language – namely, by reweighting the probabilities of certain linguistic choices being taken up (i.e. by putting different kinds of meaning at risk).

Halliday and Matthiessen suggest a framework for modelling semiotic change according to the 'time depth' involved. For relatively short time frames such as that involved in the unfolding of a text, they suggest the term logogenesis[5] (Matthiessen mimeo); for the longer time frame of the development of language in the individual, they use the term ontogenesis

(Painter 1984); and for maximum time depth, phylogenesis (as in Halliday's reading of the history of scientific English; Halliday and Martin 1993). This framework is summarized in Table 1.1.

**Table 1.1** Framing semiotic change

| logogenesis | 'instantiation of the text/process' | unfolding |
|---|---|---|
| ontogenesis | 'development of the individual' | growth |
| phylogenesis | 'expansion of the culture' | evolution |

In a model of this kind, phylogenesis provides the environment for ontogenesis which in turn provides the environment for logogenesis; in other words, the stage a culture has reached in its evolution provides the social context for the linguistic development of the individual, and the stage this development has reached in the individual provides resources for the instantiation of unfolding texts. Conversely, logogenesis provides the material (i.e. semiotic goods) for ontogenesis, which in turn provides the material for phylogenesis; in other words, texts provide the means through which individuals interact to learn the system, and it is through the heteroglossic aggregation of individual (always already social) systems that the semiotic trajectory of a culture evolves (Figure 1.6). Language change in this model is read in terms of an expanding meaning potential, a key feature of semiotic systems as they adapt to new discursive and non-discursive (physical and biological) environments.

**Semogenesis: kinds of change**

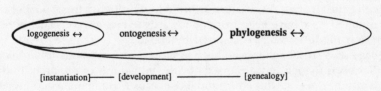

**Figure 1.6** Time frames and semogenesis

At this point in the discussion we might resume the question of ideology, passed over above. The fundamental issue here has to do with the ways in which social subjects are positioned in a culture. To interpret this semiotically, we need to be able to model the meaning potential available to social subjects and, as well, the different ways in which they draw on this potential as they interact with each other. Traditionally, the variables which affect this positioning are generalized under headings such as gender, ethnicity, class and generation. SFL research in this area has been strongly influenced by Bernstein's notions of coding orientation (e.g. Cloran 1989; Hasan 1990), with Martin (1992a) suggesting that ideology

might be conceived as the system of coding orientations engendering subjectivity – at a higher level of abstraction than genre.

One of the dangers inherent in modelling subjectivity along these lines
is that of locking subjects in and eliding agency, thereby effacing their
potential for resistance and transformation. One way to defuse this
danger might be to approach subjectivity dynamically, from the perspective of the genesis theory just outlined. This would enable us to foreground the ways in which subjects engage dynamically with texts as they
unfold (logogenesis), the ways in which they are positioned and re-
positioned socially throughout their life (ontogenesis) and the ways in
which a culture reworks hegemony across generations (phylogenesis). In
a model of this kind, it would be more natural to interpret language, register and genre as the projection of semohistory (across all three time
frames) than as realizing an abstract and reified ideology (as Martin's
model has at times been read to imply). In these terms, language, register
and genre constitute the meaning potential that is immanent, from
moment to moment as a text unfolds, for the social subjects involved, at
the point in the evolution of the culture where meanings are being made.
An outline of this perspective is presented as Figure 1.7, including some
indication of the way in which links might be drawn with the work of
central post-structuralist theorists in a model of this kind. In Figure 1.7
Halliday's (1985a) α β' notation for projecting clause complexes has
been borrowed to represent one of the senses in which history (i.e. semogenesis) gives meaning to synchronic (albeit always changing) semiosis.

### A glance at register

Since the early 1980s, researchers involved in developing the model of context outlined here have been working towards a semiotic construal of field,
tenor and mode variables – inspired by Halliday's (e.g. 1978) reading of
language as a social semiotic. This has proved an ambitious undertaking,
and has been shaped in various ways by the availability of research funding
and consumer needs, with educational concerns compelling a good deal of
the work. The descriptive responsibilities of the field, tenor and mode
analyses assumed is essentially that outlined in Martin (1992a).

Field is concerned with systems of activity, including descriptions of the
participants, process and circumstances these activities involve. From the
perspective of field, the principles for relating activities to one another
have to do with the institutional focus of the activities – the ways in which
the activities co-articulate everyday and public institutions such as domestic life, bridge, rugby, information technology, sociology, science, bureaucracy and so on. The co-articulating activities of a field tend to share
participants, which are organized taxonomically – via hyponymy (class/
subclass) or meronymy (part/whole). Participants enter into activities by
bonding with processes and circumstances, so that when we hear that
*Waugh has just notched up a double century at Sabina Park* we know the field

of cricket is at stake[6] (or, if outsiders, we simply have no idea what is going on). For illustrative work on activity sequences and taxonomies in the field of science see Rose *et al.* (1992), Halliday and Martin (1993) and Martin and Veel (to appear).

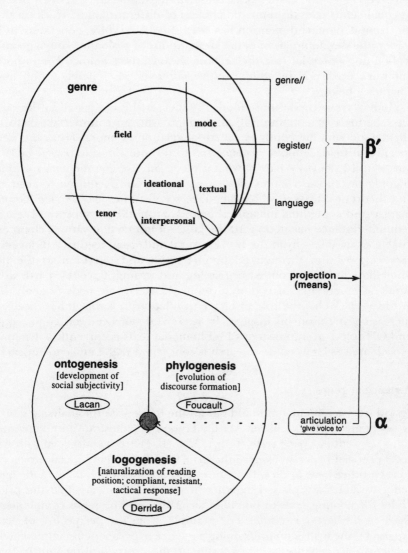

**Figure 1.7** Language, register and genre as the projection of their semohistory – across time frames

Tenor is concerned with social relations, as these are enacted through the dimensions of power and solidarity. Following Poynton (1985/1989), work on the 'vertical' status dimension has focused on reciprocity of semiotic choice – taking up her suggestion that interlocutors of equal status have access to the same kinds of meanings whereas interlocutors of unequal status take up semantic choices of different kinds. Work on the 'horizontal' contact dimension has been slower to evolve, dependent as it was on the development of better descriptions of evaluative language and its bonding potential (see the section on APPRAISAL below). For important work on tenor in administrative contexts see Iedema (1996 and Chapter 3 below).

Mode is concerned with semiotic distance, as this is affected by the various channels of communication through which we undertake activity (field) and simultaneously enact social relations (tenor). From the perspective of field, semiotic distance has to do with the role played by language in the activity – part of what is going on, live commentary on what is going on, reconstruction of what was going on . . . and on to abstract and theoretical texts in which language reconstitutes activity (see 'Grammatical and contextual metaphor' below). From the perspective of tenor, semiotic distance has to do with the kinds of interaction various channels enable or disable – from the two-way aural and visual feedback of face-to-face conversation through telephone, radio and television to the no immediate feedback context of reading and writing. Recently, partly as a result of emergence of communication via electronic texts (e-mail; the World Wide Web), the role of image in relation to verbiage has received increasing attention (as inspired by Kress and van Leeuwen 1990, 1996 and O'Toole 1994); the study of multi-modal texts is currently a dynamic growth area as far as mode research is concerned (e.g. Lemke to appear).

## A glance at genre

As with register (field, tenor and mode) the framework for analysing genre is essentially that outlined in Martin (1992a; for illustrative implementations see Ventola 1987, 1988, 1995). As such, genre is concerned with systems of social processes, where the principles for relating social processes to each other have to do with texture – the ways in which field, mode and tenor variables are phased together in a text. This means that the principles for relating texts to one another at the level of genre complement those at the level of register. For example, from the perspective of field (register), the instructions for doing a science experiment are immediately related to actually doing the experiment, the procedural recount of that experiment, the explanation the experiment is designed to illustrate (and so on; see Veel, Chapter 6). From the perspective of genre, on the other hand, the instructions are immediately related to a range of procedural texts (e.g. directions, recipes, instruction manuals) with closely related texture (i.e. a sequence of commands, potentially prefaced by a list of tools, ingredients, or relevant apparatus, potentially headed by the purpose of the procedure and so on; see Rose, Chapter 2).

In Australian educational linguistics, genres have been defined as staged, goal-oriented social processes (e.g. Martin *et al.* n.d./1987), a definition which flags the way in which most genres take more than a single phase to unfold, the sense of frustration or incompletion that is felt when phases don't unfold as expected or planned, and the fact that genres are addressed (i.e. formulated with readers and listeners in mind), whether or not the intended audience is immediately present to respond. In these terms, as a level of context, genre represents the system of staged goal-oriented social processes through which social subjects in a given culture live their lives.

Recent work has foregrounded the question of modelling relations among genres and the nature of generic structure. The impetus for the concern with modelling genres relations stems from two sources: (1) the availability of descriptions of an ever-widening range of genres, especially in educational contexts (families of stories, procedures, explanations, etc.), and (2) countering resistance to the notion of a distinct level of genre as part of a model of social context (as voiced by Hasan 1995).

### Genre agnation

As far as strategies for modelling genre as system are concerned, two approaches have been explored. One involves the traditional SFL approach to agnation, via **typology**. With this approach, categorical distinctions are set up as oppositions and used to factor out similarities and differences among genres. For simple sets of oppositions, a paradigm can be used to display the relevant valeur, as in Table 1.2[7] (from Martin in press).

**Table 1.2** Using a paradigm to express genre agnation

|  | particular | generalized |
|---|---|---|
| **activity focused** | procedural recount [1] | historical recount [2] |
| **entity focused** | description [3] | descriptive report [4] |

Paradigms quickly become saturated as a display mechanism as additional oppositions are taken into account and more complicated typologies are better imaged as system networks. In Figure 1.8 (taken from Martin in press), procedural genres are added to the picture. The network shows procedures to be immediately agnate to historical recounts with which genres they share a generalized focus on activity; but whereas histor-

ical recounts make a statement about the past, procedures direct activity
which has yet to be undertaken.

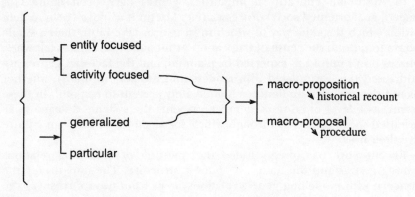

**Figure 1.8** Using a system network to model genre agnation

Typological description of this kind and its formalization in system networks is of course the cornerstone of SFL theory and description. The
categorical precision with which it sets up its oppositions and renders
meaning as valeur is at the same time its weakness. In grammar, for example, clauses are classified according to process type – and for purposes
of analysis and description they have to be one type or another. But as the
front cover of Halliday's 2nd edition of his *Introduction to Functional Grammar* illustrates, process types can also be interpreted as blending into one
another as does one colour to another in a rainbow. Behaving (*laughing,
pondering, looking*) is between acting (material processing) and sensing
(mental processing) just as purple can be read as a cline between red and
blue (for a discussion of typology and process type see Martin 1996a). As
a result it is necessary to complement typological analysis with a topological perspective. Lemke introduces the notion of topology in relation
to genre relations as follows (the significance of topology elsewhere in
the model is taken up in Martin and Matthiessen 1991):

A **topology**, in mathematical terms, is A SET OF CRITERIA FOR ESTABLISHING
DEGREES OF NEARNESS OR PROXIMITY AMONG THE MEMBERS OF SOME CATEGORY.
It turns a 'collection' or set of objects into a *space* defined by the relations of
those objects. Objects which are more alike by the criteria are represented in
this space as being closer together; those which are less alike are further apart.
There can be multiple criteria, which may be more or less independent of one
another, so that two texts, for instance, may be closer together in one dimension (say horizontal distance), but further apart in another (vertical distance).
What is essential, obviously, is our choice of the criteria, the *parameters*, that
define similarity and difference on each dimension. These parameters can be
represented as more or less alike. The same set of parameters allows us to
describe both the similarities and the differences among texts, or text-types

(genres). (From Lemke 'The topology of genre . . .' unpublished earlier draft of Lemke in press)

By way of brief illustration, consider the genre topology in Table 1.3, involving a set of secondary school history genres (as further explored and exemplified by Coffin, Chapter 7 below). The display arranges the history genres in a pedagogic developmental sequence, as a scaffolding for apprenticeship into the discipline. It begins on the left with genres that are likely to be more accessible to students because of their similarity to recounting genres in their oral cultures; it ends on the right with genres that involve a great deal of grammatical metaphor as far as text organization is concerned, and thus depend on levels of literacy commonly associated with senior secondary school.

**Table 1.3** A topological perspective on genre agnation (for secondary school history genres)

| 1 | prosodic appraisal | | periodic appraisal | | thesis appraisal |
|---|---|---|---|---|---|
| 2 | proposition | | | | proposition/ proposal |
| 3 | tell | record | explain | | |
| | | | reveal | probe | argue |
| | auto/ biographical recount | historical recount | historical account | factorial and consequential explanation | exposition/ challenge discussion |
| 4 | individual focus | group (+ hero) focus | | | |
| 5 | text time = field time | | | text time ≠ field time | |
| 6 | episodic unfolding in time | | causal unfolding | internal unfolding | |

In Table 1.3 we have boxed in the genres, but the relation of one to another needs· to be seen as a cline. For example, from the typological perspective, the categorical difference between historical recounts and accounts has to do with whether history unfolds sequentially or causally – whether one event is followed by another or leads to another. But many texts use a combination of sequential and causal relations. For purposes of typological classification, we have to define just what percentage of causal relations is required for a text to qualify as an account. The topological perspective on the other hand allows us to position texts on a cline, as more or less prototypical recounts or accounts according to the time/cause parameter.

Generally, when articulating a pedagogic sequence like that in Table 1.3, there is more than one parameter to consider. Six parameters are in fact deployed above. And note that these parameters group the history genres in different ways. The 'mood' parameter (proposition vs. proposition/proposal) opposes most of the genres to the argumentative ones on the right, since in general it is only the argumentative genres that include commands of one kind or another (e.g. exhortative appeals to redress past injustices). Conversely, the 'identification' parameter opposes most of the history genres to the autobiographical and biographical recounts, since in general it is only the auto/biographical recounts that focus on individual participants (as opposed to generic classes of participant). As with all topological parameters these distinctions are matters of degree – most mainstream history, for example, foregrounds male individuals who shape the course of history for generic classes of participant, right across the historical recount, account, explanation and argument spectrum.

We have found the topological perspective on genre agnation to be a particularly significant one in educational contexts for a number of reasons. For one thing, it facilitates the development of learner pathways (as in Table 1.3) – outlines of what kinds of developmental sequence will help students move smoothly from control of one genre to another. For another, it helps teachers and students make sense of the real-life instantiations of genres they come across in their reading and marking, which are not always prototypical examples of canonical genres. And, finally, the topological perspective provides principled tools for reasoning about genre mixing and semogenesis – as with the greening of secondary school science (Veel to appear); topologically, the new green genres can be read as involving additional ecological discourse parameters, above and beyond the traditional parameters associated with the discipline.

*Genre structure*

Turning to the question of genre structure, the main developments have involved moving away from simple constituency representations of genre staging. This development first arose in the context of dealing with longer texts, such as those comprising so much of the reading and writing in secondary school subjects. Martin (1994, 1995a) proposes the term **macro-genre** for texts which combine familiar elemental genres such as recount, report, explanation, exposition and so on. He suggests that logico-semantic relations such as those outlined by Halliday for clause complexes (elaboration, extension, enhancement) can be deployed to reason about genre complexing in longer texts. In the course of this research Martin also noted periodic and prosodic patterns ranging over combinations of genre complexes – for example, the introduction and conclusion of an essay, or the evaluative stance of a review. This raised the issue of whether the staging of elemental genres should be reconsidered in light of Halliday (e.g. 1979) and Matthiessen's work (e.g. 1988) on types of structure in grammatical description.

Martin (1996b) suggests that the structure of even elemental genres can indeed be factored out according to a range of structuring principles, and that constituency representation offers only a relatively compromised image of genre phasing. Martin's rendering of Halliday and Matthiessen's types of structure is outlined in Figure 1.9, which in addition associates

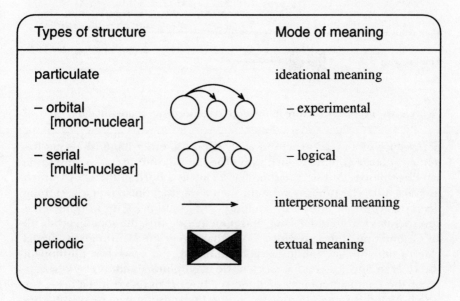

| Types of structure | Mode of meaning |
|---|---|
| particulate | ideational meaning |
| – orbital [mono-nuclear] | – experimental |
| – serial [multi-nuclear] | – logical |
| prosodic | interpersonal meaning |
| periodic | textual meaning |

**Figure 1.9** Types of structure in relation to modes of meaning

the various structuring principles with metafunctions. The basic division is between particulate, prosodic and periodic structure. Particulate structure organizes text segmentally, into either orbital or serial patterns. Orbital structure takes one segment as nuclear, and associates other segments with this nucleus as satellites (see White, Chapter 4 below); with serial structure, there is no nuclear segment on which others depend – the text unfolds step by step, with each step dependent on the immediately preceding. Prosodic structure is supra-segmental; it spreads itself across a text, more and less intensely as required, in a way akin to tone contours in phonology. Periodic structure is wave-like; it organizes a text into a rhythm of peaks and troughs, as the demands of information flow prescribe.

It follows from this factoring of kinds of structure that genre structure is best interpreted simultaneously from the perspective of particulate, prosodic and periodic representations. By way of illustration, consider the analyses of an exemplum (one of the narrative genres discussed in Rothery and Stenglin, Chapter 8 below). Read from the perspective on constituency, an exemplum like Springsteen's 'Born in the USA' (Cranny-Francis and Martin 1991) consists of an Orientation, followed by an Incident, followed by an Interpretation, followed by a Coda. Read from the

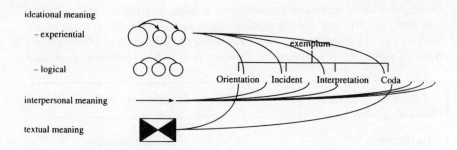

ideational meaning

 - experiential

 - logical

interpersonal meaning

textual meaning

exemplum

Orientation    Incident    Interpretation    Coda

**Figure 1.10** Types of structure in relation to constituency representation

perspective of a multi-structural analysis on the other hand, the song has
a nuclear stage (the Incident), with Orientation, Interpretation and Coda
satellites; alongside this, the song has a chorus ('Born in the USA') which
interacts with the Interpretation in such a way that Springsteen's scathing
deconstruction of America's military exploitation of its working class
reverberates through the song; and punctuating this, the song begins with
an Orientation and ends with a Coda that foreground, through relational
clauses and low-key musical accompaniment, the powerless position of
the veteran Springsteen has written the exemplum about. A crude synopsis of the complementarity of these readings is outlined in Figure 1.10,
which includes some attempt to outline the sense in which constituency
representation compromises the factored analysis.

## A brief outline of APPRAISAL

In the course of the secondary school and workplace literacy research
noted above, it became necessary to expand our analyses of interpersonal
meaning to include more work on evaluative language (building on
Martin 1992b, 1995b, 1996c). We tackled this first in the context of narrative analysis in English, moving on to the issue of objectivity in the
media and finally focusing on responses to verbal and non-verbal artefacts
in English and Creative Arts. Partly in line with this trajectory, we concentrated first on AFFECT (resources for construing emotion), then on JUDGE-
MENT (resources for judging behaviour in 'ethical' terms) and finally on
APPRECIATION (resources for valuing objects 'aesthetically'). Collectively,
we refer to these resources as APPRAISAL, including additional resources
for AMPLIFICATION and ENGAGEMENT (a more detailed discussion of these
resources is presented in Martin to appear).

Before looking at the scaffolding we developed for categorizing AFFECT,
JUDGEMENT and APPRECIATION, let's illustrate the domains of meaning at
issue here. The examples are taken from the opening scene of the movie
*Educating Rita*[8] – the first meeting between Rita and her tutor, Frank. In
the first example, Rita expresses her emotional response to the view from

Frank's window, drawing on mental processes of affection (relevant appraisal in bold face in these examples):

AFFECT (emotions; reacting to behaviour, text/process, phenomena)
Rita: I **love** this room. I **love** the view from this window. Do you **like** it?
Frank: I don't often consider it actually.

In the following example, Frank makes judgements about the propriety of his appalling teaching as far as most of his students and Rita are concerned:

JUDGEMENT (ethics; evaluating behaviour)
Frank: You want a lot and I can't give it. Between you, and me, and the walls, actually I am an appalling teacher. That's **all right** most of the time. Appalling teaching is **quite in order** for most of my appalling students. But it is **not good enough** for you young woman.

In the next example, Rita comments on the value of a book she's been reading:

APPRECIATION (aesthetics; evaluating text/process, phenomena)
Rita: Rita Mae Brown, who wrote 'Rubyfruit Jungle'. Haven't ... haven't you read it?
Frank: No.
Rita: It's a **fantastic** book, you know. Do you want to lend it?
Frank: Ah yes.
Rita: Here.
Frank: Yes. Well, thank-you very much.
Rita: That's okay.

Alongside these evaluative resources, we also considered systems for adjusting a speaker's commitment to what they are saying (ENGAGEMENT). In the following example Frank uses explicitly subjective modality metaphors (Halliday 1994: 358) to hedge his reply (exasperating Rita in the process).

ENGAGEMENT (resources for adjusting modal responsibility)
Rita: ... That's a nice picture, isn't it Frank?
Frank: Uh yes, **I suppose** it is.
Rita: It's very erotic.
Frank: Actually **I don't think** I've looked at that picture in 10 years, but, uh, yes, it is, **I suppose so**.
Rita: Well, there's no suppose about it.

Appraisal resources also include systems for grading evaluations – turning up the volume as in the first example, or playing things down as in the second.

AMPLIFICATION (resources for grading)

Rita: . . . You know like when I'm in the hair-dressers where I work, I'll say
something like um "Oh, I'm **really** fucked" **dead** loud. I mean, it does**n't half**
cause **a fuss** . . .
Frank: [laughs]

Frank: . . .What is your name?
Rita: Me first name?
Frank: Well, that would **at least** constitute **some sort of** start, wouldn't it?
Rita: Rita.
Frank: Rita. Uh, here we are. Rita. It says here "Mrs S White."

Grading is an essential feature of APPRAISAL, which means that a
number of related resources for negotiating solidarity are treated separ-
ately, under the heading INVOLVEMENT. These resources include the use
of names, slang and taboo lexis, specialized and technical terms, standard
and non-standard features and the like to orchestrate group membership.

INVOLVEMENT (lexical in/exclusion; not graded)
Rita: It's a fantastic book, you know. Do you want to **lend** it?

Rita: Yes, but with educated people, they don't worry, do they? It's the aristocracy
that swears more then anyone. It's all 'Pass me the **fucking** pheasant' with
them . . .

Rita: . . . And oh what do they call you round here?
Frank: **Sir**. But you may call me **Frank**.
Rita: Okay, **Frank**. That's a nice picture, isn't it **Frank**?

A rough outline of interpersonal resources is presented as Table 1.4,
organized by strata. In the table, NEGOTIATION refers to MOOD-based
resources for exchanging information and goods/services, as outlined in
Martin (1992a). The APPRAISAL and INVOLVEMENT systems are designed
to complement the traditional focus on dialogue into terms of turn-
taking and exchange. They are of special relevance to work on the discourse dynamics of solidarity.

Unfortunately, space does not permit a detailed presentation of
APPRAISAL resources. Our framework for AFFECT stabilized around the
variables outlined in Table 1.5. Note that at this stage it does not include
resources for desire (wanting, wishing, longing, etc.), which is elsewhere
grouped with modality (modulations of inclination); nor does it include
resources for surprise (being shocked, startled, taken aback, etc.). AFFECT
variables consider:

(i)    Are the feelings popularly construed by the culture as positive (good
       vibes that are enjoyable to experience) or negative ones (bad vibes
       that are better avoided)?

**Table 1.4** A survey of interpersonal resources (across strata)

| register | discourse semantics | lexicogrammar | phonology |
|---|---|---|---|
| TENOR | NEGOTIATION<br>– speech function<br>– exchange | – mood<br>– tagging<br>– polarity | – tone (and 'key') |
| power (status) | APPRAISAL<br>– engagement<br>– affect<br>– judgement<br>– appreciation<br>– amplification | – 'evaluative' lexis<br>– modal verbs<br>– modal adjuncts<br>– pre/numeration<br>– intensification<br>– repetition<br>– manner; extent | – loudness<br>– pitch movement<br>– voice quality<br>– [formatting] |
| solidarity (contact) | INVOLVEMENT<br>– naming<br>– technicality<br>– anti-language<br>– swearing | – vocation/names<br>– technical lexis<br>– specialized lexis<br>– slang<br>– taboo lexis | – 'accent' . . .<br>– whisper . . .<br>– acronyms<br>– 'pig latins'<br>– secret scripts |

     – positive affect     the boy was HAPPY
     – negative affect    the boy was SAD

(ii) Are the feelings realized as a surge of emotion involving some kind of embodied paralinguistic or extra-linguistic manifestation, or more prosodically experienced as a kind of predisposition or ongoing mental state?

     – behavioural surge   the boy LAUGHED
     – mental disposition  the boy LIKED the present

(iii) Are the feelings construed as directed at or reacting to some specific external agency or as a general ongoing mood for which one might pose the question 'Why are you feeling that way?' and get the answer 'I'm not sure'?

**Table 1.5** A framework for analysing English AFFECT (with examples)

| | SURGE (of behaviour) | DISPOSITION |
|---|---|---|
| UN/HAPPINESS | | |
| **unhappiness** | | |
| misery<br><br>[mood] | whimper<br>cry<br>wail | down [low]<br>sad [median]<br>miserable [high] |
| antipathy<br><br>[directed feeling] | rubbish<br>abuse<br>revile | dislike<br>hate<br>abhor |
| **happiness** | | |
| cheer | chuckle<br>laugh<br>rejoice | cheerful<br>buoyant<br>jubilant |
| affection | shake hands<br>hug<br>embrace | fond<br>loving<br>adoring |
| IN/SECURITY | | |
| **insecurity** | | |
| disquiet | restless<br>twitching<br>shaking | uneasy<br>anxious<br>freaked out |
| apprehension | tremble<br>shudder<br>cower | wary<br>fearful<br>terrorized |
| **security** | | |
| confidence | declare<br>assert<br>proclaim | together<br>confident<br>assured |
| trust | delegate<br>commit<br>entrust | comfortable with<br>confident in/about<br>trusting |
| DIS/SATISFACTION | | |
| **dissatisfaction** | | |
| ennui | fidget<br>yawn<br>tune out | bored<br>fed up<br>exasperated |
| displeasure | caution<br>scold<br>castigate | cross<br>angry<br>furious |
| **satisfaction** | | |
| engagement | attentive<br>busy<br>flat out | interested<br>absorbed<br>engrossed |
| admiration | pat on the back<br>compliment<br>reward | satisfied<br>impressed<br>proud |

- reaction to other      the boy LIKED the present/the present PLEASED the boy
- undirected mood      the boy was HAPPY

(iv) How are the feelings graded: towards the lower valued end of a scale of intensity or towards the higher end; or between?

- low            the boy LIKED the present
- 'median'      the boy LOVED the present
- high          the boy ADORED the present

(v) The final variable in our typology of affect groups emotions into three major sets. The in/security variable covers emotions concerned with eco-social well-being – anxiety, fear, confidence and trust; the dis/satisfaction variable covers emotions concerned with telos (including frustration) – ennui, anger, curiosity, respect; the un/happiness variable covers emotions concerned with sadness, antipathy, happiness and love.

- in/security      the boy was ANXIOUS/CONFIDENT
- dis/satisfaction the boy was FED UP/ABSORBED
- un/happiness    the boy was SAD/HAPPY

Our framework for JUDGEMENT is outlined in Table 1.6 (for a partial exemplification see Martin 1995c). Judgement can perhaps be thought of as the institutionalization of feeling, in the context of proposals (norms

**Table 1.6** A framework for analysing JUDGEMENT in English

| SOCIAL ESTEEM 'venial' | POSITIVE [admire] | NEGATIVE [criticize] |
|---|---|---|
| **normality** [fate]<br><br>'is s/he special?' | lucky, fortunate, charmed...;<br>normal, average, everyday...;<br>in, fashionable, avant garde... | unfortunate, pitiful, tragic...<br>odd, peculiar, eccentric...;<br>dated, daggy, retrograde... |
| **capacity**<br><br>'is s/he capable?' | powerful, vigorous, robust...;<br>insightful, clever, gifted...;<br>balanced, together, sane... | mild, weak, whimpy...;<br>slow, stupid, thick...;<br>flaky, neurotic, insane... |
| **tenacity** [resolve]<br><br>'is s/he dependable?' | plucky, brave, heroic...;<br>reliable, dependable...;<br>tireless, persevering, resolute | rash, cowardly, despondent...;<br>unreliable, undependable...<br>weak, distracted, dissolute... |

| SOCIAL SANCTION 'mortal' | POSITIVE [praise] | NEGATIVE [condemn] |
|---|---|---|
| **veracity** [truth]<br><br>'is s/he honest?' | truthful, honest, credible...;<br>real, authentic, genuine...;<br>frank, direct... | dishonest, deceitful...;<br>glitzy, bogus, fake...;<br>deceptive, manipulative... |
| **propriety** [ethics]<br><br>'is s/he beyond reproach?' | good, moral, ethical...;<br>law abiding, fair, just...;<br>sensitive, kind, caring... | bad, immoral, evil...;<br>corrupt, unfair, unjust...;<br>insensitive, mean, cruel... |

about how people should and shouldn't behave). Like AFFECT, it has a positive and negative dimension – corresponding to positive and negative judgements about behaviour. Our media research led us to divide judgements into two major groups, social esteem and social sanction (Iedema *et al.* 1994). Judgements of esteem have to do with normality (how unusual someone is), capacity (how capable they are) and tenacity (how resolute they are); judgements of sanction have to do with veracity (how truthful someone is) and propriety (how ethical someone is).[9]

Social esteem involves admiration and criticism, typically without legal implications; if you have difficulties in this area you may need a therapist. Social sanction on the other hand involves praise, and condemnation, often with legal implications; if you have problems in this area you may need a lawyer. The kinds of judgement speakers take up is very sensitive to their institutional position. For example, only journalists with responsibility for writing editorials and other comment have a full range of judgemental resources at their disposal; reporters writing hard news that is meant to sound objective have to avoid explicit judgements completely.

Our framework for APPRECIATION is outlined in Table 1.7. Appreciation can perhaps be thought of as the institutionalization of feeling, in the context of propositions (norms about how products and performances are valued). Like AFFECT and JUDGEMENT it has a positive and negative dimension – corresponding to positive and negative evaluations of texts and processes (and natural phenomena). The system is organized around three variables: reaction, composition and valuation.[10] Reaction has to do with the degree to which the text/process in question captures our attention (reaction:impact) and the emotional impact it has on us. Composition has to do with our perceptions of proportionality (composition:balance) and detail (composition:complexity) in a text/process. Valuation has to do with our assessment of the social significance of the text/process.

**Table 1.7** A framework for analysing APPRECIATION in English

|                                                  | POSITIVE                                                          | NEGATIVE                                                       |
| ------------------------------------------------ | ---------------------------------------------------------------- | ------------------------------------------------------------- |
| reaction: impact<br>'did it grab me?'            | arresting, captivating, engaging...;<br>fascinating, exciting, moving... | dull, boring, tedious, staid...;<br>dry, ascetic, uninviting... |
| reaction: quality<br>'did I like it?'            | lovely, beautiful, splendid...;<br>appealing, enchanting, welcome... | plain, ugly...;<br>repulsive, revolting...                     |
| composition: balance<br>'did it hang together?"  | balanced, harmonious, unified,<br>symmetrical, proportional...   | unbalanced, discordant,<br>contorted, distorted...            |
| composition: complexity<br>'was it hard to follow?' | simple, elegant...;<br>intricate, rich, detailed, precise...  | ornamental, extravagant...;<br>monolithic, simplistic...      |
| valuation<br>'was it worthwhile?'                | challenging, profound, deep...;<br>innovative, original, unique... | shallow, insignificant...;<br>conservative, reactionary...    |

Of these dimensions, valuation is especially tied up with field, since the criteria for valuing a text/process are for the most part institutionally specific. But beyond this, since both JUDGEMENT and APPRECIATION are in a sense institutionalizations of feeling, all of the dimensions involved will prove sensitive to field. An example of this coupling of ideational and interpersonal meaning is presented for appreciations of research in the field of linguistics in Table 1.8.

**Table 1.8** Field specific appreciation (for linguistics)

| linguistics | positive | negative |
|---|---|---|
| **reaction:** impact [noticeability] | timely, long awaited, engaging, landmark. . . | untimely, unexpected, overdue, surprising, dated. . . |
| **reaction:** quality [likeability] | fascinating, exciting, interesting, stimulating, impressive, admirable. . . | dull, tedious, boring, pedantic, didactic, uninspired. . . |
| **composition** [balance] | consistent, balanced, thorough, considered, unified, logical, well argued, well presented. . . | fragmented, loose ended, disorganized, contradictory, sloppy. . . |
| **composition** [complexity] | simple, lucid, elegant, rich, detailed, exhaustive, clear, precise . . . | simplistic, extravagant, complicated, Byzantine, labyrinthine, overly elaborate, narrow, vague, unclear, indulgent, esoteric, eclectic. . . |
| **valuation** [field genesis] | useful, penetrating, illuminating, challenging, significant, deep, profound, satisfying, fruitful. . . | shallow, ad hoc, reductive, unconvincing, unsupported, fanciful, tendentious, bizarre, counterintuitive, perplexing, arcane. . . |

Further complicating this issue is the implicit coupling of field with appraisal. This means that ideational meanings can be used to appraise, even though explicitly evaluative lexis is avoided. For example, when Rita mentions Rita Mae Brown's *Rubyfruit Jungle* in the example noted above, it is clearly the case that her tutor Frank and anyone else naïvely apprenticed into mainstream literary sensibilities is being positioned by Willie Russell to value the book as insignificant, judge Rita as ignorant and feel dislike for the book, its author and Rita as well. Mere mention of the book evokes these feelings, without any explicit appraisal having to be construed at all. Every institution is loaded with couplings of this kind, and socialization into a discipline involves both an alignment with the institutional practices involved and an affinity with the attitudes one is expected to have towards those practices.

In practical terms this means that when analysing APPRAISAL in a text, one has to take into account the APPRAISAL that is evoked by ideational tokens, alongside that which is explicitly inscribed; and beyond this it means that analysts need to declare their reading position – since the evaluation one makes of evocations depends on the institutional position one is reading from. There are many readers, for example, who would have aligned with Rita rather than Frank with respect to a popular culture

text like *Rubyfruit Jungle*. Similarly, according to reading position, formal
and functional linguists will evaluate terms in the following sets of oppositions in complementary ways – with firm convictions about what the good
guys and the bad guys should celebrate.[11]

> rule/resource:: cognitive/social:: acquisition/development:: syntag-
> matic/paradigmatic:: form/function:: language/parole:: system/
> process:: psychology and philosophy/sociology and anthropology::
> cognitive/social:: theory/description:: intuition/corpus:: knowledge/
> meaning:: syntax/discourse:: pragmatics/context:: parsimony/extrava-
> gance:: cognitive/critical:: technicist/humanist:: truth/social action::
> performance/instantiation:: categorical/probabilistic:: contradictory/
> complementary:: proof/exemplification:: reductive/comprehensive::
> arbitrary/natural:: modular/fractal:: syntax and lexicon/lexico-
> grammar. . .

By way of summary, a topological perspective on APPRAISAL resources is
offered in Figure 1.11. It tries to align types of AFFECT, JUDGEMENT and
APPRECIATION in terms of their affinities across appraisal variables. For
example, capacity is aligned with valuation, because of the close relation
between judging someone's behaviour as capable and appreciating the
text/process arising from the behaviour (e.g. a skilful cricketer/a skilful
innings; a gifted painter/an innovative painting, etc.). Similarly, reaction
is aligned with the relevant types of AFFECT. ENGAGEMENT (modality, projection, mitigation, etc.) and AMPLIFICATION (grading, intensity, etc.)
have been included as attendant resources for hedging how committed
we are to what we feel and how strongly we feel about it.

## Grammatical and contextual metaphor

At this point in the discussion I would like to return to the stratification
parameter introduced in the section above on SFL, and elaborate a little
on the way a stratified content plane (lexicogrammar and discourse
semantics) is used by Halliday to interpret abstraction, particularly in
written English. Then, in closing, I will briefly consider the way in which
analogous reasoning in relation to a stratified context plane (register and
genre) might be used to interpret one of the kinds of texts that emerge
around the issue of 'mixed genres'.

First, stratification and abstraction. Halliday has described the realization relationship between lexicogrammar and discourse semantics (modelled in images like Figure 1.3 above) as 'natural'. This reading suggests
that there is an unmarked correlation between meanings and wordings –
that all things being equal we expect, interpersonally, that statements will
be realized as declaratives, questions as interrogatives and commands as
imperatives, or, ideationally, that participants will be realized as nouns,
processes as verbs, properties as adjectives and logical relations as con-

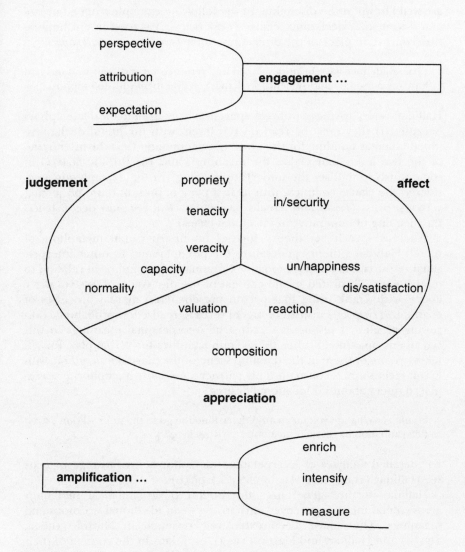

**Figure 1.11** A topological perspective on APPRAISAL resources

junctions. Things not being equal, the model allows for tensions to arise between semantics and grammar, opening up the possibility of indirect speech acts (one mood acting as another) or nominalizations (e.g. processes dressed up as nouns). Halliday refers to the realization and instantiation processes whereby meaning and wording are denaturalized along these lines as grammatical metaphor (see especially Halliday 1985a: chapter 10).

Interpersonal grammatical metaphors of the indirect speech act variety

are well known in the discipline. In the following example from a bureaucratic context, a declarative clause (*I ask that* . . .) is used in an 'imperative' context, in place of the direct imperative *Give them your full support*.

> (The guidelines have been developed as a resource for staff and students and
> have my personal endorsement.) I ask that you give them your full support.

Halliday refers to these indirect speech acts as grammatical metaphors
because: (i) they must be read on two levels, with the literal declarative
mood taken as standing for the underlying command (it is the interaction
of the two levels that makes the meaning); and (ii) the literal level in
some sense symbolizes the underlying reading (in the example just considered the clause complex, with its first person, present tense projecting
verbal process (*I ask*) and irrealis projection (*that you give*) deconstructs
the meaning of imperative in ideational terms).

Whereas speech act theory focuses on interpersonal metaphors of
mood, Halliday's theory generalizes the phenomenon to other interpersonal resources, including modality. Grammatical metaphor in relation to
modality was illustrated in the context of the discussion of ENGAGEMENT
above, with Frank using first person present tense mental processes of
cognition (*I suppose*) instead of modal verbs to realize low probability. Bor-
rowing ideational resources to construe interpersonal meanings in this
way opens up, among other things, opportunities for verbal play. Russell
takes up one of these in the opening scene of the play *Educating Rita*, with
Frank facetiously reconstruing his partner's modality metaphor as a mis-
placed query about his ideational desires.

> Frank: . . . What do you mean am I determined to go to the pub? – I don't need
> determination to get me into a pub . . . (Russell 1985: 2)

For detailed analyses of interpersonal metaphor across a range of texts
see Halliday (1982) and Martin (1992a, 1995b).

Halliday further generalizes the notion of grammatical metaphor
across metafunctions, to cover tensions between ideational wordings and
meanings. These have been extensively reviewed in Martin (1992a,
1993b) and Halliday and Martin (1993), especially in the context of their
role in constructing the uncommon sense discourses of science and
humanities. Ideational metaphors also abound in bureaucratic contexts,
as illustrated in the following example:

> The Passive Restraint Guide is designed to prevent intentional abuse by chil-
> dren. Excessive towel loop length could make intentional abuse more likely.
> Failure to follow loading instructions could result in serious injury or death.
> (Notice on towel dispenser in the men's loo in The 99er Diner, north of Van-
> couver in Canada)

If we paraphrase the second sentence as 'If you don't act as you've been instructed to when loading, you could injure yourself seriously or die', then various features of the metaphorical version are foregrounded – for example, the realization of cause as a verb (*could result in*), and processes as nouns (*failure, loading instructions, serious injury* and *death*). Note that grammatical metaphor facilitates metaphor in its more traditional literary usage – how else can playing cricket catch an ear?

> On a mid-week evening the sound of willow and leather in violent collision caught my ear and I hurried along. (Colin Luckhurst, 'I do like to be beside the seaside', *Guardian Weekly*, 21 August 1994)

Grammatical metaphor also facilitates the organization of APPRAISAL across institutions. In the following example two judgements (of tenacity and capacity) are nominalized (*courage and toughness*) and placed in a causal relationship (*contributed to*) with the success of the Long March. The advantage of nominalizing the judgements for the historian is that s/he can make them Agents in a range of causative processes whose meaning potential is subtle and differentiated enough to support the interpretation of why things happened as they did.

> This question has often been raised by historians, and a number of factors have been suggested to explain the success of the Long March . . . The courage and toughness of the young members of the Red Army, many of whom were teenagers, also contributed to its success.

The educational implications of grammatical metaphor are immense, especially in light of Halliday's suggestion (e.g. 1993c) that grammatical metaphor develops out of non-metaphorical text across all three of the time frames discussed above – tending to unfold later in text (logo-genesis), tending to develop later in the maturation of the individual (onto-genesis) and tending to evolve later in the history of a culture (phylogenesis). In other words, if we take the fracturing of glass as an example, Halliday is claiming that a series of realizations which unfolds as follows is in some sense a natural one as far as semogenesis is concerned.

> (the question of how) glass cracks, (the stress needed to) crack glass, (the mechanism by which) glass cracks, as a crack grows, the crack has advanced, will make slow cracks grow, speed up the rate at which cracks grow, the rate of crack growth, we can increase the crack growth rate 1,000 times. (Halliday and Martin 1993: 56)

If we add to this Halliday's association of the emergence of ideational metaphor with the development of writing systems (e.g. Halliday 1985b), and the association of ideational metaphor with discipline specific secondary school literacy (e.g. Martin 1993b), then we arrive at a foundational sequencing principle as far as institutionalized learning is concerned, namely, grammatically metaphorical text after non-metaphorical. The principle has certainly shaped genre-based literacy programmes in Australia (as reflected in the genre topology in Table 1.3 above). Its implications and implementations are likely to reverberate through language in education initiatives for years to come.

The move from non-metaphorical to metaphorical text is in some sense symbolized across literate cultures by the separation of primary and secondary schooling and the drift from thematically organized multi-disciplinary units of work in primary school to strongly classified discipline specific work in secondary school. Halliday (1993c) also suggests a semiotic interpretation of the beginning of school, which has been explored in detail by Painter (1993). What seems to be emerging from this research is that the move to primary schooling symbolizes the ability to deal with abstractions. The example I often draw on to illustrate this point comes from my daughter, then aged 4. At Manly Pier in Sydney, there is a famous sign which greets visitors: *7 miles from Sydney and 1000 miles from care.* Upon my reciting this on arrival, my daughter asked 'Where's care?' Over the next year or two, she learned not to ask questions like this,[12] and then to laugh at her younger brother making mistakes of just that kind.

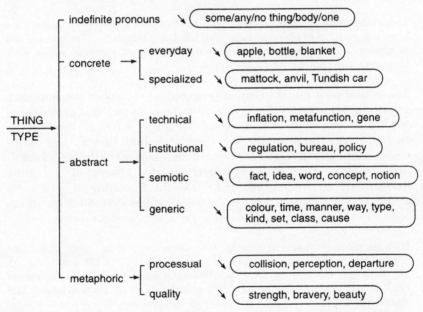

**Figure 1.12** Kinds of thing: covering abstractions and grammatical metaphors

A rough framework[13] for classifying types of thing is outlined in Figure 1.12. Note that the network distinguishes specialized and technical language. Specialized things, like everyday things, can be ostensively defined; you can point them out to apprentices. Technical things on the other hand are abstractions that have to be linguistically defined (and even if you can point to them, as with the gene in a microscope, just pointing doesn't fully explain what they mean; Halliday has referred in passing to technical terms as 'semiotic ratchets'). Alongside the technical abstraction of science, we find institutional abstractions (bureaucratic ratchets if you will) that organize our lives. Abstractions also include terms for semiosis (e.g. *fact, idea, concept, notion*) and terms for generic dimensions of meaning (such as *size, shape, colour, means, manner, way*, etc.).

Analysis of the abstract and metaphorical things is not just a matter of derivation. The noun *regulation*, for example, may refer to an institutional abstraction, as in *the regulations don't permit that activity*, or it may be a metaphorical process, as in *excessive regulation of students' behaviour may not always be in the school's best interests*. Analysis is further complicated by the fact that technical and institutional terms are engendered through grammatical metaphor – in other words, grammatical metaphor is used to define and explain these meanings, which are then intended to transcend the metaphors and carry on as abstractions in their own right. The following text from Halliday and Martin (1993: 223) illustrates this process for the terms *compression, rarefaction* and *compression wave*, leading to the definition of the once concrete, but now abstract meaning *sound*.

(a) If we look at how a tuning fork produces sound (b) we can learn just what sound is. (c) By looking closely at one of the prongs (d) you can see that it is moving to and fro (vibrating). (e) As the prong moves outwards (f) it squashes, or compresses, the surrounding air. (g) The particles of air are pushed outwards (h) crowding against and bashing into their neighbours (i) before they bounce back. (j) The neighbouring air particles are then pushed out (k) to hit the next air particles and so on. (l) This region of slightly 'squashed' together air moving out from the prong is called a **compression**. (m) When the prong of the tuning fork moves back again (n) the rebounding air particles move back into the space that is left. (o) This region where the air goes 'thinner' is called a **rarefaction** (p) and also moves outwards. (q) The particles of air move to and fro in the same direction in which the wave moves. (r) Thus **sound** is a **compression wave** that can be heard.

For purposes of analysis, these terms are probably best treated as metaphorical at their point of genesis, and as technical abstractions thereafter. In order to help clarify the boundary between metaphorical and abstract things, Halliday's inventory of types of grammatical metaphor has been included here as Table 1.9 (Halliday to appear b).

This brief discussion of the educational significance of grammatical metaphor puts us in a position to raise the issue of contextual metaphor and ask whether similar kinds of tension across strata can be found at the level of context. The following text, discussed in Cranny-Francis and Martin (1995), lends itself to an interpretation of this kind. On the surface, the text is organized as a kind of story – a psychological quest narrative; the story, however, was intended in its context to stand for an information report about dolphins – as part of an attack on genre-based

**Table 1.9** Types of grammatical metaphor

1. quality ⇒ entity      adjective ⇒ noun
   Epithet = Thing      *unstable = instability*

2. process ⇒ entity      verb ⇒ noun
   (i) Event = Thing      *transform = transformation*
   (ii) Auxiliary = Thing:
      (tense)      *will/going to = prospect*
      (phase)      *try to = attempt*
      (modality)      *can/could = possibility, potential*

3. circumstance ⇒ entity      preposition ⇒ noun
   Minor Process = Thing      *with = accompaniment; to = destination*

4. relator ⇒ entity      conjunction ⇒ noun
   Conjunctive = Thing      *so = cause/proof; if = condition*

5. process ⇒ quality      verb ⇒ adjective
   (i) Event = Epithet      *[poverty] is increasing = increasing [poverty]*
   (ii) Auxiliary = Epithet:
      (tense)      *was/used to = previous*
      (phase)      *begin to = initial*
      (modality)      *must/will [always] = constant*

6. circumstance ⇒ quality      adverb/prepositional phrase ⇒ adjective*
   (i) Manner = Epithet      *[decided] hastily = hasty [decision]*
   (ii) other = Epithet      *[argued] for a long time = lengthy [argument]*
   (iii) other = Classifier      *[cracked] on the surface = surface [cracks]*

7. relator ⇒ quality      conjunction ⇒ adjective
   Conjunctive = Epithet      *then = subsequent; so = resulting*

8. circumstance ⇒ process      <u>be</u>/<u>go</u> + preposition ⇒ verb
   Minor Process = Process      *be about = concern; be instead of = replace*

9. relator ⇒ process      conjuction ⇒ verb
   Conjunctive = Event      *then = follow; so = cause; and = complement*

10. relator ⇒ circumstance      conjunction ⇒ preposition/-al group
    Conjunctive = Minor Process      *when = in times of/in . . . times*
         *if = under conditions of/under . . . conditions*

11. [zero] ⇒ entity      *= the phenomenon of . . .*

12. [zero] ⇒ process      *= . . . occurs/ensues*

13. entity ⇒ [expansion]      noun ⇒ [various] (in env. 1, 2 above)
    Head = Modifier      *the government [decided] =*
         *the government's [decision], [a/the decision]*
         *of/by the government, [a] government(al) [decision]*
         *the government [couldn't decide/was indecisive =*
         *the government's [indecision], [the indecision] of*
         *the government, government(al) [indecision]*

\* or noun; cf. *mammal*
[*cells*]/*mammalian*
[*cells*]

literacy pedagogy, along the lines of 'Why can't students hand in a range of genres in science? Why are you trying to limit them to boring old information reports?' Informally, then, we might describe the text as a story standing for a report (analogous to informally describing an indirect speech act as a declarative standing for an imperative).

Rephrasing this in terms of stratal tension at the level of context, we could argue that the register of the text (its field, mode and tenor selections) invokes narrative, but that certain features of the story (the Socratic dialogue, the technical information about dolphins, the fact that the object of the quest is information, etc.) indicate that at a deeper level this text is intended to instantiate a report genre. As with grammatical metaphor, it is the tension between levels (between genre and register in this instance) that construes the meaning. Contextual metaphors of this kind represent an excursion of English discipline discourse across the curriculum which has been promoted by radical progressive pedagogies around the English speaking world.

Is this a report or a recount or a discussion?

Yesterday I went to the library and found a book about dolphins. I had seen dolphins on TV and I was interested in them. I wanted to find the answer to the question, why are dolphins so interesting to humans?

The book said that dolphins were sea mammals. I bet you didn't know that dolphins have to breathe air! If they don't breathe air, they will die.

I have often wondered what dolphins like to eat, so I looked in the book for information about this. Do they eat other fish, I wondered? I found out that they do.

I suppose you know what dolphins look like, of course. I found out some interesting things, such as what that dorsal fin is for and how they keep warm.

Why do we humans like dolphins so much, I often wonder. I searched in the book for the answer to this question, but could not get down to the real reason. The book talked about their tricks and stunts and their general friendliness. As I thought about it, I came to the conclusion that it had something to do with the fact that they, like us, are mammals.

It may well be that a notion of contextual metaphor, interpreted along these lines, will turn out to be as educationally significant as Halliday's work on grammatical metaphor – particularly with respect to success in secondary school. In progressive history classrooms, for example (see Coffin, Chapter 7 below), students are often encouraged to write stories from the point of view of participants in historical processes. To succeed in this task, they have to realize that the story they tell must not only be accurate in historical detail, but ought as well to symbolize and focus attention on issues the historian considers significant. The task, in other words, has to be read not as an opportunity to depart from history discourse, but as an opportunity to use a story to stand for historical interpretation.

Looking beyond education, the notion of grammatical metaphor (interpreted as stratal tension within language) has been developed by systemic linguists as an important insight into the way in which a culture increases its linguistic meaning potential (e.g. Halliday 1992a, c, 1993b,

1996a; Martin 1993b; Halliday and Martin 1993). By refocusing attention on the issue of contextual metaphor (interpreted as stratal tension at the level of context) we should be able to gain some valuable insights into one of the trajectories along which the social processes of a culture expand – by deploying register variables metaphorically (as figure), to symbolize a complementary genre (as ground).

## Notes

1 One problem with this image is that it implies that field/ideational resources are in some sense more extensive than mode/textual or tenor/interpersonal ones; theoretically, this is not the case.

2 For critique of this stratified model see Hasan (1995); Martin (in press) offers a partial reply.

3 In this sense of the term, register is thus comparable to what Halliday and Hasan (e.g. 1985/1989) refer to as context of culture; see Matthiessen (1993) for discussion.

4 In Figure 1.5, a single slash is used to represent metaredundancy, and a double slash to represent meta-metaredundancy – thus language/register//genre is read as language metaredounding with register, meta-metaredounding with genre.

5 Along this dimension Halliday and Matthiessen are refocusing a long-standing SFL interest in the dynamics of text as process (Martin 1985a; Bateman 1989).

6 For the record, Steve Waugh is an Australian cricketer, who performed the remarkable feat of scoring more than 200 runs in a single innings against the West Indies in 1995; in this field, 100 runs is considered an outstanding contribution.

7 Procedural recounts give an after-the-fact account of a procedure that has been enacted; historical recounts record two or more generations of human endeavour; descriptions characterize a specific participant; descriptive reports characterize a generic class of participants.

8 *Educating Rita*, Copyright Columbia Pictures Industries 1983, RCA/ Columbia/Hoyts PTY LTD 1985. Marketed and Distributed by CEL Home Video. RCS/Columbia Pictures International Video.

9 At this level of delicacy the types of JUDGEMENT are related to MODALITY (Halliday 1994), in the following proportions: normality is to usuality, as capacity is to ability, as tenacity is to inclination, as veracity is to probability, as propriety is to obligation.

10 These variables are relatable to the kind of mental processing (Halliday 1994) involved in the appreciation, in the following proportions: reaction is to affection, as composition is to perception, as valuation is to cognition.

11 For these complementarities, '/' stands for 'is to' and '::' stands for 'as'; they can thus be read as *rule is to resource as cognitive is to social* . . ., etc.

12 Compare from about the same period (while swinging high on a swing): 'I'm full of petrol and energy'; 'Well, Hamie, what do you reckon about the meaning of life this morning?' (daughter interrupting) 'What meeting?'; 'Daddy, what's government mean?'

13 This framework was jointly constructed in the course of research seminars involving David Butt, Carmel Cloran, Michael Halliday, Ruqaiya Hasan, Jim Martin, Christian Matthiessen and Chris Nesbitt.

# References

Bateman, J. (1989) 'Dynamic systemic-functional grammar: a new frontier'. *Word*, 40(1–2) (*Systems, Structures and Discourse: Selected Papers from the Fifteenth International Systemic Congress*), 263–86.

Bloor, T. and Bloor, M. (1995) *The Functional Analysis of English: A Hallidayan Approach*. London: Edward Arnold.

Butt, D., Fahey, R., Spinks, S. and Yallop, C. (1995) *Using Functional Grammar: An Explorer's Guide*. Sydney: NCELTR (National Centre for English Language Teaching and Research, Macquarie University).

Christie, F. (1992) 'Literacy in Australia'. *Annual Review of Applied Linguistics* 12, 142–55.

Cloran, C. (1989) 'Learning through language: the social construction of gender'. In R. Hasan and J. R. Martin (eds) *Language Development: Learning Language, Learning Culture*. Norwood, NJ: Ablex (*Meaning and Choice in Language: Studies for Michael Halliday*), 111–51.

Cope, W. and Kalantzis, M. (eds) (1993) *The Powers of Literacy: A Genre Approach to Teaching Literacy*. London: Falmer (Critical Perspectives on Literacy and Education) and Pittsburgh: University of Pittsburgh Press (Pittsburgh Series in Composition, Literacy and Culture).

Cranny-Francis, A. and Martin, J. R. (1991) 'Contratextuality: the poetics of subversion'. In F. Christie (ed.) *Literacy in Social Processes: Papers from the First Australian Systemic Linguistics Conference, Held at Deakin University, January 1990*. Darwin: Centre for Studies of Language in Education, Northern Territory University, 286–344.

Cranny-Francis, A. and Martin, J. R. (1995) 'Writings/readings: how to know a genre'. *Interpretations: Journal of the English Teachers' Association of Western Australia* 28(3), 1–32.

Eggins, S. (1994) *An Introduction to Systemic Functional Linguistics*. London: Pinter.

Eggins, S. and Martin, J. R. (1996) 'Genres and registers of discourse'. In T. A. van Dijk (ed.) *Discourse: A Multidisciplinary Introduction*. London: Sage.

Halliday, M. A. K. (1978) *Language as a Social Semiotic: The Social Interpretation of Language and Meaning*. London: Edward Arnold.

Halliday, M. A. K. (1979) 'Modes of meaning and modes of expression: types of grammatical structure, and their determination by different semantic functions'. In D. J. Allerton, E. Carney and D. Holdcroft (eds) *Function and Context in Linguistic Analysis: Essays Offered to William Haas*. Cambridge: Cambridge University Press, 57–79.

Halliday, M. A. K. (1982) 'The de-automatization of grammar: from Priestley's "An Inspector Calls"'. In J. M. Anderson (ed.) *Language Form and Linguistic Variation: Papers Dedicated to Angus MacIntosh*. Amsterdam: Benjamins, 129–59.

Halliday, M. A. K. (1985a) *An Introduction to Functional Grammar*. London: Edward Arnold (2nd edition 1994).

Halliday, M. A. K. (1985b) *Spoken and Written Language*. Geelong, Vic.: Deakin University Press (republished by Oxford University Press 1989).

Halliday, M. A. K. (1991) 'Towards probabilistic interpretations'. In E. Ventola (ed.) *Functional and Systemic Linguistics: Approaches and Uses*. Berlin: Mouton De Gruyter (Trends in Linguistics Studies and Monographs 55), 39–61.

Halliday, M. A. K. (1992a) 'How do you mean?' In M. Davies and L. Ravelli (eds) *Recent Advances in Systemic Linguistics*. London: Pinter, 20–35.

Halliday, M. A. K. (1992b) 'Language as system and language as instance: the corpus as a theoretical construct'. In J. Svartvik (ed.) *Directions in Corpus Linguistics: Proceedings of Nobel Symposium 82, Stockholm, 4–8 August 1991*. Berlin: De Gruyter (Trends in Linguistics Studies and Monographs 65), 61–77.

Halliday, M. A. K. (1992c) 'The act of meaning'. In J. E. Alatis (ed.) *Georgetown University Round Table on Languages and Linguistics 1992: Language, Communication and Social Meaning*. Washington, DC: Georgetown University Press.

Halliday, M. A. K. (1992d) 'The history of a sentence: an essay in social semiotics'. In V. Fortunati (ed.) *Bologna, la cultura italiana e le letterature straniere moderne*, Vol. 3. Ravenna: Longo Editore (for University of Bologna), 29–45.

Halliday, M. A. K. (1993a) 'Quantitative studies and probabilities in grammar'. In M. Hoey (ed.) *Data, Description, Discourse: Papers on English Language in Honour of John McH. Sinclair (on his sixtieth birthday)*. London: HarperCollins, 1–25.

Halliday, M. A. K. (1993b) *Language in a Changing World*. Canberra, ACT: Applied Linguistics Association of Australia (Occasional Paper 13).

Halliday, M. A. K. (1993c) 'Towards a language-based theory of learning'. *Linguistics and Education* 5(2), 93–116.

Halliday, M. A. K. (to appear a) 'On language in relation to the evolution of human consciousness'. Paper prepared for Nobel Symposium 92 'The relation between language and mind'. Stockholm, 8–12 August 1994.

Halliday, M. A. K. (to appear b) 'Things and relations: regrammaticizing experience as technical knowledge'. In J. R. Martin and R. Veel (eds) *Reading Science: Critical and Functional Perspectives on Discourses of Science*. London: Routledge.

Halliday, M. A. K. and Hasan, R. (1976) *Cohesion in English*. London: Longman (English Language Series 9).

Halliday, M. A. K. and Hasan, R. (1980) *Text and Context: Aspects of Language in a Social-semiotic Perspective*. Sophia Linguistica VI. Tokyo: the Graduate School of Languages and Linguistics and the Linguistic Institute for International Communication, Sophia University. (New edition published as Halliday, M. A. K. and Hasan, R. (1985) *Language, Context and Text: Aspects of Language in a Social-semiotic Perspective*. Geelong, Vic.: Deakin University Press (republished by Oxford University Press 1989).)

Halliday, M. A. K. and Martin, J. R. (1993) *Writing Science: Literacy and Discursive Power*. London: Falmer (Critical Perspectives on Literacy and Education).

Halliday, M. A. K. and Matthiessen, C. M. I. M. (to appear) *Construing Experience through Language: A Language-based Approach to Cognition*. Berlin: De Gruyter (Foundations of Communication and Cognition).

Hasan, R. (1987) 'The grammarian's dream: lexis as most delicate grammar'. In M. A. K. Halliday and R. P. Fawcett (eds) *New Developments in Systemic Linguistics*, Vol. 1: *Theory and Description*. London: Pinter, 184–211.

Hasan, R. (1990) 'Semantic variation and sociolinguistics'. *Australian Journal of Linguistics* 9(2), 221–76.

Hasan, R. (1995) 'The conception of context in text'. In P. Fries and M. Gregory (eds) *Discourse in Society: Systemic Functional Perspectives*. Norwood, NJ: Ablex (*Meaning and Choice in Language: Studies for Michael Halliday*, Advances in Discourse Processes, Vol. L), 183–283.

Iedema, R. (1996) *Administration Literacy* (Write It Right Literacy in Industry Research Project, Stage 3). Sydney: Metropolitan East Disadvantaged Schools Program.

Iedema, R., Feez, S. and White, P. (1994) *Media Literacy* (Write It Right Literacy in Industry Research Project, Stage 2). Sydney: Metropolitan East Disadvantaged Schools Program.

Kress, G. and Threadgold, T. (1988) 'Towards a social theory of genre'. *Southern Review* 21(3), 215–43.

Kress, G. and van Leeuwen, T. (1990) *Reading Images*. Geelong, Vic.: Deakin University Press (Sociocultural Aspects of Language and Education).

Kress, G. and van Leeuwen, T. (1996) *Reading Images: The Grammar of Visual Design*. London: Routledge.

Lemke, J. L. (1995) *Textual Politics: Discourse and Social Dynamics*. London: Taylor & Francis (Critical Perspectives on Literacy and Education).

Lemke, J. (in press) 'Typology, topology, topography: genre semantics'. *Network* 22.

Lemke, J. (to appear) 'Multiplying meaning: visual and verbal semiotics in scientific text'. In J. R. Martin and R. Veel (eds) *Reading Science: Critical and Functional Perspectives on Discourses of Science*. London: Routledge.

Lock, G. (1996) *Functional English Grammar: An Introduction for Second Language Teachers*. Cambridge: Cambridge University Press (Cambridge Teacher Education Series).

Martin, J. R. (1985a) 'Process and text: two aspects of human semiosis'. In J. D. Benson and W. S. Greaves (eds) *Systemic Perspectives on Discourse*, Vol. 1: *Selected Theoretical Papers from the 9th International Systemic Congress*. Norwood, NJ: Ablex, 248–74.

Martin, J. R. (1985b) *Factual Writing: Exploring and Challenging Social Reality*. Geelong, Vic.: Deakin University Press (republished by Oxford University Press 1989).

Martin, J. R. (1991) 'Intrinsic functionality: implications for contextual theory'. *Social Semiotics*\* 1(1), 99–162.

Martin, J. R. (1992a) *English Text: System and Structure*. Amsterdam: Benjamins.

Martin, J. R. (1992b) 'Macroproposals: meaning by degree'. In W. A. Mann and S. A. Thompson (eds) *Discourse Description: Diverse Analyses of a Fund Raising Text*. Amsterdam: Benjamins, 359–95.

Martin, J. R. (1993a) 'Genre and literacy: modelling context in educational linguistics'. *Annual Review of Applied Linguistics* 13, 141–72.

Martin, J. R. (1993b) 'Technology, bureaucracy and schooling: discursive resources and control'. *Cultural Dynamics* 6(1), 84–130.

Martin, J. R. (1994) 'Macro-genres: the ecology of the page'. *Network* 21, 29–52.

Martin, J. R. (1995a) 'Text and clause: fractal resonance'. *Text* 15(1), 5–42.

Martin, J. R. (1995b) 'Interpersonal meaning, persuasion and public discourse: packing semiotic punch'. *Australian Journal of Linguistics* 15(1), 33–67.

Martin, J. R. (1995c) 'Reading positions/positioning readers: JUDGEMENT in English'. *Prospect: A Journal of Australian TESOL* 10(2), 27–37.

Martin, J. R. (1996a) 'Metalinguistic diversity: the case from case'. In R. Hasan, C. Cloran and D. Butt (eds) *Functional Descriptions: Theory in Practice*. Amsterdam: Benjamins (Current Issues in Linguistic Theory), 323–72.

Martin, J. R. (1996b) 'Types of structure: deconstructing notions of constituency in clause and text'. In E. Hovy and D. Scott (eds) *Burning Issues in Discourse: A Multidisciplinary Perspective*. Heidelberg: Springer.

Martin, J. R. (1996c) 'Evaluating disruption: symbolising theme in junior secondary narrative'. In R. Hasan and G. Williams (eds) *Literacy in Society*. London: Longman, 124–71.

\* This journal in functional linguistics, semiotics and critical theory can be ordered from: Professor David Birch, Communication and Media Studies, Central Queensland University, Rockhampton, Queensland 4702, Australia.

Martin, J. R. (in press) 'A context for genre: modelling social processes in functional linguistics'. In R. Stainton and J. Devilliers (eds) *Communication in Linguistics.* Toronto: GREF (Collection Theoria).

Martin, J. R. (to appear) 'Beyond exchange: APPRAISAL resources in English'. In S. Hunston and G. Thompson (eds) *Evaluation in Text.* Oxford: Oxford University Press.

Martin, J. R., Christie, F. and Rothery, J. (n.d.) 'Social processes in education: a reply to Sawyer and Watson (and others)'. In I. Reid (ed.) *The Place of Genre in Learning: Current Debates.* Geelong, Vic.: Centre for Studies in Literary Education (Typereader Publications 1), 46–57. (More fully published in *The Teaching of English: Journal of the English Teachers' Association of New South Wales* 53 (1987), 3–22.)

Martin, J. R. and Matthiessen, C. M. I. M. (1991) 'Systemic typology and topology'. In F. Christie (ed.) *Literacy in Social Processes: Papers from the Inaugural Australian Systemic Linguistics Conference, Held at Deakin University, January 1990.* Darwin: Centre for Studies in Language in Education, Northern Territory University, 345–83.

Martin, J. R., Matthiessen, C. M. I. M. and Painter, C. (1996) *A Workbook in Functional Grammar.* London: Edward Arnold.

Martin, J. R. and Veel, R. (eds) (to appear) *Reading Science: Critical and Functional Perspectives on Discourses of Science.* London: Routledge.

Matthiessen, C. M. I. M. (1988) 'Representational issues in systemic functional grammar'. In J. D. Benson and W. S. Greaves (eds) *Systemic Functional Approaches to Discourse.* Norwood, NJ: Ablex, 136–75.

Matthiessen, C. M. I. M. (1991) 'Language on language: the grammar of semiosis'. *Social Semiotics* 1(2), 69–111.

Matthiessen, C. M. I. M. (1992) 'Interpreting the textual metafunction'. In M. Davies and L. Ravelli (eds) *Advances in Systemic Linguistics.* London: Pinter, 37–81.

Matthiessen, C. M. I. M. (1993) 'Register in the round: diversity in a unified theory of register analysis'. In M. Ghadessy (ed.) *Register Analysis: Theory and Practice.* London: Pinter, 221–92.

Matthiessen, C. M. I. M. (1995) *Lexicogrammatical Cartography: English Systems.* Tokyo: International Language Sciences Publishers.

Matthiessen, C. M. I. M. (mimeo) 'Instantial systems and logogenesis'. Paper presented at the Third Chinese Systemic-functional Linguistics Symposium, Hangzhou, 17–20 June 1993.

Matthiessen, C. M. I. M. and Halliday, M. A. K. (in press) 'Systemic Functional Grammar: a first step into theory'. In J. Ney (ed.) *Current Approaches to Syntax.* Tokyo: International Language Studies.

Nesbitt, C. and Plum, G. (1988) 'Probabilities in a systemic-functional grammar: the clause complex in English'. In R. P. Fawcett and D. Young (eds) *New Developments in Systemic Linguistics*, Vol. 2: *Theory and Application.* London: Pinter, 6–38.

O'Donnell, M. (1990) 'A dynamic model of exchange'. *Word* 41(3).

O'Toole, M. (1994) *The Language of Displayed Art.* London: Leicester University Press (a division of Pinter).

Painter, C. (1984) *Into the Mother Tongue: A Case Study of Early Language Development.* London: Pinter.

Painter, C. (1993) 'Learning through Language: a case study in the development of language as a resource for learning from 2½ to 5 years'. PhD thesis, Department of Linguistics, University of Sydney.

Poynton, C. (1985) *Language and Gender: Making the Difference*. Geelong, Vic.: Deakin University Press (republished by Oxford University Press 1989).

Ravelli, L. (1995) 'A dynamic perspective: implications for metafunctional interaction and an understanding of Theme'. In R. Hasan and P. Fries (eds) *On Subject and Theme: A Discourse Functional Perspective*. Amsterdam: Benjamins (Current Issues in Linguistic Theory 118), 187–234.

Rose, D., McInnes, D. and Korner, H. (1992) *Scientific Literacy* (Write It Right Literacy in Industry Research Project, Stage 1). Sydney: Metropolitan East Disadvantaged Schools Program.

Rothery, J. (1994) *Exploring Literacy in School English* (Write It Right Resources for Literacy and Learning). Sydney: Metropolitan East Disadvantaged Schools Program.

Rothery, J. and Stenglin, M. (1994a) *Spine-Chilling Stories: A Unit of Work for Junior Secondary English* (Write It Right Resources for Literacy and Learning). Sydney: Metropolitan East Disadvantaged Schools Program.

Rothery, J. and Stenglin, M. (1994b) *Exploring Narrative in Video: A Unit of Work for Junior Secondary English* (Write It Right Resources for Literacy and Learning). Sydney: Metropolitan East Disadvantaged Schools Program.

Rothery, J. and Stenglin, M. (1994c) *Writing a Book Review: A Unit of Work for Junior Secondary English* (Write It Right Resources for Literacy and Learning). Sydney: Metropolitan East Disadvantaged Schools Program.

Russell, W. (1985) *Educating Rita*. London: Longman (Longman Study Texts).

Threadgold, T. (1991) 'Postmodernism, systemic-functional linguistics as metalanguage and the practice of cultural critique'. In F. Christie (ed.) *Literacy in Social Processes: Papers from the Inaugural Australian Systemic Linguistics Conference, Held at Deakin University, January 1990*. Darwin: Centre for Studies in Language in Education, Northern Territory University, 60–82.

Threadgold, T. (1993) 'Performing genre: violence, the making of protected subjects, and the discourses of critical literacy and radical pedagogy'. *Domains of Literacy, Changing English* 1(1), 2–31.

Threadgold, T. (1994) 'Grammar, genre and the ownership of literacy'. *Idiom* XXIX (2), 20–8 (reprinted in *The Teaching of English* 3, 62–70).

Veel, R. (to appear) 'Being green and going grey: the language of environmentalism in the classroom'. In J. R. Martin and R. Veel (eds) *Reading Science: Critical and Functional Perspectives on Discourses of Science*. London: Routledge.

Ventola, E. (1987) *The Structure of Social Interaction: A Systemic Approach to the Semiotics of Service Encounters*. London: Pinter (Open Linguistics Series).

Ventola, E. (1988) 'Text analysis in operation: a multilevel approach'. In R. P. Fawcett and D. Young (eds) *New Developments in Systemic Linguistics*, Vol. 2: *Theory and Application*. London: Pinter, 52–77.

Ventola, E. (1995) 'Generic and register qualities of texts and their realization'. In P. Fries and M. Gregory (eds) *Discourse in Society: Systemic Functional Perspectives*. Norwood, NJ: Ablex (*Meaning and Choice in Language: Studies for Michael Halliday, Advances in Discourse Processes*, Vol. L), 3–28.

# 2 Science, technology and technical literacies

*David Rose*

My aim in this chapter is to explore the relationships between technical literacies learned in the stages of a science education and employed at various levels of industry. The data on which the discussion is based are drawn from the findings of a major literacy research project which examined discursive practices in both these fields (Rose *et al.* 1992). Linguistic and cultural relationships are explored using the tools of systemic functional linguistics (SFL) to describe the features of texts collected in industry and school contexts, and Bernstein's (1990) models of relations between the fields of economic production and education in modern industrial societies. These two perspectives enable us systematically to relate commonalities and differences found in the texts to their institutional macrocontexts.

The chapter begins with a discussion of the relationships between the stratified production systems of Western economies, and the highly stratified outcomes of their education systems. This is followed by a discussion of the nature of technical discourse at each stratum of education and industry. Discursive relationships between the two fields are then exemplified with comparative analyses of written texts from one industry stratum, the skilled operator/vocational level, and the corresponding stage of secondary school science curriculum. The conclusion discusses the functionality of different types and degrees of technical literacy in the reproduction of social stratification, its apparent dysfunctionality in emerging post-Fordist economies and the potential for change that this opens up.

The description of industrial and educational contexts is based on research in Australia, but is broadly applicable to most Western economies and state education systems. The key features include a rapid shift from Fordist production modes, involving rigidly stratified skill levels of workers in heavily capitalized industries, to the flattened hierarchies of cell-production, multi-skilling and the communications revolution associated with 'flexible modes of capital accumulation' (Harvey 1989: 141 ff.). Since the 1980s Western governments have recognized the need for education systems to provide a better trained workforce to meet this changed economic environment, and they have attempted to weaken the strong insulation between school and work that has become a feature of industrial societies, no matter what their ideologies (Bernstein 1990: 203-4).

## Context

From the mid-1980s the social democratic Labour government in Australia has promoted a programme of restructuring Australia's industrial base, the key to which is a major restructuring of education and training for workers and students at all levels of industry and education. The literacy research reported on here was conducted as an element of this process. The post-Second World War development of manufacturing industry in Australia has relied on a strongly stratified workforce, consisting essentially of five layers of workers:

1. post-graduate-trained research scientists
2. professionally trained applied scientists and production managers
3. vocationally trained tradespeople and supervisors
4. industry-trained operators and supervisors
5. minimally trained process workers

The ideal process line production system entailed a maximum separation of 'mental' and 'manual' labour. Minimal planning, design or decision-making was carried out on the factory floor; as many of these tasks as possible were transferred to management or technical positions. This distinction effectively meant that manual labour required minimal reading and writing skills.

The structure and outcomes of formal education have until now reflected the demands of manufacturing for a strongly stratified workforce. A small cohort of secondary students achieve well in senior secondary science and go on to science and technology degrees at tertiary level. A still smaller number go on to post-graduate research. A larger group leave secondary school before the final year and go into vocational training. Another large group may or may not complete junior secondary school and enter the workforce as manual labourers.

## Technological and scientific English

Our research found a strong correspondence between the literacy demands at each level of the traditional manufacturing hierarchy, and the level and type of literacy offered at each stage of the secondary and tertiary science curricula. Two general categories of written English were found in the texts analysed that differed in systematic ways from the grammar and subject matter of everyday spoken English: **technological** English and **scientific** English.

Technological English is concerned with the processes and technology of industrial production. It uses specialized terms and grammar to describe technology and systematically organizes the manufacturing process in written texts for the purposes of apprenticing trained workers and reporting on the production process. Reading and writing technological texts involves both an understanding of its grammatical forms and a step-by-step apprenticeship into the subject matter – the particular field of technology. This apprenticeship typically involves work experience as well as reading and writing. Typical text types used in these fields included various types of procedures and manuals, as well as reports and technical notes.

Scientific English is concerned with the chemical, physical and biological processes involved in explaining, classifying and manipulating natural phenomena, with the goal of applying these explanations and classifications to industrial production. Part of each scientific field is the construction of large numbers of technical terms that are systematically related to each other, and this feature of scientific English is easily recognized. However, what is harder to recognize (and also harder to learn) is that the grammar of scientific English also becomes highly abstract as its subject matter diverges from everyday common-sense experience. Reading and writing scientific texts depends on a long apprenticeship into science in general and then into particular scientific fields. At each stage of this apprenticeship, knowledge of the field and ability to read and write the grammar become more and more specialized. Typical texts in these fields include reports, explanations, discussions, technical notes and research articles.

Most of the texts analysed involved both technological and scientific English, even at the level of machine operator, depending on the degree of scientific knowledge required to operate the technology. Both types of written English are closely related, particularly at the vocational to undergraduate levels, and an apprenticeship into science will give access to technological as well as scientific literacy.

## Science recontextualized as pedagogy: stages of apprenticeship

The stages of apprenticeship into a scientific field were analysed, from junior secondary to post-graduate research level, in terms of both depth of specialized field knowledge and forms of written English in which it is expressed. At each stage the field is embodied in published texts, systematically organized to apprentice students into the field, and culminates in scientific reference texts used by researchers, and in the research articles by which research scientists contribute to the body of field knowledge.

What students are learning at each stage is information that has been produced at the research level but is not the same body of information that research scientists work with. Rather the knowledge system and the methodological skills taught at each stage of an apprenticeship constitute a recontextualized discourse. It has been taken out of one context – the social environment where scientific discourse is produced – and given a new form for a different context – the social environment where science apprentices are trained. The system of knowledge and skills that science students learn is a pedagogic discourse, different in its subject matter foci, role relations of participants, and mode of realization as texts and grammar, from the scientific discourse that is produced and applied by graduates of the apprenticeship.

Scientific discourse and practice at the research level are recontextualized at the undergraduate level as curriculum in each of the disciplines. This curriculum is systematically organized to cover the classification systems of the discipline, with enough detail within each category for graduates to be able to apply it usefully in work as applied scientists, engineers, doctors, educators, or to go on to further post-graduate specialization. But this apprenticeship does not begin at tertiary level. Pedagogic science at the secondary level has evolved to prepare students for entry to undergraduate science. In senior secondary science, the scientific classifications and the detail in which they are studied are determined by the needs of the tertiary faculties for recruits with an adequate knowledge of each field to cope with the tertiary curriculum. At senior secondary level, the age and consequent learning patterns of students becomes more significant, and the competing demands of the other secondary curriculum areas must also be compensated for. So the degree of detail within each classification is much broader than at undergraduate level, and the level of abstraction is tailored to what adolescent students are able readily to process.

The same processes of recontextualization apply again at the junior secondary level, with significant differences. At this stage, students are just learning to read and reproduce scientific writing, many of them for the first time. These forms of written English are very different from the forms that most junior students are familiar with, and they are used to express complex chains of reasoning and classification that are remote from the students' everyday experience. So the pedagogic science that senior secondary students learn is once again recontextualized for a different set of educational conditions. Nevertheless, the organization and detail of the science that junior secondary students learn must give them a foundation for progression to the senior level, or the apprenticeship sequence will fall down.

This brings in another factor in junior secondary science – the fact that only a minority of students go on to senior science for matriculation. Part of the pedagogic function of junior science is to sort out this minority of 'able' students from the rest, and to give them the curriculum content required for entry to senior science. The curriculum given to the remaining majority has different goals which are related more to the needs of a Fordist economy for less highly skilled workers and to educational ideas promulgated in Australia since the 1970s known as 'progressivism'.

Bernstein defines pedagogic discourse as 'a recontextualising principle, which transforms the actual into the virtual or imaginary . . . a signifier for something other than itself' (1990: 183). Pedagogic discourse, in this model, consists of two general components: *instructional discourse*, which transmits 'specialized competences', and *regulative discourse*, which transmits 'principles of order, relation, and identity'. Bernstein insists that regulative discourse is dominant, and that instructional discourse is 'embedded' in it. The nature of this recontextualizing principle is the concern of this chapter. Our contention is that the multiple demands on the education system to provide stratified specializations for Fordist economies are what generates the recontextualizing principle, whether the dominant pedagogic theory is 'traditional' or 'progressive'. The stratified acquisition of specialized competences, professional, vocational or manual, depends on students' positioning in regulative discourse. In particular, it depends on the degree to which they are able to identify with the instructional discourses of science. In other words, the degree to which the features of these discourses resonate with students' subjective experience of natural and social reality is likely to influence how meaningful it is to them.

### Science recontextualized as production: levels of industry

Scientific discourse produced at the research level is not only translated into educational curriculum. Its primary function is to be applied to industrial contexts – to be translated into economic production. Industrial development continually demands new ways of producing material goods and services, and it is the role of the research scientist to provide industry with new processes – chemical, physical, biological – that can be applied to production of goods and services. These new processes are developed into industrial applications by the next level of scientist – applied scientists and engineers – who design products and manage the processes of manufacture. There is then a demand for a stratum of trained technicians to construct the manufacturing plant, maintain the machinery and supervise the workers who operate the machinery. This latter group of machine operators may have trades or on-the-job training, and if so they may be responsible for an area of production and possibly for a group of other operators who are not so highly trained. The last group are the process worker stratum whose jobs are rapidly disappearing in post-Fordist economies.

Each of these strata of manufacturing workers has different degrees of training in science and technology. Each stage of training, as we have seen, is related both to the preceding training stage and to a level in the industrial hierarchy. The relationship between the stages of the educational sequence and the levels in the industrial hierarchy can be interpreted in terms of supply and demand. Manufacturing industry demands work to be carried out with different levels of technical specialization, and the educational sequence supplies workers with appropriate levels of training in science and technology. These correspondences, between the demands of industry for workers trained to various levels, and the jumping-off points in the science education sequence, are illustrated in Figure 2.1.

Note that there is a direct relationship between science training and scientific work roles only at the tertiary level, and that senior secondary science is an explicit training ground for matriculation into the professions. Both the subject matter – the 'content' – and the scientific method – the 'process' – of the tertiary and senior secondary curricula are directly related to the demands of a science oriented profession. On the other hand, the relationship between the *bottom* two jumping-off points – at the end and in the middle of junior secondary – and the jobs that students go into is only indirect. These students are generally not going on to professions where scientific knowledge and method are required. The content of the secondary science curriculum has no direct relationship to these students' future needs. However, our research into the language of science in school and industry has shown that the junior secondary curriculum may be equally functional with respect to industrial vocations as it is to the industrial professions – although less directly and less obviously because the content itself is not directly related.

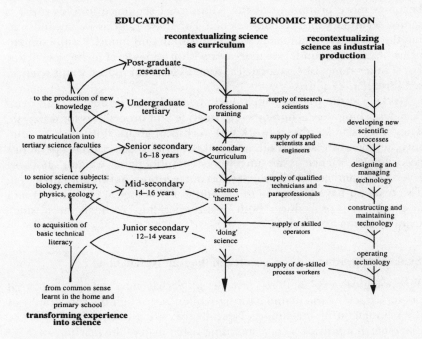

**Figure 2.1** Stages in science education and levels in industry (from Rose *et al.* 1992)

What is carried over from the junior stages of secondary science to industrial vocations is an orientation to technical literacy. Text types employed in junior secondary science textbooks, such as explanations, reports and procedures, are closely related to text types used in non-professional industrial vocations. As well, the features of grammar that encode these genres are closely related between junior secondary science texts and non-professional industry texts. This finding represents a modification of Bernstein's contention that 'recontextualising rules . . . exclude manual discourse from [education's] dominant modalities' (1990: 203). Rather, there are intermediate stages between 'mental' and 'manual' occupations and their discourses, and the need to accommodate training for these intermediate occupations contributes to the forms of recontextualizing rules of pedagogic discourse, at least in the science classroom.

The pivotal stage in a science education is in junior secondary school. It is here that many students meet the features of scientific discourse for the first time, and it is at this point that they are evaluated and streamed towards different specializations, depending on their level of acquisition of scientific literacy: as matriculation candidates, as technical tradespeople, or as manual workers. The technological English used in technical vocations is similar to much of the writing that students meet in the first stages of junior secondary science, while scientific English gradually becomes more prominent as the educational sequence unfolds towards senior secondary and tertiary science. For these reasons we are illustrating the discursive relations between education and industry with comparisons of junior secondary science texts with trades-level technology texts. For a fuller range of text analyses from all levels of industry and science, see Rose *et al.* (1992).

Workers at the trades/skilled operator level must be able to read manuals describing the technology they operate and procedures for doing so. They must also be able to work with technical abstractions such as pressure, temperature and so on, and make decisions about their operations accordingly. Science is an increasing component of training at these levels, and familiarity with science discourse a prerequisite for entry to it. The texts we have chosen here include a technological explanation and a conditional procedure, both from operating manuals in a steel-manufacturing enterprise.

## Explaining production systems: technological explanations

Technological explanations provide a 'verbal map' of an industrial process, tracking the manufacturing sequence through the topography of the manufacturing machinery. Typically they are accompanied by a set of diagrams that provide a corresponding visual map of the machinery.

The goal of this genre is to enable skilled operators to perform complex tasks involving informed decisions by giving them information about the manufacturing technology. These operators are required to intervene at certain points in the manufacturing sequence, and the technological explanation is accompanied by written procedures which set out the steps for doing so.

Technological explanations and their accompanying procedures typically occur as part of manuals which describe the composition and operation of plant and equipment. The text we will examine here is from one such manual describing the gas cleaning system in a blast furnace operated by the Australian manufacturing and mining company BHP. BHP's *No. 4 Blast Furnace Gas Cleaning System Manual* is organized as a composition taxonomy of the stages of machinery that makes up the system. Each chapter in the manual consists of a technological explanation describing the parts and operation of one of the sections of the system:

1.0 Introduction
2.0 Dustcatcher
3.0 Brassert
4.0 Septum Valve
5.0 Semi-clean Gas Main
6.0 Precipitators
7.0 Goggle Valves
8.0 Effluent System

To identify the structure and grammatical resources used in a technological explanation, we will look at an extract from chapter '3.0 Brassert'. In the transcript below, marked Themes (realized in prepositional phrases and dependent clauses) are in bold-face type. Each sentence (i.e. clause complex) in this extract is numbered 1, 2, 3, . . . Dependency relations within each clause complex are analysed as paratactic 1, 2, . . . or hypotactic α, β, γ, . . .

### Text 1: Brassert

1      The brassert washer is the 2nd mechanism used in the No. 4 BF gas cleaning system.

2      It is located between the dustcatcher and the electrostatic precipitators.

3      The main function of the brassert is [[to cool down the blast furnace gas [[discharged from the furnace [[and to also partially remove dust and grit from the gas]] ]] ]].

4 β      **To achieve this increased gas cleanliness,**
  α      the gas must pass through the brassert at a reasonably slow velocity.
5      Thus, the semi clean gas enters the bottom section of the brassert via a main from the dustcatcher.

6 β      **Before the gas enters the brassert,**
  α      it is cleaned by 16 water sprays (8 in each ring main)

γ   located on the neck of the main.
7   The gas and water then flow into the brassert.
8   The gas then travels from the bottom of the brassert to the top and out into the precipitators via the septum valves.

9   **Inside the brassert** two ring mains (top and bottom sprays) supply salt water to the brassert sprays.
    . . .
10  1   The water sprays in the brassert cools the gas stream
    2   and also combines with the gas, dust, etc.,
    3   and precipitates (by gravity) at the base of the brassert.
11  α   The mud precipitated is periodically removed by the brassert dump valves
    β   located at the base of the brassert.

(from Abeysingha 1991)

The explanation represents the unfolding manufacturing process as a sequence of material processes which follow one after the other, linked by temporal succession, reason or purpose. This type of activity sequence closely resembles those found in scientific explanations described by Wignell *et al.* as an 'implication sequence', in which 'each step through the sequence implies what has gone before' (1992: 157); in other words, each step is an effect or outcome of preceding steps. In the technological explanation, material processes typically unfold in concrete spatial locations, and each of these locations (realized as prepositional phrases) realizes a new part of the manufacturing technology. The explanatory functions of the technological explanation are simultaneously to explain the manufacturing process as an activity sequence and to build up the composition taxonomy of the manufacturing technology.

## Textual organization: Theme and New

The unfolding of the implication sequence and the construction of a composition taxonomy of the technology are organized by the resources of the textual metafunction. The following re-presentation of the procedure indicates the elements functioning as Theme in each clause (underline), and those functioning as New information (italics). Marked Themes, i.e. prepositional phrases or dependent clauses in thematic position, are in bold face.

1   <u>The brassert washer</u> is the *2nd mechanism used in the No. 4 BF gas cleaning system.*
2   <u>It</u> is located between *the dustcatcher and the electrostatic precipitators.*
3   <u>The main function of the brassert</u> is *to cool down the blast furnace gas discharged from the furnace and to also partially remove dust and grit from the gas.*

4 β   **To achieve this increased gas cleanliness,**
α   the gas must pass through the brassert *at a reasonably slow velocity.*
5   Thus, the semi clean gas enters *the bottom section of the brassert via a main from the dustcatcher.*
6 β   **Before the gas enters the brassert,**
α   it is cleaned by *16 water sprays*
γ   located *on the neck of the main.*
7   The gas and water then flow *into the brassert.*
8   The gas then travels *from the bottom of the brassert to the top and out into the precipitators via the septum valves.*
9   **Inside the brassert** two ring mains (top and bottom sprays) supply *salt water to the brassert sprays.*
10 1   The water sprays in the brassert cools *the gas stream*
2   and also combines *with the gas, dust, etc.,*
3   and precipitates (by gravity) *at the base of the brassert.*
11 α   The mud precipitated is periodically removed *by the brassert dump valves*
β   located *at the base of the brassert.*

Topical Themes are generally the brassert itself, or the gas, while News generally foreground parts of the technology, mostly expressed as circumstances of Location. The exceptions are 4β, 10 and 11, in which the New information from the preceding clauses is picked up and re-presented as Themes.

While elements known to the reader, the brassert, the gas and so on, are starting points for each clause, those elements that are unknown, the technology components to which the reader must pay attention, are focused on in final position of each clause as News. These components occurring as News are set out in the following list.

the No. 4 BF gas cleaning system
the dustcatcher and the electrostatic precipitators
the furnace
the bottom section of the brassert via a main from the dustcatcher
16 water sprays
the neck of the main
the bottom of the brassert
the top
the precipitators
the septum valves
the brassert sprays
the base of the brassert
the brassert dump valves

## Marked Themes and text staging

Because the function of a technological explanation is to lead the reader through the manufacturing technology, the staging of the text corresponds to the stages in the manufacturing process. In this text there are four stages, the second, third and fourth of which are announced by a marked Theme – either a dependent clause realizing time or purpose (i.e. enhancing), or a prepositional phrase realizing spatial location (also enhancing):

| stage | marked Theme | logical relation | type of structure |
|---|---|---|---|
| 2 | To achieve this increased gas cleanliness, | purpose | dependent clause |
| 3 | Before the gas enters the brassert, | succession | dependent clause |
| 4 | Inside the brassert | location | prepositional phrase |

## Ideational metaphor and Theme/New structure

Ideational metaphor is an essential resource in technical writing for organizing text as sequences of messages that predict and accumulate information as they go. Nominalization enables clauses to be reconstrued as participants of other clauses, so that they may be re-packaged as Theme or New, particularly in relational clauses (Halliday and Martin 1992: 54 ff.).

While most of the technological explanation is made up of congruent material processes involving concrete things in concrete locations, the first three clauses differ. These constitute the 'macro-Theme' of the text, which predicts the messages to follow (for macro-Theme see Martin 1992, traditionally the 'introduction'). Their experiential elements include:

(1) the classification of the brassert washer in the gas cleaning system;
(2) its physical location; and
(3) its function in the system.

These are expressed as relational identifying clauses, the most common clause type in technical writing, particularly report writing, of which this macro-Theme is a typical example. In 2 and 3, embedded clauses function as participants, while in 3 the other participant is an abstraction *the main function of the brassert*.

| 1 | The brassert washer | is | the 2nd mechanism [[used in the No. 4 BF gas cleaning system]]. |
|---|---|---|---|
| | Token | Pr | Value |
| 2 | It | is | [[located between the dustcatcher and the electrostatic precipitators]]. |
| | Token | Pr | Value |
| 3 | The main function of the brassert | is | [[to cool down the blast furnace gas [[discharged from the furnace]] and [[to also partially remove dust and grit from the gas]] ]] ]] |
| | Value | Pr | Token |

In each clause the brassert is Theme, while its classification, location and function are New information, located in the Rheme. This Theme/New pattern is changed in the following clause 4β, which picks up the Rheme of clause 3 and further nominalizes it, so that it can function as Theme of a hypotactic clause complex.

| 4β   To achieve this increased gas cleanliness    xα    the gas must pass through the brassert . . . | |
|---|---|
| Theme | New |

Figure 2.2 illustrates how the congruent wording of the material clause is 'translated' into the metaphorical wording of the nominal group. (1) the adverb *partially* becomes an Epithet *increased,* (2) the Location *from the gas* becomes a Classifier *gas,* and (3) the Process plus Goal *remove dust and grit* becomes a Thing *cleanliness.* The logical relation between clauses 3 and 4 is one of purpose. It links the statement of function in 3, *to partially remove dust and grit from the gas,* to the activity sequence that starts with clause 4α. In other words, the activity sequence follows logically as effect follows intention. In doing so it sets up an expectation for whole text as an implication sequence.

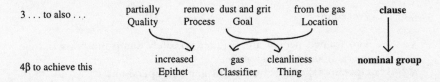

**Figure 2.2** Clause translated into nominal group

Note that the resource of nominalization is also employed in the last step of the procedure, with the process of 'precipitating' embedded as Qualifier to 'the mud'. Here it serves to distil information presented in three clauses, 10.1–3, and re-presents it as Theme of 11. The New information presented in this penultimate clause 11α assigns agency to 'the brassert dump valves'. This follows the general transitivity pattern (illustrated in Figure 2.5) of 'agentive technology' acting on the gas, etc. as Medium. Sentence 11 is the macro-New of the text, its 'point of arrival'.

This is the point at which the reader is required to intervene in the manufacturing sequence, to operate the brassert dump valves. The agency of the technology here becomes conflated with the agency of its human operator. Both person and machine are elements of the institutional context of steel production, and within this context the agency of each is determined not by themselves, but by the power of the institution to inform and command. The power to inform is realized in the technological explanation, while the power to command is realized in its accompanying procedures.

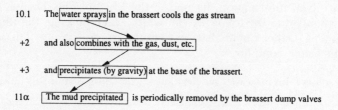

**Figure 2.3** Distilling information by nominalizing

Thus the macro-New of the technological explanation is picked up as the macro-Theme of a procedure. The following is a brief extract from the procedure enabling readers to operate the brassert dump valves, in which the macro-Theme is expressed under '1.0 Purpose'.

**Text 2: Dumping brassert washer**

**1.0      Purpose**
            The purpose of this procedure is to establish or outline the steps required in dumping the brassert washer under normal conditions. `
. . .
**5.0      Procedure**
. . .
5.2        Two trained people are required to safely dump the brassert (one operator and one gas watcher).
5.3        Operators should liaise with the general supervisor
. . .        (steps in the procedure)

                                                        (from Abeysingha 1991)

Here the institutional roles of the readers are made explicit, thematized in 5.2 as *Two trained people.* Their status in the institution is generalized in this clause by explicitly objective obligation *are required to,* locating the source of the command in the institutional context. The operators' position in the chain of command is then specified in 5.3 with implicitly objective obligation *should liaise with the general supervisor,* before the steps they are required to perform are spelled out. We will return to this discussion of institutional role relations following analysis of the experiential and logical features of the technological explanation.

**Tracking the product through the technology: implication sequences**

The activity sequence of technological production is realized as a succession of material processes linked by temporal and causal relations. The circumstances of Location occurring as News in each clause construe a composition taxonomy of the technology. Figure 2.4 represents the composition taxonomy that is constructed by the text.

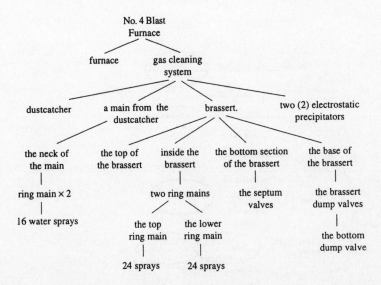

**Figure 2.4** Composition taxonomy of the blast furnace gas cleaning system

Figure 2.5 attempts to capture the way the implication sequence construes the manufacturing process. Most processes are material ones of movement, and these are represented by arrows leading from the Actor (on the left) to a Goal and/or circumstance of Location (in bold outline on the right); effective processes are indicated by bold lines. Logical relations are represented by curved lines, linking each figure to the next. The conjunctions that realize these relations are in bold type, with implicit conjunctions in parentheses. The types of logical relations they realize are set out to the left. The gas is identified by shading.

As far as transitivity roles are concerned, the gas is Actor in middle (non-effective) clauses, while elements of the technology, the brassert, water sprays and the brassert dump valves are agentive Actors in effective clauses, acting on the gas, water and dust. Other elements of the technology, from, through, into and at which these processes occur, are realized by circumstances of Location.

Logical relations between each step in the sequence are generally temporal, but several are modulated by purpose or reason. Only two of these causal relations, between steps 3, 4 and 5, are made explicit; the rest must be inferred by the reader. In particular implicit causal relations include:

- three of purpose (Intention^Effect), relating the statement of functions in the macro-Theme to steps 6, 10 and 11, and
- two of reason (Cause^Effect), relating the sequence to the macro-New of the text.

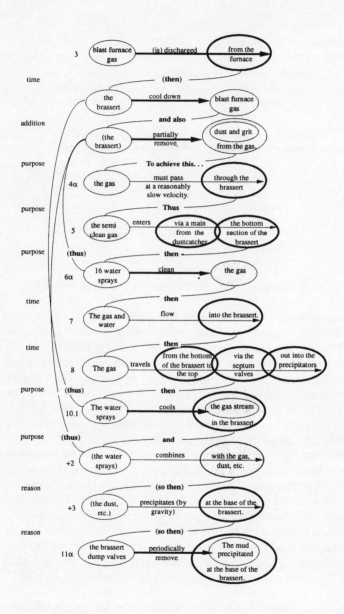

**Figure 2.5** Brassert washer implication sequence

While the macro-Theme of the technological explanation predicts the implication sequence by means of purpose, the macro-New distils it as implicit reason. The latter implicitly encodes an obligatory relation between the manufacturing sequence and its effect as 'mud precipitated'. The obligation on the reader to act at this point is then made explicit in the accompanying procedure. These two manifestations of obligation, as cause and command, are both projected by the institutional context, expressed in instructional manuals.

Simple procedures typically express explicit obligation on the reader by means of sequences of commands in imperative mood. But the implicitness of causality in the technological explanation is an expression of another set of tenor relations. Here readers are expected to be able to interpret obligatory relations between events, and their judgement of and role in the events. The following discussion of secondary school science learning suggests possible contexts in which students learn to identify the logic of causality in technical English.

## Explaining natural systems: scientific explanations

We have identified the general textual, ideational and interpersonal features of technological explanations which are common at the trades and skilled-operator level of industry. Traditionally workers at these levels completed no more than the first three or four years of secondary schooling before they commenced employment or workplace-based training. Yet to be able to operate and maintain the level of technology described in such procedures, and to recognize their roles in them, they must be able to read the specialized manuals which are composed of such explanations. Our question is how they learn to do so.

In our comparative study of workplace and secondary science texts, we found that technological implication sequences are closely related to similar sequences in scientific explanations, common in junior secondary science textbooks. The following is an example of a scientific explanation from Wignell *et al.* (1992).

### Text 3: Alluvial fans

| | | |
|---|---|---|
| 1 | | After flash floods, desert streams [[flowing from upland areas]] carry heavy loads of silt, sand and rock fragments. |
| 2 | β | As they reach the flatter area of desert basins, |
| | α1 | they lose speed |
| | 2 | and their waters may also soak quickly into the basin floor. |
| 3 | | The streams then drop their loads, the heaviest materials first – the stones – then the sand and finally the silt. |
| 4 | β | Choked by their own deposits, |
| | αα | these short lived streams frequently divide into a maze of channels, |
| | β | spreading their load in all directions. |
| 5 | | In time fan or cone shaped deposits of gravel, sand, silt and clay are |

formed around each valley or canyon outlet.
6           These are called alluvial fans.

(from Sale *et al.* 1980)

This text exhibits similar resources to the technological explanation for tracking something – in this case *desert streams* through time and space.

(1) Textual organization: (a) one participant, *streams*, is tracked, typically in Theme position in most clauses; (b) Locations generally occur as News; (c) stages of the sequence are announced by marked Themes, i.e. enhancing dependent clauses or prepositional phrases.
(2) Field construction: (a) there is a causally related implication sequence of material and relational processes of movement; (b) one element of the field, *streams*, is Actor in most processes; (c) the sequential movements of this Actor are tracked *from*, *in*, *into* and *around* circumstances of Location in space, construing a composition taxonomy of the landscape.
(3) Tenor relations: (a) the relation between writer and reader is implicitly one of apprenticeship, mediated by the field, with *streams* as Subject of each clause; (b) causal relations between each step in the sequence are left implicit for the apprentice to interpret for herself.

## Textual organization

The following re-presentation of the explanation identifies Themes, marked Themes and News.

1           **After flash floods**, desert streams [[flowing from upland areas]] carry *heavy loads of silt, sand and rock fragments.*
2    β      **As they reach *the flatter area of desert basins*,**
     α1     they lose speed
     2      and their waters may also soak quickly *into the basin floor.*
3           The streams then drop *their loads, the heaviest materials first – the stones – then the sand and finally the silt.*
4    β      **Choked by *their own deposits*,**
     αα     these short lived streams frequently divide *into a maze of channels,*
     β      spreading *their load in all directions.*
5           **In time** fan or cone shaped deposits of gravel, sand, silt and clay are formed *around each valley or canyon outlet.*
6           These are called *alluvial fans.*

The analysis makes it clear that streams (and their waters) are Theme of most clauses, while the loads carried by the streams, or the Locations through which they flow, are News. These are presented in the following list.

heavy loads of silt, sand and rock fragments

the flatter area of desert basins
the basin floor
their loads, the heaviest materials first – the stones – then the sand and
    finally the silt
their own deposits
a maze of channels
their load in all directions
each valley or canyon outlet
alluvial fans

The final New element, *alluvial fans*, combines the two strands occurring as News in the preceding clauses, the streams' loads, and elements of the landscape. By the end of the text, 'their loads' have become a landscape feature named by a technical term. While flash floods, streams and their load is macro-Theme of the text, its macro-New is the formation of alluvial fans – a technical term that fits into the classification system of the scientific field. This definition is achieved by means of an identifying relational clause, with the technical term as its New.

| 6 | These (fan or cone shaped deposits of gravel, sand, silt and clay) | are called | alluvial fans |
|---|---|---|---|
| | Value/Theme | Process | Token/New |

This is comparable with the technological explanation in which 'the function of the brassert . . . to remove dust and grit from the gas' is macro-Theme, and removing 'the mud precipitated' is macro-New. The difference is that one explains a natural sequence so the reader knows what a technical term refers to, while the other explains a technological sequence so the reader knows what action to perform.

Each stage of the natural sequence is clearly indicated, as in the procedure, by temporal circumstances or dependent clauses, as marked Themes. And at each of these temporal stages a new stage of the process occurs.

| marked Themes | News |
|---|---|
| After flash floods | desert streams . . . carry heavy loads |
| As they reach the flatter area of desert basins | . . . drop their loads |
| Choked by their own deposits | . . . spreading their load |
| In time | . . . alluvial fans |

**Field construction**

Since the scientific explanation is an explanation of a natural sequence, each step is related (implicitly) by reason, rather than purpose. And because the function of the science explanation genre is to teach about landscape formation, the circumstances are spatial locations. While not as significant as in the technological explanation they do construe a composition taxonomy of elements of a landscape through which desert streams flow, and transform as they do so. Figure 2.6 interprets this composition taxonomy.

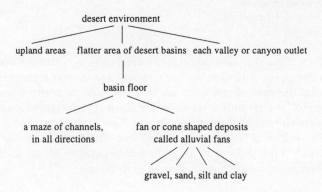

**Figure 2.6** Composition taxonomy of desert streams' environment

The activity sequence is unpacked in Figure 2.7, using the same conventions as with the technological explanation. Again Actors are circled to the right, and these are 'streams' in almost every case. Circumstances of Location are circled in heavy lines, and the loads that streams carry, and the deposits they form, are shaded.

This school science explanation has a simpler logical structure than the technological explanation, with relations between adjacent clauses only. However, the majority of causal relations are similarly implicit. As with the procedure they can only be inferred if the reader recognizes the genre as an implicational explanation, and knows that it is an answer to a 'why' question in a scientific field. This recognition enables the overall pattern of logical relations to be inferred as *reason*.

### The logic of cause and institutional role relations

The implicit causality in both technological and science explanations must be recognized by the reader for the logic of the texts to be comprehensible. Causality is a domain of English grammar in which ideational and interpersonal meanings come together. Martin (1992) interprets causal/conditional relations in English along interpersonal lines, as *modulating* and *modalizing* relations of temporal succession between events; that is, they incorporate the interpersonal resources of MODALITY into the logical system of INTERDEPENDENCY. These metafunctional relationships are outlined in Table 2.1.

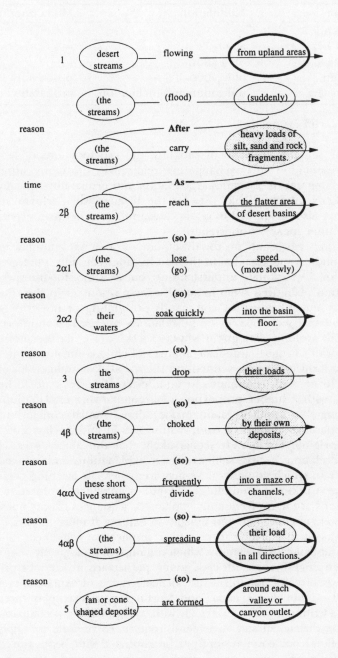

**Figure 2.7** Activity sequence represented in desert streams

**Table 2.1** Consequential logic and modality

| Logical relation | Modulation | Modalization |
|---|---|---|
| Time (when, while) | – | – |
| Manner (thus, by) | ability | – |
| Reason (so, because) | obligation | – |
| Condition (then, if) | obligation | probability |
| Purpose (so that) | obligation and inclination | probability |

*Source:* from Martin (1992: 94)

Thus, in the semantic domain of causality, the two functions of language as representation and exchange are realized in the same causal motif: whereas degrees of obligation, inclination and probability typically **grade** a speaker's intention that s/he or the listener will perform an action, they may also be applied to grade causal relations between events that involve neither speaker nor listener.

Painter's (1994) case study on the development of causal grammar in middle-class children suggests that in the first instance causality 'emerged not as a tool for dispassionate understanding, but as a tool for interpersonal negotiation'. Children seem to acquire these resources in the context of reasons and purposes for commands prohibiting or prescribing behaviours, and that sequences of causal relations emerge first in efforts to control and prolong dialogue ('why? ... why? ...'). Furthermore, Hasan and Cloran's (1990) large-scale analyses of child control strategies reveal significant differences dependent on the social class and gender of the children. In general, commands in middle-class families tend to be more implicit, with a higher proportion of accompanying explanations than in working-class families. Malin (1990) draws similar conclusions from her comparative analysis of control strategies in middle-class European and Aboriginal families. It seems likely that the ability to read implicit causal relations in texts such as science explanations is influenced by the manner in which students have acquired them in learning their mother tongue. Children of middle-class families, in which prohibitions and prescriptions are more frequently explained, sequences of why questions and answers encouraged, and obligation expressed more implicitly, may be advantaged in learning to recognize implication sequences and interpret the implicit causal relations which organize them logically.

In the written English of middle-class adults, particularly in scientific discourse, the lexis of cause realizes a vast, delicate range of expressions of obligation and evidentiality. Halliday and Martin (1992) exemplify these from Maxwell's writing in 1881, externally with 'cause, lead to, accompany, follow, produce, dictate, stimulate, demand, require, correspond to, apply to, arise from, flow from, cover, result from, be associated with, be measured by', and internally with 'prove, show, predict, illustrate, suggest, attest, be explained by, indicate, confirm'. Such elaborate resources for expressing cause mirror the elaborate resources for expressing modality that have evolved in modern English to facilitate the continual negotiation of status and solidarity that is a feature of middle-class discourse for example, and academic discourse in particular.

While the ability to interpret logical relations has traditionally been interpreted in cognitive psychological terms, in fact there appears to be a close link between degree of identification within the role structures of an institutional network, and understanding of the logic of cause expressed in the texts generated by the institution.

## Making decisions: conditional procedures

Written workplace procedures may become very complex when operators need to make choices about potential courses of action that depend on multiple variables in the manufacturing process. At each point in such a procedure, there are a number of possible decisions to take. In other words, the action the operator takes depends on a number of conditions. This type of procedure has been labelled a **conditional procedure**.

As in the technological explanation and scientific explanation, conditional procedures depend on an interplay between logical and textual organization. However, in the latter, the interweaving of these two metafunctions becomes even more critical, since the activity sequence follows a number of pathways simultaneously.

To achieve this, conditional clauses are presented as marked Themes of hypotactic clause complexes, announcing a new stage in the procedure – a point at which a decision must be made before the task can continue. These decisions depend on information presented in the opening sentences of the procedure.

Potential courses of action are then realized as a sequence of commands, presented as New elements in the clause complex. For each stage in the following conditional procedure, there are up to three possible courses of action. These are numbered i, ii, iii, but the logical meaning of the numbers is actually **variation** 'either . . . or'.

### Text 4: Stop gas flow through precipitator

5.3.1　　Check the number of the tar precipitators on line to assure an uninterrupted gas flow. Currently four (4) tar precipitators are the minimum number that have to be on line to maintain an acceptable back pressure range of 8–14 kPa.

If after this precipitator is isolated:
i.　　　　There will be fewer than four (4) tar precipitators in operation, go to step 5.3.2.
ii.　　　　There are four (4) or more tar precipitators in operation, go to step 5.3.3.

5.3.2       Open tar precipitators by pass gas valve (5 or 6 turns).
5.3.3       Close the inlet gas valve slowly,
            and tag, 'OUT OF SERVICE' in two positions . . .
If when the precipitator by pass gas valve is open:
i.          Pressure range is OK,
            go to step 5.3.7
ii.         Pressure range is too high,
            go to step 5.3.5
iii.        Pressure range is too low,
            go to step 5.3.6.
5.3.5       Open the precipitator by pass gas valve
            until exhauster back pressure is in range.
5.3.6       Close tar precipitator by pass gas valve
            until exhauster back pressure is in range.
5.3.7       Close the outlet gas valve slowly,
            and tag, 'OUT OF SERVICE' in two positions . . .

(from BHP Coke Ovens By Products Dept 1991)

## Announcing decision points: logical relations as marked Themes

Text 4 begins with a command, qualified by a *purpose* for why this task must be done:

5.3.1  α   Check the number of the tar precipitators on line
       β   to assure an uninterrupted gas flow.

An operator at this level has to understand the effect of her actions on the technology, and thus the purpose for each step in the procedure. This is followed by a statement giving the two pieces of information that are needed to decide the next course of action in the procedure.

Currently four (4) tar precipitators are the minimum number [[that have to be on line to maintain an acceptable back pressure range of 8–14 kPa]].

This clause picks up the New information of 5.3.1α, *the number of the tar precipitators on line*, and re-presents it as Theme, specifying *the minimum number*. It then presents the reason for this number as New, specifying a *back pressure range* which the operator must monitor, employing the nom-inalizing resource of an embedded clause complex. The number of tar precipitators is critical for the first set of decisions to follow, while the pressure range is critical for the second set of decisions.

The first decision point depends on a particular action having been completed, *after this precipitator is isolated*. It begins with this provision, but is preceded with a conditional conjunction:

α     **If** <<**after** this precipitator is isolated>>
ββ    there will be fewer than four tar precipitators in operation,
βα    go to step 5.3.2.

In the complex thematic structure of this clause complex, the conjunction **if** is the starting point for the whole message. However the 'after' clause (α) must also be marked Theme because its completion is the starting point for the following pair of choices. To achieve this, it is nested within the 'if' clause (ββ), so that the combination of the two becomes Theme for the message as a whole, with the command *go to step 5.3.2* presented as its New (βα). The condition of completed action is Theme, and the command is New, as illustrated in Figure 2.8. But logically, the conjunction **if** actually relates clause ββ to βα, while **after** relates α to ββ. The message could have read:

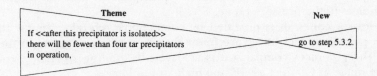

**Figure 2.8** Nested β clause complex as marked Theme

α      **After** this precipitator is isolated,
ββ     **if** there will be fewer than four tar precipitators in operation,
α      go to step 5.3.2.

But in this version, the conditional **if** is not the starting point. This condition refers to two choices, which lead to two alternative commands:

i    β      (**either if**) there will be fewer than four (4) tar precipitators in operation,
     α      go to step 5.3.2
ii   β      (**or if**) there are four (4) or more tar precipitators in operation,
     α      go to step 5.3.3.

By making the conjunction **if** the starting point for the whole message, the writer has emphasized the condition as the point of departure for the message. The meaning of this marked Theme is firstly 'I'm going to give you a choice', and secondly 'you've already isolated this precipitator'.

The second decision point depends on the outcome of the first, specifically that *step 5.3.2* has been completed, *when the precipitator by pass gas valve is open*. It also is announced by the conditional **if** as starting point. This conditional clause complex gives three alternatives for action:

      α      **If** <<when the precipitator by pass gas valve is open>>:
i    ββ     (**either**) pressure range is OK,
     α1     go to step 5.3.7
ii   2β     (**or**) pressure range is too high,
     α      go to step 5.3.5
iii  3β     (**or**) pressure range is too low,
     α      go to step 5.3.6.

## Logical relations, lexical cohesion and comparative reference

To this point we have examined the logical relations and textual organization of Text 4 step by step. We can now expand our point of view to cover
the text as a whole, to discover how each step is related to the whole.
There are two more sets of resources that achieve this, lexical cohesion in
combination with comparative reference.

As we mentioned earlier, the <u>minimum number of tar precipitators</u>,
and the <u>acceptable back pressure range</u> were presented in the text's
macro-Theme. These constitute the circumstances for the following decisions. The two sets of choices refer back to these by means of **repetition**,
the first pair of choices to the number of precipitators, and the second
three choices to the pressure range.

This lexical cohesion is qualified by comparative reference items. In
the first pair of choices, these are **fewer than** in contrast to **more**. In the
second three choices comparison is achieved by <u>grading Attributes</u> (of
pressure range as Carrier) as **OK**, **too high**, or **too low**.

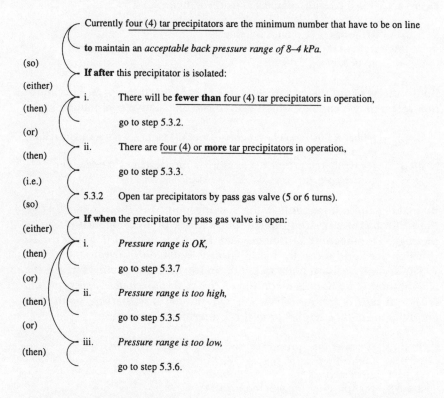

Currently <u>four (4) tar precipitators</u> are the minimum number that have to be on line
**to** maintain an *acceptable back pressure range of 8–4 kPa.*

(so)

(either)       **If after** this precipitator is isolated:

(then)         i.       There will be **fewer than** four (4) tar precipitators in operation,

(or)                    go to step 5.3.2.

(then)         ii.      There are four (4) or **more** tar precipitators in operation,

(i.e.)                  go to step 5.3.3.

(so)           5.3.2    Open tar precipitators by pass gas valve (5 or 6 turns).

(either)       **If when** the precipitator by pass gas valve is open:

(then)         i.       *Pressure range is OK,*

(or)                    go to step 5.3.7

(then)         ii.      *Pressure range is too high,*

(or)                    go to step 5.3.5

(then)         iii.     *Pressure range is too low,*

                        go to step 5.3.6.

**Figure 2.9** Conjunction, lexical cohesion and comparative reference in Text 4

The overall pattern of logical relations, lexical cohesion and comparative reference is presented in Figure 2.9. Because its logical structure is a sequence of conditions and alternatives, it is illustrated differently from the implication sequences in Texts 1 and 3. In Figure 2.9, implicit conjunctions are set out to the left, with curved lines indicating relations, while explicit conjunctions are in bold. Lexical relations are indicated by underlining for number of <u>tar precipitators</u>, and italics for *pressure range*. Comparative reference items are also in bold type.

There are also longer implicit relations of purpose (not shown above), from the last and second last commands, back to the second line – the function of steps 5.3.5 and 5.3.6 being to 'maintain an acceptable back pressure range'. The text here is only an extract from a much longer conditional procedure which repeats the same pattern over and over again. It is a common type of procedure in workplaces where operators need to make decisions about alternative possible actions.

## Complex conditional relations in secondary science texts

Although the complex conditional relations in a conditional procedure are remote from everyday spoken English, and may be difficult to follow, similar complexity of conditions is a common feature of secondary school science texts, at junior and senior levels. The genres where these types of conditions are found are explanations of abstract physical phenomena, such as pressure, upthrust in a fluid, flotation, etc. The following is an extract from one such explanation, from a unit on fluid mechanics from an Australian secondary science textbook. We will call this genre a **conditional explanation**.

### Text 5: Buoyancy and density

. . .

| | | |
|---|---|---|
| 1 | β | If the object is completely submerged |
| | α | it displaces its own volume of fluid. |
| 2 | | The weight of displaced fluid, and therefore the upthrust, will depend on the density of the fluid. |
| 3 | β | If the density of the fluid is less than the average density of the object, |
| | α1 | the weight of the displaced fluid will be less than the weight of the object |
| | 2 | and the object will sink. |
| 4 | β | If, on the other hand, the density of the fluid is greater than the average density of the object, |
| | α | the weight of the displaced fluid will therefore exceed the weight of the object. |
| 5 | α | The net upward force will then cause the object to rise to the surface |
| | β | where it will float. |

(from Heading *et al.* 1972)

### Textual organization and logical relations; lexical cohesion and comparative reference

As with the conditional procedure, this text depends on the interplay of logical relations with Theme/New structure, and of lexical cohesion with comparative reference.

To begin with, the distilling of information through nominalization, which we noted in the macro-New of the technological explanation ('the mud precipitated'), is reflected here in the macro-Theme. The lexical content of sentence 1 is nominalized and re-presented as Theme in 2, *The weight of displaced fluid*, except that the abstract entity 'volume' is replaced by its co-hyponym, 'weight', and a third co-hyponym 'upthrust'. These contrastive lexical relations lend textual prominence to the Theme, fore-grounding the message as 'Now I'm talking about <u>weight</u> and <u>upthrust</u> (as opposed to <u>volume</u>)'.

The fourth co-hyponym, 'density', is then presented as New in 2. This in turn is picked up in the marked Themes of 3 and 4, as the background condition for the following alternatives. As in the conditional procedure, alternatives are expressed as conditional clauses in marked Theme position, that organize the text in three stages:

| | | |
|---|---|---|
| 1 | β | **If** the object is completely submerged |
| 3 | β | **If** the density of the fluid is less than the average density of the object, |
| 4 | β | **If**, on the other hand, the density of the fluid is greater than the average density of the object, |

Between the first stage and the following two, there is an implicit logical relation of exemplification, 'e.g.'. Clause 2 introduces causal relations between three abstract entities '<u>weight</u> . . . therefore . . . <u>upthrust</u>, will depend on . . . <u>density</u>', and this is exemplified by the following two stages, the first example explicitly contrasted with the second, 'on the other hand'. Within each example stage there is an explicit conditional relation 'if', followed by an implicit one of reason, i.e. clause 3 'and (so) . . . sink', clause 5 '(so) then . . . rise to the surface'.

But the stages are also related lexically, and these lexical relations harmonize with the logical relations. Thus the New element of 1β, *completely submerged*, introduces a lexical field which is picked up as New in the first example as a synonym, *sink*, and in the contrasting example as antonyms, *rise to the surface* and *float*.

The general relationship between density and weight, of the object and the fluid, introduced in 2, is exemplified contrastively in the second and third stages, by means of comparative reference. The density and weight of the <u>fluid</u> are Themes of β and α clauses in 3 and 4, while the density and weight of the <u>object</u> are their News. The latter are referred to as **less than**, in contrast to **greater than** and **exceeds**, respectively.

The representation in Figure 2.10 highlights the patterns of logical relations, lexical cohesion and comparative reference. Explicit conjunc-

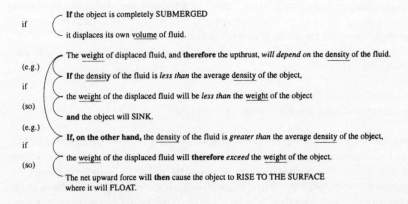

**Figure 2.10** Conjunction, lexical cohesion and comparative reference in Text 5

tions are bold, the lexical group submerge, sink and float are in caps, while the abstract entities are underlined. Implicit conjunctions are bracketed to the left. In general the intricacy of this text is similar to that of the conditional procedure. In both cases the reader is expected to **imagine alternative possible eventualities**. In the science explanation, these imagined events are intended to lead to the students' understanding of an abstract physical relationship – that 'buoyancy' is dependent on 'density'. And the way this understanding is achieved is through the grammatical resource of conditional relations between clauses in tandem with similar Theme/New patterns, and lexical cohesion combined with comparative reference. In the conditional procedure, the imagined events are possible outcomes of actions the operator might take, and similar patterns of interweaving resources are used to create its texture.

Both texts display features of the written mode of English. In these written texts, the grammar is constructing possible worlds that are independent of the immediate context in which they are being read. It enables scientifically literate readers and writers to generalize across different possible contexts, and to construct abstract models of reality. These abstractions can then be translated back into concrete situations, whether it is to make operating decisions, or to design industrial technology.

## Abstract entities

Both the conditional procedure and explanation assume familiarity with abstract entities including gas flow, pressure, volume, weight, upthrust and density. Grammatically these abstract things are modelled on 'mass nouns' such as water, air and so on, and like these are potentially quantifiable by means of measure 'of' structures. Historically they are nominalizations of processes and qualities in common-sense registers, including flowing, pressing, big/little, heavy/light, pushing up, and thick/thin (liquid). But semantically they are only distantly related to these common-sense meanings; they are now terms in technical fields and their meanings are specialized to these registers.

Within the first two sentences of the conditional procedure are two nominalizations:

> an uninterrupted gas flow
> an acceptable back pressure range of 8–14 kPa.

In the first the material process 'gas is flowing' is nominalized so that 'flow' functions as Thing with 'gas' as its Classifier. Within the technical field the second nominal group is lexically cohesive, with 'pressure' a hyponym of 'gas flow'. Pressure is an abstraction deriving from the material process of 'gas pressing'. Nominalizing the process enables it to be identified, judged, classified and quantified in a single nominal group.

| an | acceptable | back | pressure | range | of 8–14 kPa |
|---|---|---|---|---|---|
| Deictic | Epithet | Classifier | Classifier | Thing | Qualifier |

The technical abstraction in the conditional procedure derives from the physical sciences, which have then been applied to the field of technology. To read and carry out this procedure, an operator needs to be able to read instruments that measure *back pressure* and translate what s/he sees into appropriate action. In order to understand the processes that the instruments and figures represent, the operator needs to be able to read the grammar of technical discourse, and must also understand the technical/scientific field which includes the abstract phenomenon of **gas pressure**. This field is first taught in the junior secondary science curriculum. The following is an extract from a junior secondary school text defining gas pressure:

**Text 6: Gas pressure**

| 1 | 1 | Put some lead shot into a small tin |
|---|---|---|
| | 2 | replace the lid |
| | 3α | and then shake the tin about |
| | β | so that you can feel the shot [[rattling or moving about inside [[and knocking against the walls]] ]]. |

| 2 | α | We said that the gas in a closed container is very similar |
|---|---|---|
| | β1 | with its molecules rapidly moving about in all directions |
| | 2 | and knocking against the walls. |

| 3 | 1 | It is in this way [[that a gas in a container exerts an outwards force on the walls of the container]] |
|---|---|---|
| | 2β | or to be more specific |

α    there is a certain force outwards on each unit area of the walls
[[which is the pressure of the gas inside the container]].

(from Messel 1965)

Text 6 begins with a mini-procedure that is intended to link the technical
definition of gas pressure to the students' sensual experience. This concrete event is then compared ('very similar') to an event that cannot be
sensually experienced, the movement of molecules. This does not constitute an explanation of the movement of molecules; it is simply an analogy,
designed for the student to *imagine* the virtual world of molecules, and
identify her own experience with this virtual world that science claims to
be *equally real.*

However, the goal of the text is to arrive at a definition of gas pressure,
and in order to do so it suddenly shifts from the everyday language of a
simple procedure to highly abstract terms such as 'exerts an outwards
force'. Again the relation with common sense/virtual reality is one of *similarity* 'it is in this way', with the abstraction expressed as a causal identifying process, embedded as a projected fact.

From here it leaps to the definition of gas pressure. This is expressed as
an existential clause with an identifying clause embedded in the Existent.
This device presents the whole definition as New information ('a certain
force . . . which is the pressure . . .'). The Token/Value structure of the
definition is paraphrased as follows:

| a certain force outwards on each unit area of the walls | is | the pressure of the gas inside the container |
|---|---|---|
| Value | Pr | Token |

In three steps the text has jumped from sensual reality to virtual reality to
technical definition. However, although it is an extremely common learning sequence in science classrooms, this is not an explanation of gas pressure. The function of the procedure is to *engage* the student physically in
an activity with which she can *identify*, sensually and semiotically. The next
step is to persuade the student that this subjective experience is the same
as an event from scientific discourse, 'molecules rapidly moving about'.
Once the student has been made to identify subjectively with the scientific
event, even though she has not personally experienced it, scientific discourse is introduced in the form of abstract participants in identifying
clauses. The abstract entities and their causal relations have nothing to do
with the sensual experience of shot rattling in a tin; the latter is a device
to make the student identify with the discourse of science, in which
common sense has no place.

The function of the activity is not to 'explain' scientific concepts as
causal sequences. Rather, apprehending the relation between subjective
experience, its representation as common-sense discourse, and the

abstractions of science requires a leap of faith. The student is being persuaded to accept the scientific construal of reality as similar to, and just as real as, the one she knows from her mother tongue.

There is not necessarily anything sinister about this process. Comparison is a common, if not the most common, educational device. And the goal of the learning experience is to apprentice the student in scientific discourse, for employment and further education. The point here is that the device relies on the student's degree of identification with the scientific construal of reality, and we know that students differ in the degree to which they do identify with it.

## Conclusion

I would like to propose that students' positioning within the regulative discourse of the science classroom, the school and their community determines the degree to which they will accept and acquire scientific discourse as a valid representation of reality, and thus their opportunities for training and future employment. To understand how this works we have to recognize that there are at least three components to the recontextualized scientific discourse of junior secondary school. The first is the simple procedures directing students to perform activities ostensibly related to the topic they are studying. The second is the range of genres including explanations and reports which explain, describe and classify features of the natural world. These are currently learnt within the recontextualized scientific 'themes' of junior secondary science in Australia. And the third component is the features of abstract scientific discourse in which identifying processes predominate, relating abstract entities by degrees of obligation and evidentiality.

The first component is accessible to the majority of students because it reflects their subjective experience of the natural reality of home, community and the classroom, and of the interpersonal reality of family life, in the form of sequences of direct commands, sometimes accompanied by reasons and purposes. The second component is accessible to a smaller majority of students because they are able to interpret (a) the implicit causal relations in implication sequences, and (b) the technical taxonomies constructed in explanations and reports (see Bernstein 1990: 56–7 for a discussion of class differences in children's classification systems). The third component is accessible only to a minority of students who are prepared to accept the comparisons, proposed by pedagogic science, between their subjective experience and the abstractions of scientific discourse, and to identify personally with the latter. This abstract construal of natural reality has evolved simultaneously with the systems of institutional role relations of modern bourgeois culture. Access to these roles and the discourses associated with them tend to be restricted to members of tertiary educated middle-class families, and the theory of reality that these highly metaphorical discourses represent is likely to resonate with domains of their social experience within and beyond the family.

The first group of students, who acquire little more than the 'doing' component of recontextualized scientific discourse, are not able to enter technical vocations or the science education sequence; they will tend to be evaluated out of education into 'manual' occupations. These occupations are rapidly changing in post-Fordist economies, forcing both schools and industry to address the problem of enabling all workers to acquire basic technical literacy. The second group of students, who acquire the technical literacy skills associated with the causal/conditional sequences of explanations and taxonomizing functions of explanations and reports, are able to enter technical or workplace training for 'vocational'-level positions. The third group are able to identify with, and acquire, the abstract construals of scientific fields, enabling them to go on to senior secondary and tertiary science, and thence out into 'professional' design and managerial positions in industry.

These latter positions include roles in Bernstein's 'recontextualizing field' of the culture's pedagogic device, such as pedagogy theorists, teacher educators, and curriculum and textbook writers. These positions are associated with the 'new middle class' of information workers, or 'agents of symbolic control' in Bourdieu's terms (e.g. Bourdieu and Passeron 1977). Whether or not the stratified outcomes of secondary science education are a result of conscious intention by individual agents of the recontextualizing field, the outcomes of their communal practices ultimately privilege the economic interests of their class across generations by restricting access to the discursive resources which are their means of livelihood. Current struggles over control of the recontextualizing field, catalysed by post-Fordist economic changes, and exemplified by Australia's labour initiated training agenda, threaten to weaken the insulation between education and production, and between the 'specialised forms of consciousness' that Bernstein associates with mental and manual labour. This movement has, perhaps for the first time in the history of Western pedagogy, the potential for redistributing access to the privileging semiotic resources of technical discourse.

## References

Abeysingha, K. (1991) *No. 4 Blast Furnace Gas Cleaning Manual.* BHP Steel, Slab & Plate Products Division, Port Kembla.

Bernstein, B. (1990) *Class, Codes and Control: The Structuring of Pedagogic Discourse.* London: Routledge.

BHP Coke Ovens By Products Dept (1991) *Isolate No. 12 Tar Precipitator.* BHP Steel, Slab & Plate Products Division, Port Kembla.

Bourdieu, P. and Passeron, J. C. (1977) *Reproduction in Education, Society and Culture.* Beverly Hills: Sage.

Halliday, M. A. K. and Martin, J. R. (1992) *Writing Science: Literacy and Discursive Power.* Pittsburgh: University of Pittsburgh Press.

Harvey, D. (1989) *The Condition of Post-Modernity.* Oxford: Basil Blackwell.

Hasan, R. and Cloran, C. (1990) 'Semantic variation: a sociolinguistic interpretation of everyday talk between mothers and children'. In J. Gibbons, H. Nicholas and M. A. K. Halliday (eds) *Learning, Keeping and Using Language: Selected Papers from the 8th World Congress of Applied Linguistics.* Amsterdam: Benjamins, 67–99.

Heading, K. E. G., Provis, D. F., Scott, T. D., Smith, J. E. and Smith, R. T. (1972) *Science for Secondary Schools,* 2. Adelaide: Rigby.

Malin, M. (1990) 'Why is life so hard for Aboriginal students in urban classrooms?' *The Aboriginal Child at School* 19(1).

Martin, J. R. (1992) *English Text.* Amsterdam: Benjamins.

Messel, H. (1965) *Science for High School Students.* Sydney: Government Printer.

Painter, C. (1994) 'Learning through Language: the development of language as a resource for learning'. Doctoral dissertation, University of Sydney.

Rose, D., Korner, H. and McInnes, D. (1992). *Write It Right: Scientific Literacy in Industry.* Sydney: NSW Dept of Education, Disadvantaged Schools Program, Metropolitan East.

Sale, C., Friedman, B. and Wilson, G. (1980) *Our Changing World.* Book 1: *The Vanishing Natural Ecosystem.* Melbourne: Longman Cheshire.

Wignell, P., Martin, J. R. and Eggins, S. (1992) *The Discourse of Geography: Ordering and Explaining the Natural World.* In Halliday and Martin (1992).

# 3 The language of administration: organizing human activity in formal institutions

*Rick Iedema*

## 1 Administration and bureaucracy

### *1.1 Introduction*

Administrative and bureaucratic practices and institutions constrain, in that we are required to do things according to pre-established rules in particular ways, at particular times, and in particular places. However, these practices and institutions also enable: they facilitate complex social processes, such as democratic elections, redistribution of wealth through taxation and provision of social welfare, and non-violent trials. Accordingly, institutional discourses can be typified as concerned with the realization of constraint, or 'shouldness', on the one hand, and with the construal of levels of institutional enablement and power on the other. Realizing 'shouldness' according to prevailing institutional conventions makes possible hierarchical structures of power and authority, or the range of institutional positionings. [1]

This chapter will look at the ways in which 'shouldness' is realized in bureaucratic–administrative settings. It will consider how differences in realization suggest differences between positionings. The analysis will take contextual, semantic as well as lexicogrammatical aspects into account (cf. Hasan 1985: 11). The purpose of the chapter is not just to provide a typology of the linguistic resources most frequently called on in those settings, but also to set up a semantic topology to provide a contextualized perspective on the resources in question.

The chapter is set up as follows. First I will look at the structure of directives, and at how those structures are suggestive of context. Then I will set up a typology of directives and distinguish four main types. I will finish by placing the directive in a topology to highlight its commonalities with other text types.

## 2 Directives: structure

### *2.1 The linguistic construction of authority*

Hierarchical control is naturalized by 'recontextualizing' the Command, i.e. by transferring it from an immediate to a reported context. If you command me by saying 'Go get it', you can rely on no more legitimacy than is evident from your status, or from our affinity, or from the urgency of the situation. 'Depersonalized' orders, on the other hand, such as 'Staff are required to obtain leave forms from their supervisor', tend to be 'reported' on behalf of others. This greatly enhances the domain (and duration) of influence of the original source of the shouldness (if such could be isolated!). This creates institutional distance, which, by limiting the 'space for dialogue, disagreement, or differing points of view' (Lemke 1987: 6), tends to legitimize the Command involved (for compliant readers! Kress 1985: 42). Figure 3.1 illustrates this distancing. It presents a line from a government brochure and a rewrite, the Command realized as imperative, 'Complete form 932!'.[2]

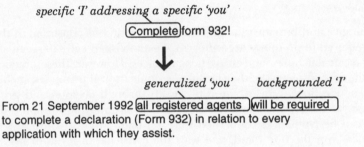

*specific 'I' addressing a specific 'you'*

Complete form 932!

*generalized 'you'*     *backgrounded 'I'*

From 21 September 1992 all registered agents will be required to complete a declaration (Form 932) in relation to every application with which they assist.

**Figure 3.1** From personalized to depersonalized Command

The original brochure backgrounds the source of the Command ('will be required') and generalizes its addressees ('all registered agents'). The rewrite encodes greater directness in that both commander and commandee are presumed involved in the exchange. The displacement of the original source from the Command both creates and consolidates the hierarchical distance between the commander(s) and the commandee(s). At the same time, it presumes that the hearer/reader knows the source of the Command, or is at least aware of its relevance to her/his action within the organization. In short, the depersonalized Command renders itself less negotiable and contestable, makes use of specialized language, and demands a high degree of contextual knowledge.

### 2.2 Directives

Commands occur as texts which are referred to here as **directives**. Directives are concerned with organizing action in social institutions. Directives contain the obligatory Command, i.e. the request for action, and perhaps background information, as well as reasons. In Fordist institutional cultures directives were most likely to reflect the unproblematized power difference between management and workforce. It is likely that such power difference would have been realized by (more or less) direct Commands and minimal background information. Post-Fordism, on the other hand, with increasing industrial democracy and task negotiability (Harvey 1989: 141), makes use of more personalized techniques to achieve organization and effect control (cf. Fairclough 1992: 219[3]). The post-Fordist directive is more likely to contain an interpersonalized Command in addition to paragraphs elaborating or justifying the Command, or offers of assistance for the carrying out of the Command (see section 2.3 below).

Given that, it is not possible to map issues of power and solidarity unproblematically and categorically on to particular linguistic tokens (Tannen 1993: 167); directness and bluntness may code extreme power as well as high solidarity. Hence, the 'interpretation will face both ways' (Halliday 1984: 13), down from context and up from the grammar, to talk about directives and their characteristics.

Consider directive 1:

**Directive 1**

**Memo from the EO**

To:      Jane[4]
Date:    Fri 7/12
Topic:   Notices – Dec
Please prepare a draft of the December Notices.
Ta
John

This directive is realized in the form of a memo with the appropriate headings. It is quite formal, suggesting distance rather than familiarity. The action requested is 'prepare', coded as an imperative. The imperative is the most direct kind of Command realization, or what Brown and Levinson refer to as 'bald' Command (Brown and Levinson 1988: 94). It suggests that the 'commander' does not have to 'do much work'[5] in order to command the addressee. The directive is mitigated, however, by 'Please'. In the institutional context, 'please' codes respect and may realize status difference. In the directive above, it relates to 'prepare a draft' by way of conciliation. 'Please' is the short form of the older 'if it pleases you',[6] which might be read as providing the addressee with the opportunity to say 'it doesn't please me, so I won't comply'. Further below we will see other realizations of conciliatory moves (section 2.3).

Commands can be realized in more elaborated ways as well. Consider directive 2:

**Directive 2**

To:      Barbara and Shane
Date:    31 August 1993
Topic:   BTS Support Package

We need to develop BTS Support Packages for schools in 95.
Would you prepare a proposal for us to discuss on Friday.
Ta
John

In this directive, the Command realization 'Would you prepare a proposal
. . .' has the structure of an interrogative, but it has not been given a question mark. Punctuation is played off here against grammatical realization,
and in that way codes a subtle shade of meaning intermediate between
the highly polite realization of the Command as interrogative and its
somewhat less polite realization as declarative. The extra 'work' involves
the addition of 'Would you' to the bald Command:

| Would you | prepare a proposal . . . |
|-----------|--------------------------|
| extra 'work' | bald Command form |

The Command as it is realized in directive 2 involves slightly more work
than its realization in directive 1. The tension between the structure and
the punctuation, and the hypotheticalness implied by the oblique
'would', both point towards a greater linguistic investment in directive 2,
and to its higher degree of (negative) politeness.[7]

Another difference between directives 1 and 2 is that directive 1 consists of a mere (admittedly slightly mitigated) Command, while directive 2
has an additional element: 'We need to develop BTS Support Packages
for schools in 95.' This clause may be read as providing background or a
legitimation for the Command that is to follow. The conjunctive 'so'
could be inserted, to emphasize its legitimizing role (see Figure 3.2).
Leaving open whether 'We need to develop BTS Support Packages for
schools in 95' provides background information to enable the addressees
to carry out the Command or whether it functions as a reason legitimizing the request, we can schematize the structure of directive 2 as in
Figure 3.3.[8] Directive 1 does not feature a background or legitimizing
element: it consists of only a 'bald' Command and 'Ta' (Figure 3.4).
Directive 2 does not only do more 'work' in realizing its Command, but
also in setting it up as part of the text. The institutional relationship
realized in directive 1 suggests a relatively large hierarchical distance (a
high status differential) due to its formal appearance and linguistic
directness. Directive 2 would suggest a relationship which, in comparison
to that coded by directive 1, requires a (slightly) greater need for politeness, and therefore a smaller hierarchical distance (a smaller status differential). In fact, these texts were collected in a small government office
whose Executive Officer uses relatively formal means of communication
(written memos) with his staff. This formality colours his imperatives as
realizations of power and distance rather than of familiarity. Moreover, he
uses different grammatical resources for different addressees, thus
marking, or *construing,* different degrees of power: directive 1 was

We need to develop BTS Support
Packages for schools in 95.

[so]

Would you prepare a proposal
for us to discuss on Friday.

**Figure 3.2** Making the conjunctive relation 'so' explicit

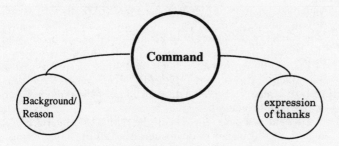

**Figure 3.3** Schematic representation of directive 2

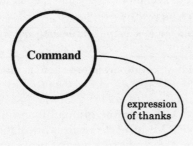

**Figure 3.4** Schematic representation of directive 1

addressed to the secretary-receptionist; directive 2 to two educational consultants.

In my discussion of directives so far I have focused on two issues: the way in which the Command has been realized (direct or indirect; congruently or metaphorically),[9] and the presence of legitimizing or enabling elements supporting the Command. A third issue, which I will focus on in the next section, is to see *where* the Command occurs in relation to additional legitimizing and/or enabling elements at the level of text.

## 2.3 Directives: two basic structural principles

The following directive (3) contains a Command (the shaded row) that is
again different from the two seen above. Here, the writer takes recourse
to emphasizing that he (a male Qantas engineer) 'would be grateful' if
the request were to be complied with. The oblique 'would' is coupled to
an attribute which behaves like a projecting mental process 'I would be
grateful for . . .', all of which represents quite a bit of 'work' on the part of
the writer.

**Directive 3**

**Payroll/EMSTAFF Interface**

| | |
|---|---|
| ORIENTATION | A pre-requisite to achieving the benefits of implementing the new corporate Payroll system is to develop an interface which will automate the transfer of data from EMSTAFF to the payroll system. |
| LEGITIMATION | The benefit of this interface to E&M is that data will be input to the Payroll system sooner and without risk of transcription errors, resulting in more timely and more accurate payroll adjustments. The corporate benefit is that it enables the company to achieve an overall staff reduction of 18 in the processing of payroll information. |
| BACKGROUND | To design, test and implement the EMSTAFF interface will require approximately two man-months of effort from a Production Systems Analyst between now and the end of October, and |
| CONCILIATION | I am aware that Production Systems does not have the resources at present to meet all of its demands. |
| LEGITIMATION | Payroll replacement is one of the key information technology projects in the lead up to privatisation and |
| COMMAND | I would be grateful for your help in facilitating Bob's efforts to support this project. |
| FACILITATION | Please call me if I can provide any information on this matter. [signed] |

The Command used in directive 3, 'I would be grateful for your help in
facilitating Bob's efforts to support this project', realizes low status due to
the work invested. It is phrased not in terms of a mental process of desire
('want' or 'need'), but in terms of a modalized ('would') mental process
of reaction ('appreciate', 'like'), construing less 'mental' influence. The
core of the Command ('help in facilitating Bob's efforts'!) has been backgrounded (moved down into a Circumstantial element) and the oblique
'would' realizes hypotheticalness (cf. Brown and Levinson 1988: 144;
Figure 3.5). The text begins like a report on the benefits of the new payroll system. When we reach the end of the text, however, we realize its
concern is to 'effect change'. The directive has backgrounded, or de-
emphasized, its Command in favour of several other elements. Thus, not
only has the essence of the Command been backgrounded in the clause,
but also at the level of text.

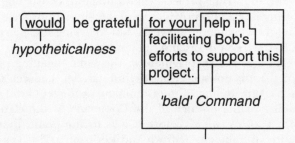

**Figure 3.5** Delaying and metaphorizing the Command

Directive 4 below reverses the Legitimation-Command order encountered in directive 3. Directive 4 begins with articulating its purpose 'I am writing to confirm'. The Command itself is projected by 'confirm'. This is not surprising, since the memo repeats a regulation already outlined in the 'Company's Graphic Standards Application Manual'. Although the projection suggests the memo is merely a record of previous announcements, the immediacy established by the use of 'I' and 'you' tells us we are dealing with a directive that is a response to 'unacceptable' behaviour.

**Directive 4**

| COMMAND | I am writing to confirm that the painting of all Qantas vehicles should conform with those guidelines outlined in the Company's Graphic Standards Application Manual. |
|---|---|
| LEGITIMATION | As you may be aware, the Graphic Standards Application Manual was one of the elements approved by the Board of Qantas when the company embarked on its new corporate identity program 10 years ago. It remains the standard for all applications of Qantas graphic disciplines worldwide. |
| LEGITIMATION | It is particularly important that our vehicles present a consistent look as they are very visible, especially in and around airports where our imagery is applied to many elements and consistency is paramount. |
| FACILITATION | If you wish to clarify the application of the Qantas branding to all of the vehicles, please contact our Production Coordinator Melissa Madden and she will gladly assist you.<br>Regards<br>[signed] |

The essence of directive 4's Command is 'all Qantas vehicles should conform with those guidelines . . .' We might regard the projecting clause 'I am writing to confirm that' as creating a dissociation between the writer and the institution as such. Had the first line of the text read 'All Qantas vehicles must conform with those guidelines . . .' the identification of writer with institutional power would have been absolute, which in this time of institutional democratization might have been considered inappropriate. Instead, the writer projects the Command, construing himself as merely reporting it. He also provides several legitimations (reasons) for it, not preceding the Command, however, but following it. The result is a tension between construed status and politeness.

Since both clause and text 'originate in the same meaning potential' (Halliday 1980: 38) it is not surprising to find parallels between them. In directive 3, the backgrounding of the Command at the text level parallels the backgrounding of the essence of the Command at the clause level. Directive 3 does a lot of 'work' before it gets to the point, thereby signalling respect for its audience (Brown and Levinson 1988: 132). Directive 4, on the other hand, foregrounds its Command, if not convincingly at the clause level, then certainly at the text level. The legitimizing elements following its Command are the textual parallel of expansion of the Command at the clause level. Overall, directive 4 is far more direct in formulating its point.

Directive 3's pattern suggests the text is written by somebody presuming (or construing) low status. It is generally used by workers writing 'up' to higher-level officials or by higher-level officials aiming to generate a 'collegial' atmosphere (cf. Kabanoff 1992). The second pattern, which foregrounds the Command at the text level and at the clause level, suggests that the writer (or speaker) is not concerned with delaying or mitigating the purpose of her/his text. This strategy minimizes reciprocity, and tends to signal high(er) status.[10]

## 2.4 Directives: Nucleus–Satellite relations

The interplay between the obligatory Command and additional optional elements as well as the dynamic unfolding of the texts may be modelled as follows. In section 2.3 two patterns were identified, showing the parallels between text and clause structure (Halliday 1980: 38). The first pattern foregrounded interpersonal meanings and backgrounded the Command. Directive 3 exemplifies this first pattern, and the text can be modelled as in Figure 3.6 to highlight the pivotal role of the Command.

To acknowledge the pivotal role of the Command in directives as a genre I will refer to it as the 'Nucleus' (cf. Martin in press; Iedema *et al.* 1994; Iedema 1996). The legitimizing elements and enabling elements will be referred to as 'Satellites'.[11] The Nucleus–Satellite model is essentially an 'orbital' model (Martin in press), with the Command-Nucleus as its centre. The model thus presumes a homology between the experiential orbitality of process and medium at the clause level and the Command-legitimation/enablement structuring principle at text level.

However, if we accept that a text is like a clause (Halliday 1980), we must account for all the metafunctional principles (experiential, logical, interpersonal and textual) which equally underlie clause and text (Thibault 1988; Martin 1995). The orbital Nucleus–Satellite model highlights the experiential contribution to the structuring of the text, but it does not acknowledge other metafunctional contributions. Although many of the institutional texts conformed to the orbital model proposed above (Iedema 1996), a sufficient number showed the presence of other metafunctional influences and hence required a different analysis. These other metafunctional contributions, resulting in different structuring principles, and redounding with different contextual prerogatives, will be described in the next section.

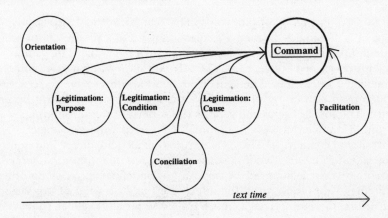

**Figure 3.6** Modelling directive 3

*2.5 The interplay of experiential, logical, interpersonal and textual meaning in text structure*

The orbital model presented in section 2.4 presumes the existence of a single and discrete Command-Nucleus, as has been the case in the directives considered so far. Not all directives contain a neatly localized Command-Nucleus, however; nor do all directives contain only one Command. The memorandum below (directive 5) was sent from a Controller of Finances of a large hotel to peers and subordinates, to instruct them in how to go about 'month end reporting'.

**Directive 5**

        To: [list of names]
        From: [name]
        Date 5th May, 1993
        Subj: Month end reporting

BACKGROUND    Attached is the format that is required to be followed when you report variances from your monthly financial statements.

COMMAND    Explanations are required if actual results exceed budget by more than $700 for any line item.

COMMAND    Please keep comments brief but accurate.

COMMAND    The variance report for the month ending April 30th must be

|            | provided to Chris Sharpe no later than midday on Monday 10th of May. |
|------------|---------------------------------------------------------------------|
| COMMAND    | Please also provide your Activities Report for the month by midday on Wednesday, 12th May. |
| COMMAND    | This report should contain a brief overview of your department's performance for the month and highlight any significant results. |
| THANKS     | Thank you for your assistance. |

Directive 5 contains five Commands. The first backgrounds its source by means of a nominalized action ('Explanations') and a passive construction ('are required'). It also sets up a condition which necessitates the action ('if actual results exceed budget . . .'). The second Command is a 'bald' imperative mitigated by 'Please'. The third Command also backgrounds its source through passivization, but it modulates the required action ('must be provided'). The fourth Command repeats the pattern of the second one, while the fifth Command makes a nominalized verbal process Subject: 'This report should contain . . .' These Commands are all quite direct, and none of them is mitigated by reasons, consequences, conditions or judgements. Neither are they legitimized by appeals to guidelines, policies or official requirements. In other words, the directive is merely a series of Commands. Its structure, therefore, is not so much orbital as 'serial' (Halliday 1978: 139), and this Command series sets up a multi-nuclearity, in contrast with the directives seen so far. For directives like directive 5 which do not conform to the orbital model (one Nucleus-Command and a number of supporting Satellites, in whatever order) an alternative account needs to be found.

The analysis employed for directives 1–4 is particulate: it isolates discrete elements, or constituents, and labels them according to their structural contribution. Martin (in press) shows that particulate analysis draws categorical boundaries in texts (i.e. 'staging'), and that this ignores other metafunctional influences on text structure. A purely particulate analysis, in that view, presumes that the text's main structural principle is ideational and this may lead to reductive accounts of text structure. Following Halliday's (1980) suggestion that the four kinds of meaning (ideational (i.e. experiential/logical), interpersonal and textual meanings) are responsible for different structuring principles both at the clause level and the text level, the various contributions made to text structure by the different metafunctions need to be accounted for. An informed account 'of the text-clause relationship must be able to show how [the] various modes of meaning (i.e. the semantic metafunctions) are integrated into the organisation of both clause and text' (Thibault 1988: 21).

Halliday (1978: 139) relates the different metafunctions to different structuring principles at both the level of clause and text. He associates ideational (experiential–logical) meanings with particulate realizations, interpersonal meanings with prosodic realizations, and textual meanings with periodic realizations. Martin (in press) models these principles, suggesting that experiential meaning revolves around one main element, its nucleus, and several dependent elements, the satellites; logical meaning involves multiple (and serial) nuclei; interpersonal meaning is realized prosodically and 'reverberates' through the text, and textual meaning sets up undulations, or waves of prominence.[12]

Directive 5 above can now be described as follows: it has two 'orbital' Satellites (the background and the expression of thanks), but it is structured principally on the basis of seriality which allows the linking of the five Command-Nuclei.

The Minute below (directive 6) shows again a slightly different structure. It contains several 'Commands' varying in realization, and located at various points in the text. The text is not serial, because the 'Commands' realize one and the same request: 'The workplace must be kept smoke-free.' To understand the structure of this text, we need to take account of a dynamically unfolding interpersonal prosody.

**Directive 6**

### Internal Minute

Subject Non-smoking policy – Implications of court judgment in Scholem v Department of Health – General Circular 92/5 – Date 16/7/92

| | |
|---|---|
| BACKGROUND | Most staff will be aware of the District Court judgment in favour of Liesel Scholem in her case against the NSW Department of Health. No appeal has been lodged. |
| LEGITIMATION [+ COMMAND TRACE] | While the department has had a non-smoking policy for some time, this judgment makes it even more important for the policy to be fully complied with. |
| LEGITIMATION [+ COMMAND TRACE] | Some staff may have been under the impression that the policy did not apply on special celebratory occasions. It must be emphasised that this is not the case and the workplace, especially if there is an air-conditioning system, must be kept smoke-free at all times. |
| LEGITIMATION | In addition to highlighting the issue of the danger of passive smoking, the judgment puts everyone on notice of potential liability for passive smoking in the workplace. |
| LEGITIMATION | There are serious implications for organisations, both financially and in respect of adverse publicity, including the prospect of prosecution under the OHS Act, 1983. |
| LEGITIMATION | It is stressed that liability under the OHS Act can extend to employees generally (S19) and to Managers (S50). |
| LEGITIMATION | In terms of the departmental policy and the Scholem judgment, a court is unlikely to accept lack of knowledge or inability to influence conduct as defences to prosecution. |
| COMMAND | All staff are urged to ensure the non-smoking policy is observed completely and the workplace is kept entirely smoke-free. |
| FACILITATION | Staff requiring additional information or advice in terms of QUIT programs should contact the Manager Administrative Support . . . |

First of all, directive 6 is interdictive: 'stop smoking'. It starts with a background element mentioning the Scholem case. One could argue that 'Most staff will be aware . . .' codes more than mere background information because of 'will' and all the imperative meanings that attach to that modal auxiliary. For the purposes of this analysis, however, we shall take this opening Satellite at face value.

The second Satellite is glossed Legitimation in the analysis above. Mention is made both of the department's non-smoking policy and of the judgment, which has now gained status of institutional (legal) instrument, backgrounding those who originally uttered it. The 'judgment' is construed in the grammar as modally responsible Subject in the clause, acting on an elided 'doer'. The more congruent rewrite 'This judgment means/says that staff must comply with the policy' brings out the shouldness that is buried in the original 'This judgment makes it even more important for the policy to be complied with'. The construction 'this judgment means staff must comply with the policy' partly de-metaphorizes a Command which was originally an embedded (non-finite) clause. The rewrite in Figure 3.7 foregrounds the non-finite clause which represents a 'Command trace' if we accept that its meaning is related to that of the more congruent version above.

The third Satellite ('this is not the case') embodies another 'Command trace'. This Command trace de-emphasizes the commandee, the commander, as well as the required action: 'the workplace . . . must be kept smoke-free'. Whereas our ideational reading treats this Command trace as embedded within a Legitimation (positing the later Command-Nucleus as the focal point of this text), there is an interpersonal prosody building up within these 'traces' which culminates in the Command-Nucleus.

The next four elements are Satellites which make alternate reference to legal instruments, 'the judgment', and 'the Occupational Health and Safety Act, 1983', 'the OHS Act', and appeal to causes, 'serious implications', and 'a court is unlikely to accept lack of knowledge . . .' This alternation between appeals to legal instruments and appeals to causes provides a rhythmic to and fro between authoritative appeals to non-negotiable institutional entities and more interpersonally coloured reasons. I interpret this as hesitancy or uncertainty with regard to interpersonal positioning, and will come back to this below.

The final Nucleus is a Command which foregrounds the addressees (the 'doers'). It is a more grammatically independent, more congruent

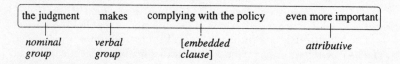

**Figure 3.7** Unpacking the clause in Satellite 2

and direct realization than that encountered in earlier Command realizations (which is why I labelled it Nucleus). Analysed orbitally, the text can be represented as in Figure 3.8. This representation does not account for three problematic issues, however. First, there is an ambiguity in the way the text addresses its audience. The required action is 'to ensure' that 'the non-smoking policy is observed [by ?]', thereby construing the elided writer of the text as carrying ultimate responsibility, and 'Staff' as carrying immediate responsibility. Those who are actually being targeted by this minute (smokers) are not grammatically realized, however (see Figure 3.9). As the analysis shows, the text is constructed in such a way that immediate responsibility for action lies with all staff. The text addresses itself not directly to those whom it, in the final analysis, targets: smokers who breach the non-smoking policy. By not directly addressing smokers with the request not to smoke in the building, the text creates an ambiguity, an uncertainty about who is responsible for doing what.

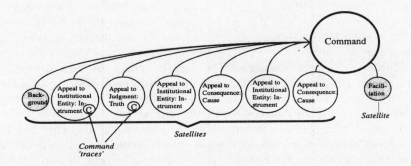

**Figure 3.8** Modelling directive 6

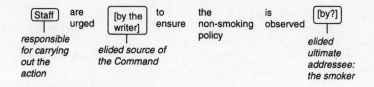

**Figure 3.9** Analysing the Command of directive 6

Second, at the level of clause structure, as well as at the level of text structure, this directive displays an indirectness, or an ambivalence of purpose. The request 'not to smoke' is realized in three different ways (Command 'traces' in Satellite 2, Satellite 3 and the Command-Nucleus), all of which elide the commandee (those 'guilty' of smoking in the workplace). At the same time, and standing in marked contrast with this elision of commandee, the directive uses no fewer than six legitimizing Satellites, which betrays a strong concern with legitimation. Then the text undoes this 'interpersonal work' (i.e. giving reasons) by calling on institutional entities three times for legitimation, emphasizing the non-negotiability of the Command at stake.

Third, the Command traces reverberate; they 'smear' the message 'Don't smoke inside the building!' across the text. The first 'Command trace' starts at a relatively low volume: it is a downranked non-finite clause, further backgrounded by the cleft construction ('this judgment makes it even more important for the policy to be fully complied with') which places immediate responsibility with the 'judgment'. The obligation is realized incongruently as Attribute 'important'. The second 'Command trace' is set up as a projected clause ('It must be emphasised that . . .'; a 'metaphenomenon'; Halliday 1985: 229), and it makes the desired action into an Attribute ('smoke-free'). This second trace constructs the addressees as at the same time elided and as carrying immediate responsibility. The Command-Nucleus is the most congruent, i.e. realizes the least 'stratal tension',[13] although it at the same time undermines its own directness for reasons outlined above. The three Command traces may be seen as becoming increasingly congruent or 'direct', and thereby realizing an amplifying prosody.

The first two issues raised may be seen to reflect the high degree of uncertainty that in fact characterized the management–staff relationship in the institution from which the text was obtained. The third issue may be seen to reflect the concern to counter this uncertainty through repetition or, as in this case, even amplification. To display this Directive by means of an orbital model does not do full credit to these interpersonal currents operating through the text. In Figure 3.10 only the Command realizations are captured. Since prosodic patterns in phonology revolve around strands realizing volume, pitch and duration, their representation may be better served by using an iconicity associated with tonal patterns.

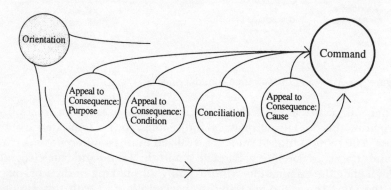

**Figure 3.10** Interpersonal Command prosody in directive 6

Periodic realizations create the wave–trough pattern found at the level of the clause in the form of Theme leading up to New. Hyper-Themes and hyper-News form 'crests' of meaning at the level of the paragraph, as do macro-Themes and macro-News at the level of text (see Martin 1993c). Directive 3 above was shown to contain an Orientation ('A pre-requisite to achieving the benefits of implementing the new corporate Payroll system is to develop an interface which will automate the transfer of data from EMSTAFF to the payroll system') which predicted the mean-ings in the Satellites to follow. It may therefore be labelled macro-Theme. The macro-Theme 'predicts' what is to come, thus representing the crest of a wave. The text proceeds to legitimize and conciliate in anticipation of the next 'crest' of meaning, the Command which represents the culmina-tion of the text, or its hyper-New.[14] Still using the orbital model, we could adapt the representation slightly to highlight the enhanced textual period-icity. The Orientation and the Command are textual prominences; the other Satellites are a textual 'trough' (Figure 3.11).

As they do at the level of the clause, the three[15] structuring principles conflate at the level of text. However, in some texts textual periodicity may prove to be the overriding structuring principle, while in others experiential orbitality (or logical seriality) or interpersonal prosody may predominate. Directive 6 above displayed clear signs of being predomin-antly subject to an interpersonal prosody. The principle of interpersonal prosody predominated there in the conception of the text's structure, 'outbidding' ideational and textual structuring influences.

I would suggest that each structuring principle has a particular contex-tual valeur, and that the social/institutional context will redound in some way with the prevailing structuring principle. The predominance of par-ticular structuring principles, in other words, is indicative of particular institutional relations. Thus, the uncertain relationship between manage-ment and staff in the institution in which the non-smoking text was issued

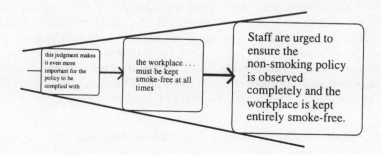

**Figure 3.11** Modelling directive 3

may account for the text's apparent interpersonal ambivalence and for its prosodic (i.e. repeated) realization of meanings of imposition.

If logical meaning is the founding principle for a text, resulting in serial structure, the concerns of the speaker/writer are extension (addition; see Halliday 1985: 202) rather than elaboration (specification of the Command) or enhancement (qualification of the Command). Serialization suggests that the speaker/writer has no need for exemplification, specification, explanation or justification, and in that sense serial directives realize a large status difference. The text considered above, directive 5, contained no legitimizing elements. This redounds with the special status Finance Controllers and their departments enjoy in current corporate life.

Predominantly orbitally organized texts foreground enhancing meaning relations at the level of the clause (between clauses) as well as at the text level (between Satellites and the Nucleus), in that Satellites tend to be concerned with giving reasons ('Do it, because . . .') or other forms of enablement. The presence of legitimations and enabling elements reflects the perceived need for extra 'work'. These types of directives therefore tend to be found especially in post-Fordist organizations with 'shallow' hierarchies and whose structure is less subject to internal segregation and more open to negotiation. Orbitality, as seen above, either foregrounds or delays extra 'work', allowing subtle mitigation of authority and emphasis on solidarity.

Finally, texts which set up waves of prominence and thus rely primarily on the periodic structuring principle are textually oriented. Textual meaning is concerned with relevance, cohesion, and information structure (Halliday 1978; Martin 1992). It is thus a metafunction primarily devoted to orienting the text co-textually as well as contextually, and is therefore primarily reader/listener-focused. Accordingly, this structuring principle is concerned with elaborating and specifying the (historical as well as grammatical) relevance of meanings for the benefit of the reader/listener. This tends to involve beginning–middle–end structures (e.g. thesis–arguments–conclusion) which foreshadow what is to come, present their point, and then again rephrase that point, making use of both generalization (construing distance) and interpersonality (construing solidarity). With this in mind, it will not be surprising that the periodic principle tends to prevail in situations where speakers or writers lack power, and where considerable 'work' is required for the text to be seen to be appropriate. Directive 7 is an example. The structure of directive 7 will be addressed in more detail in the following sections.

## 3 A semantic view of shouldness: four types of directives

So far I have discussed directives without generalizing about the semantics of the Command. The distinctions here turn on whether directives aim to limit the behaviour of workers, achieve change, or whether they repeat

**Directive 7**

|  |  | John, |
|---|---|---|
| (PROJECTED) LEGITIMATION | | I have commented before that I think our efforts at marketing to schools are very poor – the attached articles make that point. |
| LEGITIMATION (CAUSE) | THESIS | The sorts of programs which [company name 1] and [company name 2] have established are the type of thing we should be doing. |
| | ARGUMENTS | I believe the fact that we are not comes back to the effectiveness of our marketing approach and this is flawed because [section of own company] persists in ignoring wealthy private schools, and because they don't have a background in education. |
| | CONCLUSION | Through its efforts [section of own company] has established among the schools a very positive attitude towards this company. We should be able to capitalise on this in both public relations and marketing terms but we are clearly failing in the latter and this failure impinges negatively upon the former. |
| | CAUSE 1 | I believe that schools will become a very large market for telecommunications as well as an increasingly important avenue for positive corporate image building. |
| | CAUSE 2 | We will only gain maximum benefit from both areas if we perform well in both areas. |
| 'COMMAND' | | For this to happen we need a change in our marketing approach and either a substantial amount of staff training or a change of personnel. |
| | | [signed] |

previous Commands. In that sense, directives may be *reactive, proactive,* or *iterative.* Reactive directives proscribe actual or suspected behaviour (cf. Halliday 1985: 86). Directive 8 below is essentially negative in that way ('all such offers should be declined and gifts returned'). Directive 8 both interdicts current (or past!) behaviour ('many invitations are received') and prohibits potential future behaviour ('offers should be declined').

**Directive 8**

**Memo to all staff**

Conflict of interest

ORIENTATION        At around this time of year many invitations are received

|                | from companies and consultants to Christmas drinks/dinner. Gifts are also sometimes received. |
|----------------|-----------------------------------------------------------------------------------|
| CONCILIATION   | I am sure that such offers only eventuate from a job being well done and it is certainly pleasing to know that the level of service provided by staff is appreciated. |
| LEGITIMATION   | The acceptance of any offers of entertainment or gifts can however lead to either a real or perceived conflict of interest. |
| LEGITIMATION   | To ensure that a real or perceived conflict of interest does not arise |
| COMMAND        | all such offers should be declined and gifts returned. [signed] |

Directives can also be positive. They can suggest changes to current practices by 'prescribing' behaviour, as does directive 7 above. Directive 7 starts with a projected 'I have commented before that . . .', indicating the writer sees this text as part of previous attempts to prescribe what he sees as the appropriate course of action. Then follows an appeal to a cause (to legitimize the command which is to follow) and this comprises an embedded argument, or 'exposition' (Martin 1985: 16; Callaghan 1991: 20). The thesis of this exposition ('The sorts of programs which [name company 1] and [name company 2] have established are the type of thing we should be doing'[16]) argues in favour of taking specific action and attributes failure to take action to a certain section of the company. Then the writer again appeals to a cause, the first part of which, 'I believe that schools will become . . .', supports 'We will only gain maximum benefit from areas if we perform well in both areas'. The embedded exposition and the appeals to cause all scaffold the final Command: 'For this to happen we need a change in our marketing approach . . .', which aims to renovate existing practices. This directive therefore is proactive.

Directive 7 can be read as either realizing an argument (as e.g. a newspaper editorial does) or as realizing an order. In view of its use in context we know this text was not a hortatory exposition (Martin 1985) but 'an order realized as argument'. It is not uncommon for those who are commanding 'up' (i.e. possessing less status than their audience) to realize shouldness as a hortatory exposition (see section 4 below).

Both reactive and proactive directives represent the initiating move of an administrative exchange. Directives may also represent follow-up moves within administrative exchanges (as does directive 7 in a sense). They may merely *reiterate* an earlier Command, or iterate it and *elaborate* it, as occurs in directive 4 seen above. Directives may also be mitigated, of course, or cancelled altogether. The different types of directives have been summarized in a system network (Figure 3.12) and explanatory instantiations have been added to gloss the distinctions.

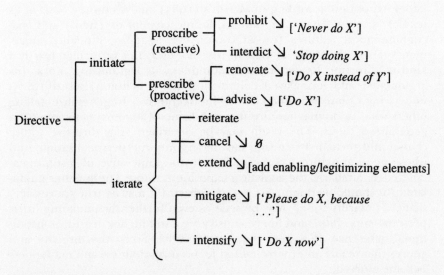

**Figure 3.12** Different types of directives

## 4 Construing authority and solidarity: a broader perspective

Above I focused on the different kinds of elements directives may comprise, and on that recurring and necessary element which is instrumental in realizing the directive, the Command. I linked the order of occurrence of obligatory and optional elements to the social or institutional discourse in which the communication occurred, and linked the structuring principle dominating the directive to aspects of context. In this section I will look at the construal of institutional authority and solidarity and take a broader view of the resources that may come into play in contexts of institutional positioning. Again, I will focus on two 'drifts': the one oriented towards interpersonalization (the proliferation of meaning which delays impact) and the other towards experientialization (the progressive shedding of interpersonal elements which achieves factualness).

The directive as presented above represents only one kind of realization of the Command. Contexts (discourses) may involve degrees of indirectness which the texts discussed above fail to achieve. Conversely, contexts may require a level of directness beyond that which the directives seen above provide. Clausally, 'Would it be possible at all for you to do it?' may be seen as interpersonalizing the Command 'Do it!' and 'Your doing it is highly necessary' as experientializing it. Following Halliday's clause–text homology, and keeping in mind contextual factors, certain texts may be treated as 'interpersonalized directives' while others may be seen as 'experientialized directives'.

As already seen in section 2.5, directive 7 could be categorized as a hortatory exposition according to Martin's (1985) analysis on the basis of its textual (staging: Thesis, Arguments, Reinforcement of Thesis) and lexicogrammatical features (causal conjunctive relations, modality, judgement). From the point of view of use, however, this particular text is a kind of directive. Its generalized shouldness, its legitimizing 'work' (its arguments) and its delayed culmination (its conclusion) all affirm its underlying Command, albeit in very indirect terms. To generalize, telling others what to do may require the mobilizing of arguments to support a generalized thesis. The result may be described as a directive whose clausal and textual structuring has undergone interpersonalization, and whose generic nature has succumbed to the imperative of institutional deference. Similarly, the analytical exposition, whose Thesis is not modulated ('it should be done . . .') but modalized ('it may be true (necessary) that . . .'; Martin 1985), may be seen as even further dissimulating interpersonal imposition, and hence construing a still higher degree of institutional deference. It is here that boundaries between the directive and genres that realize interpersonalized forms of shouldness and maybe-ness become blurred.

Moving in the other direction, the experientialization of shouldness allows 'Commands' to become buried in yet other, this time more authoritative, text types. Here the directive becomes associated with genres comprising non-negotiable expressions of certainty and fact, such as explanations or reports. Directive 9 below (extract) may be treated as either explanation (providing 'the rationale') or a report (listing the 'major changes'; cf. Callaghan 1989: 16). The text's concern with organizing human activity is evident from the shouldness which it rankshifts down into the nominal group ('a high priority') and the requested action which it buries within a circumstantial ('to the reform of . . .'). The text also shifts responsibility from specific people to impersonal entities, such as 'the Government', or 'the Treasury', further enhancing institutional distance.

**Directive 9**

**Accrual accounting**
Session 4: The Financial Reporting Code – the rationale and major changes Background

ORIENTATION     [1] In recent years, the Government of New South Wales has given a high priority to the reform of financial and management practices in the State's public sector.

BACKGROUND     [2] To this end, a number of significant initiatives have been taken, or are planned for implementation in the short term, with the aim of:
(a) establishing clear objectives for public sector organisations;
(b) providing managers of public sector organisations with greater autonomy to pursue those objectives;

        (c) creating a disciplined approach to the evaluation of the performance of public sector organisations and improving the quality of the financial information available concerning the financial performance and position of both individual organisations and the State as a whole;

        (d) introducing a scheme of remuneration for managers in the public sector which is based upon rewards and sanctions commensurate with performance; and

        (e) exposing public sector organisations to competition and creating an environment of competitive neutrality.

LEGITIMATION    [6] The major thrust of these efforts, however, has been on technical and systems matters, rather than on creating an appreciation of the conceptual elements of effective financial and resource management.

COMMAND    [7] Accordingly, the Treasury believes that it is now appropriate to provide further impetus to the reform of financial and resource management practices within Inner Budget Sector entities by:

        (a) establishing, amongst the Chief Executives and Senior Finance Executives of these entities, an awareness of and commitment to the elements of excellent financial and resource management;

        (b) providing financial officers in these entities with an appreciation of the approaches needed to achieve effective financial and resource management; and

        (c) relating the financial and resource management model to the broader model of an Integrated Management System, as described above.

Directive 9's 'Command' locates modal responsibility with 'Treasury' who 'believes it is now appropriate to provide further impetus to the reform' of certain practices. Shouldness ('impetus') as well as the requested action ('reform') are here realized nominally and this construes control in terms of what 'the government provides', not what certain individuals want other individuals to do (see Hasan 1985 on the close resemblance of Offers and Commands). This rankshifting of the constituent element of the canonical directive (its Command) reopens the choice potential at both the clause and text level. It is here that the boundaries between directives and other genres which contain experientialized shouldness become blurred.

Besides describing the directive as a discrete text type, therefore, it is also useful to look at the ways in which it is agnate[17] with, or 'topologically' related to, other genres. Using a topological perspective, the occurrence of either interpersonalized or experientialized modulation in genres which are ostensibly concerned with facts (explanations, reports), modalization (analytical expositions) or generalized modulation (hortatory expositions) can be traced. In that view, shouldness may pervade various genres agnate to the directive in rankshifted[18] form.

Figure 3.13 sets out a topological representation of five main genres involved (report, explanation, analytical and hortatory exposition, directive) from the perspective of modality and its use in context. Two comments are important here. First, the meaning of a text is inseparable from its use and how it is read. Criteria for categorization are therefore ultimately embedded in both practice and text. So what the diagram presents is a range of resources *likely* to be employed to achieve directive force in formal institutions (Iedema 1996). Second, the agnation of analytical and hortatory expositions has been recognized and described on the basis of structural similarities (staging, lexicogrammar) as well as contextual ones ('to persuade'; Martin 1985). Because these categorizations arose from a specific (the pedagogic) context, the labels hortatory and analytical exposition, explanation and report may need to be seen as euphemisms when used in the administrative–bureaucratic context to describe Commands, or rather, directive-like permutations. Topologically, these genres realize varying degrees of authority ('will' or 'is' versus 'maybe'; 'must' versus 'should') and of objectivity ('objective reality'; 'social reality').

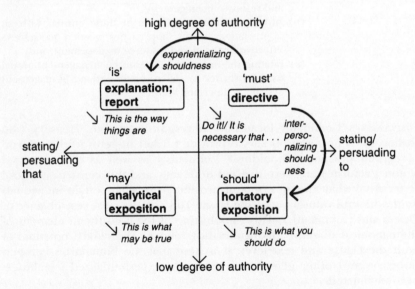

**Figure 3.13** A generic (text-type) topology of realizations of shouldness

Considered from the perspective of institutional shouldness, then, agnation between the analytical exposition and the explanation/report may be seen to derive from their shared focus on propositions (information) rather than proposals (goods and services, or action). Seen contextually, the occurrence and realization of causality (or absence of it) in these genres construe varying kinds of interpersonal (institutional) positioning.[19] Agnation between the directive and the explanation/report derives from their shared concern with authority. The explanation and report achieve authority through 'objectivity' (i.e. the suppression of interpersonal meaning and congruent causality, and the foregrounding of an 'impersonal reality'). Along similar lines, the directive achieves authority by nominalizing shouldness, by backgrounding the specific individuals involved, and by minimizing overt reasoning.

In short, these genres can realize different degrees of influence and solidarity. Whereas the directive orders others to act, the hortatory exposition attempts to convince others to act, and does so very indirectly. The analytical exposition merely aims to persuade others to believe a proposition which phrases shouldness in terms of maybe-ness. The explanation/report plainly states the truth or certainty of a proposition which has fully experientialized all references to shouldness (or phrased its Command as Offer, as in directive 9 above), thereby naturalizing a particular view on reality and on the future.

## 5 Conclusion

This chapter has considered the ways in which members of an institution realize both shouldness and institutional positioning. The analysis has tried to link elements and structures to the ways in which context is construed, and has proposed particular associations between grammatical structuring principles and the social action they may accompany. These various elements and structuring principles can be played off against one another to suit perceived positioning in context. For example, the Command can be backgrounded in the directive but the Satellites may all concern appeals to powerful institutional entities, thereby signalling respect (backgrounding the Command) as well as authority (relying on relatively non-negotiable legitimations). In a different context, we can 'work the front of the (Command) clause' (e.g. 'Would it be possible at all for you to help me?') without offering a reason, thereby combining politeness with the presumption that no legitimation is required. The great variety of linguistic devices involved allows for great subtlety (and this is not even addressing the co-variance of language with other semiotic issues such as layout or gesture).

If administrative texts are sometimes (or often!) seen as unnecessarily formal, imposing or verbose, we may be forgetting that their linguistic subtlety and complexity serves two purposes at once: the organization of human activity (shouldness) and institutional positioning (interpersonal distance). To want to make administrative/bureaucratic discursive practices more 'user-friendly' may either encourage the kind of 'synthetic' democratization Fairclough talks about,[20] or it may favour reductive kinds of linguistic 'simplicity', which end up signalling greater differences in power than the original bureaucratese. Kress, in a paper attacking the principles on which the Plain English movement grounds itself, says:

> To reduce the complexities of language is to reduce the ... complexities of practices and structures ... [C]ertain forms of thought structure, practice, which we value and on which the edifice of western technological societies depends – whether in science, the economy, bureaucracies, education systems, or the Western arts for that matter – are inextricably interlinked with certain forms of language. Without the one the others would not exist. (Kress 1993b: 132)

Thus, the complexity of administrative texts is functional: it represents the 'discursive augmentation' of human faculties (Hunter 1994: 103); administrative texts enable sophisticated forms of social organization, and they transcend physical (i.e. violent) modes of interaction. Rather than dismissing the principles and complexities of an institutional culture *a priori*, and rather than trying to reduce discursive diversity to an ideal of perceived accessibility, we need to come to a better understanding of the prevailing principles of institutional organization and communication. Thus, future linguistic and discourse analytic research should not dismiss the complexities of institutional culture, either on the grounds that these matters are already understood by those concerned (even if 'outsiders' often fail to understand them), or on the grounds that such matters are convoluted and bedevilled by obscurity. On the contrary, such research, properly mindful of the issues, should address the question: what exactly are the semiotic principles of cultural and institutional complexity and power?

## Notes

1 There is a small body of work which looks at how administrative discourse deals with these two objectives linguistically. An insightful analysis of administrative discourse is given in Hodge *et al.* (1979), where it is shown how institutional participants construe their institutional identity (or 'habitus'; Bourdieu 1990: 52) by adopting specific ways of talking (see also Kress 1995). The way in which the middle manager construes her/his identity (i.e. 'realizes habitus') reflects a particular reading of the institutional hierarchy and thus indicates a particular positioning within it (Iedema 1996). Fowler and Kress (1979) focus on the realization of administrative rules and regulations, and distinguish between 'enacting' and 'institutionalizing' administrative control – a categorization which becomes important when distinguishing between here-and-now commands on the one hand, or personalized shouldness, and commands conveyed from other (usually more distant) spheres within an institution on the other, or depersonalized shouldness. Martin (1993a) provides an account of how shouldness is ideationalized in the bureaucratic context (and thereby 'institutionalized' in Fowler and Kress's sense) and thus placed beyond negotiation.

2 'The imperative is at best a fringe category, teetering between finite and non-

finite (in languages which make this distinction), having either no distinct clause or verb form or else one that is only minimally distinguished; and even when a distinct imperative form does exist it may be rarely used, with other, non-congruent forms taking over the command function' (Halliday 1984: 20).

3 See especially his notion 'synthetic personalization'.

4 All the names used here are fictitious.

5 'Work' here refers to the grammatical 'work' the situation requires one to perform on an expression. It is assumed that the expression form which is simplest (i.e. which matches its purpose most directly to its realization) is the most congruent. In that sense, 'Do it' is simpler, it involves less 'work', and is therefore more congruent than 'Is it possible for you to do it?' or even 'Please do it'.

6 Compare 'S'il vous plaît' in French. 'Please', in the adult–child context, may have the function of intensifier. Hasan (1985: 58), however, offers an alternative account of 'please'.

7 'The outputs [of negative politeness] are all forms useful in general for social "distancing"' (Brown and Levinson 1988: 130).

8 The memo heading and sign-off are set aside here as features of the channel of communication, not of the directive *per se*.

9 For a more in-depth description of Command realizations see Iedema (1996).

10 Compare Windshuttle and Windshuttle's 'inductive' (foregrounding the Command) and 'deductive' (backgrounding the Command) memo structure (Windshuttle and Windshuttle 1990).

11 The Nucleus–Satellite terminology is borrowed from Thompson, Mann and Matthiessen's 'Rhetorical Structure Theory' which aims to explain the links between ideas in texts. See also the 'Media Literacy Report', volume II in the Write It Right Industry Research series (Disadvantaged Schools Program, Metropolitan East, New South Wales) for an extended discussion on Nucleus–Satellite modelling of media texts.

12 For discussion see Halliday (1985), Matthiessen and Thompson (1988) and Martin (1992).

13 Stratal tension occurs when processes are realized as nouns, conjunctive relations as verbs, and nouns as modifiers (see Martin 1993b: 152).

14 'The hyper-New . . . pulls together and summarises the information built up in the rest of the paragraph' (Martin 1992: 453/4).

15 Since ideation includes experiential and logical meaning, and since a structure must be seen as either multivariate (experiential) or univariate (logical), the relevant structuring principles (orbitality, seriality) are alternative, not simultaneous.

16 Not a 'do it' but a 'let's!', i.e. not a jussive imperative, but a suggestive imperative (Matthiessen n.d.: 358).

17 Agnation, in a typology, refers to items which share features within a specific network.

18 Shouldness may be rankshifted up from the clause to the text level and thus determine the choice of genre (interpersonalization), or it may be rankshifted down into the group opening up a whole new range of clausal and textual choices (experientialization).

19 For an account of the close relationship between causality and modality see Martin (1992: 193–5).

20 'Among the many types of marker which may tend to be eliminated are: asymmetrical terms of address; "bald" (e.g. imperative) directives, in favour of more indirect and "face"-sensitive forms (Brown and Levinson 1988); asymmetries in rights to make certain sorts of contribution, such as initiating topics, and asking questions; use by powerful participants of specialized vocabulary inaccessible to others ... It is also arguable that as overt markers become less evident, covert markers of power asymmetry become more potent, with the result that power asymmetry becomes more subtle rather than disappearing' (Fairclough 1992: 203).

## References

Bernstein, B. (1990) *The Structuring of Pedagogic Discourse.* London: Routledge & Kegan Paul.

Bourdieu, P. (1990) *The Logic of Practice.* Cambridge: Polity.

Brown, P. and Levinson, S. (1988) *Politeness: Universals in Language Usage.* Cambridge: Cambridge University Press.

Callaghan, M. (1989) *The Report Genre.* Sydney: DSP (Disadvantaged Schools Program) Metropolitan East.

Callaghan, M. (1991) *A Brief Introduction to Genre.* Sydney: DSP Metropolitan East.

Fairclough, N. (1992) *Discourse and Social Change.* Cambridge: Polity.

Fowler, R. (1986) 'Power'. In T. van Dijk, *Handbook of Discourse Analysis*, Vol. 4: *Discourse Analysis in Society*. London: Academic Press, 61–82.

Fowler, R., Hodge, B., Kress, G. and Trew, T. (1979) *Language and Control.* London: Routledge & Kegan Paul.

Fowler, R. and Kress, G. (1979) 'Rules and regulations'. In R. Fowler, B. Hodge, G. Kress and T. Trew (eds) *Language and Control.* London: Routledge & Kegan Paul, 27–45.

Halliday, M. A. K. (1978) *Language as Social Semiotic.* London: Edward Arnold.

Halliday, M. A. K. (1980) 'Text semantics and clause grammar: some patterns of realisation'. In J. E. Copeland and P. W. Davies (eds) *The Seventh LACUS Forum 1980.* Columbia, SC: Hornbeam Press, 31–59.

Halliday, M. A. K. (1984) 'Language as code and language as behaviour: a systemic-functional interpretation of the nature and ontogenesis of dialogue'. In R. P. Fawcett, M. A. K. Halliday, S. M. Lamb and A. Makkai (eds) *The Semiotics of Culture and Language*, Vol. 1: *Language as Social Semiotic.* London: Frances Pinter, 3–35.

Halliday, M. A. K. (1985) *An Introduction to Functional Grammar.* London: Edward Arnold (2nd edition 1994).

Halliday, M. A. K. and Martin, J. R. (eds) (1993) *Writing Science: Literacy and Discursive Power.* London: Falmer Press.

Harvey, D. (1989) *The Condition of Post-Modernity.* Oxford: Basil Blackwell.

Hasan, R. (1985) 'Offers in the making: a systemic-functional approach'. Revised/enlarged version of paper presented at the XIIth International Systemic Workshop, August 1985, Ann Arbor, MI.

Hodge, B. and Kress, G. (1993) *Language as Ideology.* 2nd edition. London: Routledge.

Hodge, B., Kress, G. and Jones, G. (1979) 'The ideology of middle management'. In R. Fowler, B. Hodge, G. Kress and T. Trew (eds) *Language and Control.* London: Routledge & Kegan Paul, 81–93.

Hunter, I. (1994) *Rethinking the School.* Sydney: Allen & Unwin.

Iedema, R. (1993) 'The language of administration: creating institutional identity'. Paper given at the Communication in the Workplace Conference 'Cultural Language and Organisational Change', Sydney, 1–4 September 1993.

Iedema, R. (1996) *The Language of Administration* (Write It Right Industry Research Report No. 3). Sydney: NSW Department of Education, Disadvantaged Schools Program Metropolitan East.

Iedema, R., Feez, S. and White, P. (1994) *Media Literacy* (Write It Right Industry Research Report No. 2). Sydney: NSW Department of Education, Disadvantaged Schools Program Metropolitan East.

Kabanoff, B. (1992) *An Exploration of Organisational Culture in Australia (with a Closer Look at the Banking Sector).* The Centre for Corporate Change, Australian Graduate School of Management, Sydney, University of New South Wales.

Kress, G. (1985) *Linguistic Processes in Socio-cultural Practice.* Geelong, Vic.: Deakin University Press.

Kress, G. (1993a) 'Genre as social process'. In B. Cope and M. Kalantzis (eds) *The Powers of Literacy.* London: Falmer Press, 22–37.

Kress, G. (1993b) 'Participation and difference: the role of language in producing a culture of innovation'. In A. Luke and P. Gilbert (eds) *Literacy in Contexts.* Sydney: Allen & Unwin, 127–35.

Kress, G. (1993c) 'Against arbitrariness: the social production of the sign as a foundational issue in critical discourse analysis'. *Discourse and Society* 4(2), 169–91.

Kress, G. (1995) 'The social production of language: history and structures of domination'. In P. Fries and M. Gregory (eds) *Discourse in Society (Systemic Functional Perspectives* Vol. L): *Meaning and Choice in Language* (Advances in Discourse Processes Series). Norwood, NJ: Ablex, 115–40.

Lemke, J. (1984) *Semiotics and Education.* Toronto: Toronto Semiotics Circle (Monographs, Working Papers and Publications No. 2).

Lemke, J. (1987) 'Technical discourse and technocratic ideology'. Paper presented at the 8th AILA Congress of Applied Linguistics, Sydney, 16–21 August 1987.

Martin, J. R (1985) *Factual Writing: Exploring and Challenging Social Reality.* Geelong, Vic. Deakin University Press (republished Oxford University Press 1989).

Martin, J. R. (1991) 'Intrinsic functionality: implications for contextual theory'. *Social Semiotics* 1(1), 99–162.

Martin, J. R. (1992) *English Text: System and Structure.* Amsterdam: Johns Benjamins.

Martin, J. R. (1993a) 'Technology, bureaucracy and schooling'. *Cultural Dynamics* 6(1), 84–130.

Martin, J. R. (1993b) 'Technicality and abstraction: language for the creation of specialised texts'. In M. Halliday and J. R. Martin (eds) *Writing Science: Literacy and Discursive Power.* London: Falmer Press, 203–20 (reprinted from F. Christie (ed.) *Writing in Schools: Reader.* Geelong, Vic.: Deakin University Press, 36–44).

Martin, J. R. (1993c) 'Genre and literacy: modelling context in educational linguistics'. *Annual Review of Applied Linguistics* 13, 141–72.

Martin, J. R. (1995) 'Text and clause: fractal resonance'. *Text* 15(1), 5–42.

Martin, J. R. (in press) 'Types of structure: deconstructing notions of constituency in clause and text'. In E. Hovy and D. Scott (eds) *Burning Issues in Discourse: A Multidisciplinary Perspective.* Heidelberg: Springer.

Martin, J. R., Christie, F. and Rothery, J. (1987) 'Social processes in education'. In
I. Reid (ed.) *The Place of Genre in Learning*. Geelong, Vic.: Deakin University
Press (Centre for Studies in Literacy Education, Typereader Publications 1),
58–82 (unabridged version published in *The Teaching of English: Journal of the
English Teachers' Association of New South Wales*, 53, 1987, 3–22).

Matthiessen, C. (n.d.) 'Lexicogrammatical cartography: English systems'. Mimeo.
Department of Linguistics, University of Sydney.

Matthiessen, C. and Thompson, S. (1988) 'The structure of discourse and subor-
dination'. In J. Haiman and S. Thompson (eds) *Clause Combining in Grammar
and Discourse*. Amsterdam: Benjamins, 275–329.

Tannen, D. (1993) 'Rethinking power and solidarity in gender and dominance'.
In D. Tannen (ed.) *Gender and Conversational Interaction*. Oxford: Oxford University Press (Oxford Studies in Sociolinguistics), 165–88.

Thibault, P. (1987) 'Interview with Michael Halliday'. In R. Steele and T. Threadgold (eds) *Language Topics: Essays in Honour of Michael Halliday*, Vol. 2. Amsterdam: Benjamins, 599–627.

Thibault, P. (1988) 'Interpersonal meaning and the discursive construction of
action, attitudes and values: some aspects of the semantics and semiotics of one
text'. Revised version of a paper presented at the International Spring Collo-
quium of the Applied Linguistics Research Group 'Relations and Functions
within and around Language', Glendon College, York University, Toronto,
Canada, 22–24 April 1988.

Thibault, P. (1992) 'Grammar, ethics and understanding: functionalist reason and
clause as exchange'. *Social Semiotics* 2(1), 135–75.

Windshuttle, K. and Windshuttle, E. (1990) *Writing, Researching, Communicating*.
Sydney: McGraw-Hill.

## 4 Death, disruption and the moral order: the narrative impulse in mass-media 'hard news' reporting

*Peter White*

### Introduction

*News reporting: genre and rhetorical objectives*

This chapter explores the genres of arguably one of the most influential textual domains in contemporary society, that of mass-media news reporting. In particular, it focuses on English-language print-media reports, since media texts display considerable generic variation across the different media and across languages and cultures. It examines both the generic organization of these mass-media reports and the social and ideological objectives which this organization acts to realize.

Texts will be explored from the domain known as 'hard news' – reports typically associated with eruptive violence, reversals of fortune and socially significant breaches of the moral order. This hard news category includes both those reports which are primarily grounded in a material event such as an accident, natural disaster, riot or terrorist attack, and those grounded in a communicative event such as a speech, interview, report or press release. The chapter will demonstrate that a significant number of reports of both types share the same generic structure, a mode of textual organization unique to the mass media which gives hard news its textual distinctiveness. Both types of hard news report will be shown to achieve their informational and rhetorical objectives through a non-linear, 'orbital' structure in which dependent 'satellites' elaborate, explain, contextualize and appraise a textually dominant 'nucleus'.

The view that the news story is a mode of 'narrative' is a commonplace in the media and cultural studies literature and the chapter will endorse this position. It will explore in detail the way the hard news report inflects the events it describes with cultural and ideological meanings, arguing that the hard news report acts to construct and to naturalize a model of social stability, morality and normality. But it will also address the apparently contradictory position typically taken by journalists themselves – the claim that the news report is an 'objective', 'neutral' and 'impersonal' mode of meaning making. While not supporting this position, the chapter will show how it is based on two key distinguishing features of the hard news report:

● the generic structure mentioned above which acts to naturalize and to obscure the operation of underlying ideological positions;
● the construction of a journalistic register in which certain interpersonally charged register variables are severely circumscribed.

### The ideational grounding of hard news: 'event' versus 'issue'

The chapter describes the structure and rhetorical purposes of two subtypes of hard news report. The first, to be labelled 'event story', describes what happened in the event of some misadventure, act of political violence, crime, economic setback and so on. The second type is grounded in a communicative event and acts typically to describe the criticisms, accusations, demands, warnings, discoveries or announcements of some authorized source such as a politician, community leader, lobbyist, professional expert or scientific researcher. These communicatively based items have been labelled 'issues reports' to reflect their role in describing the semiotic activity, the public controversies and debates which are triggered when some newsworthy event or state of affairs acquires the status of 'issue'.[1]

The two types of report are exemplified below. The first, an event story, describes a newsworthy happening – the associated set of violent actions and events which followed the testing of a nuclear weapon by the French government in August 1995. The second, an issues report, is grounded, in contrast, not in any single event but in the statements to a parliamentary inquiry by a children's magistrate in Sydney, Australia. The report describes his claims that there has been a serious increase in violent juvenile crime and his call for increased police powers to address the problem.


[Event story]

**BOMB RAGE**

**Riots sweep Tahiti**

RIOTERS carved a blazing trail of destruction through the paradise island of Tahiti yesterday in a wave of fury sparked by French nuclear bomb tests.

Tahiti airport was left a smouldering wreck after more than 1000 protesters attacked riot police, drove a mechanical digger through the terminal and set the building alight.

France sent in tough Foreign Legion troops as riots spread to the nearby capital, Papeete.

Protesters looted shops, set a perfume store on fire and stoned an office building and the Territorial Assembly building.

Opposition to nuclear testing swept around the globe just a day after France exploded the first of up to eight bombs at Mururoa atoll, also in French controlled Polynesia.

Demonstrations included one by more than 10,000 people in Chile.

The riots in Tahiti are believed to have involved independence activists and trade unions.

Foreign Affairs Minister Gareth Evans said yesterday: 'France has really reaped what it has sown.'

(*Telegraph Mirror*, Sydney, 8 September 1995. © The Daily Telegraph, Used by permission)

[Issues report]

**Ban Teens' Knives**

**Juvenile violence 'rising sharply'**

POLICE should have the power to confiscate knives from teenagers after an increase in violent offences, the State's most senior children's magistrate told a parliamentary inquiry yesterday.

Rod Blackmore, senior children's magistrate for 17 years, said violent offences had risen while others, such as car stealing and general theft, had fallen.

Mr Blackmore said violent matters accounted for 41 per cent of offences listed before him at Bidura Children's Court, Glebe, for the next two months. They included malicious wounding, armed robbery, assault with bodily harm, assault on police, personal violence and assault with intent to rob.

Offences involving knives made up 30 per cent of all violent matters before him.

Mr Blackmore said knives had become the most popular weapon used by young criminals.

He said police should be given the power to confiscate pocket knives, butterfly and flick knives.

Mr Blackmore told the all party Standing Committee on Social Issues inquiry into youth violence that five years ago car theft was the big problem.

It made up more than half of his workload but a clampdown on car theft had reduced the number, Mr Blackmore said, to less than 20 per cent.

He said there were about 17 youths charged with murder going through the court system.

'The real worry is the carrying of knives by juveniles which is very frequent in the community and schools,' he said.

Outside the inquiry, Mr Blackmore said he felt the proportion of violent offences involving knives had increased six-fold over the past five years.

'The use of knives, certainly in robberies, is a fairly frequent feature.'

Mr Blackmore said the law says a person is not entitled to carry a weapon for personal protection.

Allowing police to confiscate a knife would mean teenagers could be cautioned, rather than charged for the offence.

It may be possible children could get their knife back from police if they proved they had a proper use for the weapon or their parents knew of it, Mr Blackmore said.

Mr Blackmore also raised the possibility the anti-car stealing push may have led to the increase in violent crime.

'If people are doing things for kicks, do they now go out and wander round
streets at night looking for someone to mug rather than taking someone's car?'
he said.

(*Telegraph Mirror*, Sydney, 27 July 1994. © The Daily Telegraph, Used by
permission)

It must be noted in passing that the grounding of the event story in a
material happening does not preclude the inclusion of statements, opin-
ions, etc. of authorized sources. In fact, such communicatively based
elements are standard in the event story. Here, however, they play only a
subsidiary role, typically confined to just a few sentences and acting only
to elaborate the central description of the newsworthy material happening.

In addition, there are some reports which combine description of
material and communicative events in roughly equal measure and which
accordingly must be seen as combining event with issue. These
event/issues hybrids are found frequently in the domain of political
reporting. It must also be noted that, while the type of news story examined here occurs with high frequency in the media, the generic structure
to be set out in detail below represents only one of the choices available
for constructing event and issues reports and other patterns of textual
development are to be found within hard news reporting.

## The lead-dominated hard news story: genre analysis

*Ideational orientation: newsworthiness and the subject matter of hard news*

The subject matter of these hard news event stories and issues reports
encompasses events or situations which are construed as threatening to
damage, disrupt or rearrange the social order in its material, political or
normative guise. The sources of this social order disruption can be
grouped under the following three headings: aberrant damage, adversative rearrangements of power relations and normative breach.[2]

### Aberrant damage

Aberrant damage can result from the action of natural forces such as
storms, earthquakes and bushfires, from accidents, incompetence or care-
lessness associated with human enterprise, from outbreaks of disease,
from the harmful action of the global or local economy or from acts of
intentional violence such as riots, terrorist attacks or warfare. The
damage, therefore, can be either of a physical or an economic nature.
The notion of 'aberrant' damage is necessary to account for the fact that
certain types of damage – four local Thais dying in a bus crash in
Bangkok, the fact that around 100 people die each day in Australia of
heart disease – are not construed as warranting news coverage by, for

example, the Australian media. Such damage is seen by the mass-media's system of subject-matter assessment as a part of the natural order of things and hence 'normal'. It is only that damage which threatens the *status quo* which is hence seen as socio-culturally 'disruptive' or 'damaging' and which is viewed as warranting coverage.

## Power relations

The domain of politics, both domestic and international, is the most obvious source of reports which turn on rearrangements of power relationships. Hard news reporting provides a fine-grained coverage of the minute shifts in power associated with rises and falls in political popularity, leadership challenges, changes in alliances, factional infighting and parliamentary performance as well as the more substantive shifts associated with elections, rebellions, military coups, trade agreements and wars. But there are other sources, including the worlds of business and the bureaucracy where, for example, take-overs, senior appointments and management power struggles are all classified as providing subject matter worthy of coverage. Also associated with shifts in power relations are those items dealing with perceived changes in social roles where those changes ultimately have an impact upon power relations. Perhaps the most obvious of these changes is that associated with the role of women in society. Even today in Australia the news that a woman has been appointed to a senior management position in a major company represents newsworthy subject matter, as is the news that a group of women has decided to form an all-women surf-lifesaving lifeboat crew. The notion of a rearrangement that is 'adversative' accounts for the fact that, to be worthy of coverage, the shift in the power relationship must be seen as at odds with the interests or at least the expectations of some socially significant individual or grouping, and can accordingly be seen as socially 'disruptive' or 'damaging' in some way.

## Normative breach

The category of 'normative breach' involves events or states of affairs construed as departing from either established morality or custom. News items which involve a sense of moral breach include the obvious crime and corruption reports, where clear-cut illegality is involved,[3] but also include coverage of those acts of incompetence, negligence, arrogance, indifference, etc. which are seen to threaten society's sense of duty or propriety. Thus, a sense of 'moral breach' will underlie the newsworthiness of reports of poor performance by government agencies, of reports that the schools are failing to equip students for the workforce and of reports of the abandonment of new-born babies. Developments such as the growth of new religions, changes in a nation's dietary habits and shifts in the populace's sporting interests are examples of departures from established

custom which are newsworthy in the English language media. Frequently
such shifts in custom will acquire overtones of moral transgression as, for
example, the burgeoning interest in American basketball among the
young in Australia is construed as a betrayal of core national values and a
threat to the Australian identity.

Under all three headings, therefore, the subject matter deemed newsworthy by the media always entails some perceived threat to the social
order – natural disasters, outbreaks of disease, price rises and stockmarket
plunges disrupt the material order; elections, leadership challenges and
warfare disrupt the *status quo* of power relations; crimes and bureaucratic
bungles destabilize the moral order. In terms of informational content,
therefore, hard news reporting texts are directed towards the identification of potential or actual sources of social-order disequilibrium.

Event stories and issues reports, however, offer different representations of this social-order disruption by dint of their respective groundings
in material and communicative events. The event story purports to
describe socially disruptive events at first hand, to present a largely
unqualified, unmodulated account of what happened, as if the reporter
had been present at the time. The event is, thus, in terms of Halliday's
grammar, presented as a 'phenomenon', as a happening in external reality to which the reader is given direct access by the text. Some aspects of
the account may be qualified by modal values of uncertainty or by attribution to external sources but, as demonstrated by the 'Tahiti Riot' report
cited above, event stories act primarily to present unmediated descriptions of 'real world' happenings.

In contrast, the issues report acts, in the terms of Halliday's grammar,
to 'project' (see Halliday 1994: 250–73) the social-order disruption with
which it is concerned. That is to say, the actions and states of affairs with
which it is concerned are not described directly by the author but are
'projected' via the process of reporting the statements of some authorized
source. Thus the ontological status of the *status-quo* disequilibrium of the
issues report is fundamentally qualified or equivocal since the issues
report acts to present 'claims', not 'facts'. We can say, therefore, that the
issues report presents statements about a supposed 'reality' rather than
that 'reality' in its own right and hence represents the social-order disruption not as a 'phenomenon' but as 'metaphenomenon' (see Halliday
1994: 252).

*The interpersonal orientation: the voice of the hard news reporter*

Media training texts, practising journalists and media commentators frequently claim that the language or the 'voice' of the hard news report
should be 'factual', 'neutral' and free of 'subjectivity'. In a training text
for French journalism students, for example, Husson and Robert con-
demn much of the French print media for mixing 'fact with opinion' in
its reporting. They insist the French media should follow more closely the

model of the high-quality English-language media where, they contend, the language of hard news reporting is 'precise and 'neutral', where the reporter eliminates all subjectivity and where 'the only things on show are the raw facts' (1991: 63, my translation). Similarly, the guidelines of Australia's Special Broadcasting Service (SBS)[4] explicitly state that all SBS news reporting must be 'impartial' and 'objective'.

Although this notion of a neutral and objective voice is a problematic one requiring more extended treatment than is possible here (see Iedema *et al.* 1994: 200–36), it does, nevertheless, reflect certain systematic trends in the semantics and lexicogrammar of hard news reporting, at least in the mainstream English-language press. In a significant proportion of hard news texts, the author avoids or at least minimizes interpersonal meanings which may act to reveal or to foreground his/her subjective involvement in the meanings being made by the text.[5] The meanings typically avoided include explicit value judgements by the reporter about the morality, competence, normality, etc. of participants, explicit evaluations of events and entities in terms of their aesthetics or emotional impact, inferences about the motivations and intentions of participants and contentious claims about causes and effects.[6] All such meanings rely upon the action of the author's individual subjecthood in applying value judgements, in responding emotionally to events, in extrapolating mental states from the material actions of others and in applying theories of cause and effect. For the author to proffer these is thus to foreground their interpersonal role in the text's construction. Consequently such meanings are either avoided or confined to the quoted comments of external sources in those canonical hard news texts which seek to represent themselves as neutral and impersonal.

In avoiding such personalizing or subjective meanings on the part of the journalist–author, hard news reporting stands in contradistinction to the other primary mode of media textuality, the commentary or opinion piece. In the media commentary, the role of the author is precisely to offer up subjective interpretations in which a central role is played by explicit value judgements, aesthetic evaluations, theories of cause-and-effect and so on. The distinction between the language of hard news and commentary is illustrated by the following two extracts from the domain of politics, the first from a hard news report from the newsroom of Australia's Special Broadcasting Service and the second from a commentary from the opinion pages of the *Sydney Morning Herald* (subjectivizing meanings in the commentary piece have been underlined).

[Hard news report]
A White House aide has paid the American Navy 562 dollars for towels and bathrobes that disappeared from an aircraft carrier on which President Clinton stayed during his trip to Normandy, earlier this month.

   Communications Director Mark Gearan said White House scheduling director Ricki Seidman paid the money from her pocket 'to dispel any notion of impropriety.'

The Navy had asked the White House for reimbursement for towels and
robes missing from the USS *George Washington,* which accommodated Mr Clinton, 40 aides and 23 reporters during ceremonies marking the 50th anniver-
sary of D-Day.

The money was paid after a memo was issued to White House staffers asking
for payment for 16 bathrobes and 68 towels from the aircraft carrier, some with
the ship's insignia.

[Commentary/opinion]
His speech two nights ago was that <u>dreadful</u>. It was <u>facile</u>, <u>contrived</u>, <u>pedestrian</u>
and <u>disingenuous</u>. It had <u>no commitment</u>, <u>no passion</u> and <u>no clarity</u>. It revived
all the <u>flaws</u> that brought him undone that first time six years ago. It <u>marked
him</u>, <u>perhaps fatally, as truly yesterday's man</u>. It exposed him <u>more brutally
than ever</u> as <u>a leader locked into the past</u>, as a politician of <u>indecision</u>, of <u>no
courage</u>, <u>no guile</u>, <u>no ideas</u>, <u>no true understanding</u> of his own country in the
1990s, and <u>no feel for the future</u>. If it wasn't <u>complete humbug</u>, it was <u>an
absolute political disaster</u>.

(Commentary by Alan Ramsey on a speech by the then Australian Federal
Opposition leader, John Howard, *Sydney Morning Herald,* 10 June 1995)

The distinction between the interpersonally neutral register of the
hard news reporter and the interpersonally charged register of the com-
mentator is not, however, a simple dichotomy. There are, in practice,
many hard news texts which lie somewhere between these two texts. The
cited texts, in fact, stand at the opposite extremes of a cline on which
texts can be located according to the number and intensity of the explicit
'subjectivizing' meanings they present and hence the degree to which
they are felt to position the reader interpersonally. In the Australian
media, the texts of correspondents and specialist 'rounds' reporters, for
example, typically contain significantly more of these interpersonal meanings than those of general reporters or the international wire services.
Nevertheless, it still remains valid to characterize hard news texts by reference to the way in which they restrict or turn off, so to speak, interpersonal meanings and to see them, at least in relative terms, as texts where a
range of interpersonal values are either avoided or underplayed.

In one crucial respect, however, even the most canonical of hard news
reports depart from this general interpersonal neutrality. A recurring
feature of the hard news report is the presence of lexis which encodes a
sense of intensity or heightened involvement by the author and which
positions the reader to view the events or statements described as significant, momentous or emotionally charged. This semantics of intensification is illustrated by the event story already cited above. There the
actions by the Tahitians in response to the French nuclear test were
described as a *bomb rage* which *carved a blazing trail of destruction* through a
*paradise* island in *a wave of fury* which left Tahiti airport *a smouldering wreck.*

This intensification is, in fact, so common a feature of the register of
hard news journalism that it now acts to mark news reporting as a distinc-

tive functional variety of language. Thus it is primarily the intensifying lexis which marks the language in the following extracts from three event stories as journalistic (intensifications underlined).

> One third of the 100 senior civil servants at the Treasury have been <u>axed</u> by Mr Kenneth Clarke, in <u>one of the greatest shake-ups</u> of a Government department.
> *(Weekly Telegraph (Daily Telegraph)*, London, 24 October 1994)

> Nine people died in and around the Greek capital as <u>torrential</u> rains <u>lashed</u> the region at the weekend, causing <u>damage of 'biblical' proportions</u> and bringing a nation-wide halt to rail traffic.          (Agence France Presse, 24 October 1994)

> A man who once praised Hitler's labour policies has emerged from Austria's general election with the strongest far-right parliamentary bloc in Western Europe in <u>a shock result</u> that has <u>sent the ruling coalition parties reeling</u> to their <u>worst losses since 1945</u>.
> (Reuters, 11 October 1994)

As illustrated by these examples, this intensification in event stories most typically takes two forms:

- Lexis, which combines an informational meaning with a sense of inter-personal engagement and heightened impact – thus, *axed* for *dismissed*, *shake-up* for *reorganization* and *torrential rains lashed* for *heavy rain fell*.[7]
- Comparisons, which assert the great size, force, severity, significance, etc. of the action under consideration – thus, *one of the greatest shake-ups*, *damage of biblical proportions* and *the worst losses since 1945*.

Tellingly, the mode of intensification is never cited by the journalistic training texts or by practising journalists as damaging the interpersonal neutrality of hard news stories. It may be seen as formulaic, clichéd or even sensationalist and hence criticized, but it is never viewed as acting to personalize or subjectivize the text. (See, for example, Bagnall 1993: 90–2.)

The same lexical resources are used within the issues report for the purpose of intensification. Perhaps predictably, given the central role of 'projection' within the issues report, the intensifying impulse often informs the way the process of verbal communication is reported. Thus politicians *slam* their opponents rather than criticizing or disagreeing with them, political parties find themselves *plunged into a heated row* rather than engaging in debate and adverse findings are formulaically described as *damning indictments*.

As a result, however, of their grounding in the words of external sources rather than those of the reporter him/herself, issues reports are less limited than event stories in their choice of meanings with which to heighten impact and to engage the reader emotionally in the text. Accordingly they do not need to rely so heavily on the mode of intensi-

fication outlined above. Thus, in the following extract from an issues
report, China's orphanages can be labelled *death camps* – an explicit moral
judgement obviously capable of engaging the reader emotionally in the
text – without damaging the author's mask of interpersonal neutrality,
since the description is an attributed one.

> Thousands of Chinese orphans are being killed each year at institutions which
> are little more than death camps, according to a report by the New York-based
> group, Human Rights Watch Asia.
>
> (*The Australian*, 8 January 1996)

Issues reports also routinely exploit the vagueness inherent in the semantics of indirect speech in order to heighten the sense of both writer's and
reader's engagement in the text. Under this vagueness, it is possible to
strengthen and intensify the statements of the quoted source while at the
same time appearing to remain within the bounds of attribution and
hence to maintain the author's neutrality. Thus, in the issues report cited
above, the call by the Sydney magistrate for police to be given the
power to *confiscate* knives is restated as a call for a *ban* on knives for
teenagers. The same process is at work in the following issues report
extract.

**CHILD CARE ON TRIAL**

**Child-care standards a scandal, say experts**

By ADELE HORIN

> Many child-care centres are flagrantly breaching regulations and are operating
> with impunity because it is almost impossible to close them, say child-care spe-
> cialists. And new national child-care standards to be introduced next year are
> unlikely to improve the worsening situation.
>
> In a damning indictment, child-care experts say some centres ignore State
> Government regulations on staff numbers, health and safety issues, knowing
> they will not even be fined.
>
> (*Sydney Morning Herald*, 11 February 1995)

Although the full report describes various strong criticisms of the child-
care centres by child-care experts, there is no evidence that the experts
actually described the situation as 'a scandal' or accused centres of 'fla-
grantly' breaching regulations. Here the choice of words acts to intensify
the strength of the attributed command or moral judgement.

*The textual organization of the hard news report: generic structure*

Textual structure acts to implement the informational and interpersonal
meanings carried by a text so as to achieve certain rhetorical or communicative objectives. Thus we are interested in how a given textual structure

arranges and presents both informational and interpersonal meanings, where given meanings are located in the movement from textual opening to closure, how informational and interpersonal meanings interact and whether sets of distinct meanings operate to establish stages of textual unfolding. In the context of the hard news report, we are concerned, therefore, with how textual structure acts to implement informational meanings relating to perceived social-order disequilibrium and interpersonal meanings which act to intensify both the author's and reader's engagement in this informational content.

The hard news report can be divided into two primary phases: an opening nucleus containing the text's core informational and interpersonal meanings; a subsequent development stage which acts not to introduce new meanings but to qualify, elaborate, explain and appraise the meanings already presented in the opening 'nucleus'. The nature of these two phases and the manner in which they interact will be examined in detail in the following sections.

### The textual nucleus: headline plus lead

The nucleus of the English-language print media hard news report is most typically constituted by the combination of its headline and its opening sentence (known to journalists as either the lead or intro[8]). These two elements can be seen as representing a single unit or phase because, in the overwhelming majority of cases, the headline exactly repeats a subset of the informational content of the lead, serving simply to signpost key meanings which will be presented more fully in the following sentence. The interdependence between headline and lead is illustrated by the following examples, the first from an event story report of a hurricane which struck the United States in 1992 and the second from the issues report already cited above. (Points of interdependence have been underlined and indexed.)

Million[1] flee[2] as hurricane[3] pounds[4] Florida[5]
MIAMI[5], Monday: Hurricane[3] Andrew smashed[3] ashore south of Miami[5] early today with walls of water and the howling terror of 257 km/h winds, forcing a million[1] people to flee[2] and leaving 13 dead in the wake of what could be the biggest storm[3] to hit the United States this century.
(*Sydney Morning Herald*, 25 August 1992)

Ban[1] teens'[2] knives[3]
Juvenile[2] violence[4] 'rising sharply'[5]
POLICE should have the power to confiscate[1] knives[3] from teenagers[2] after an increase[5] in violent[4] offences, the State's most senior children's magistrate told a parliamentary inquiry yesterday.
(*Telegraph Mirror*, Sydney, 27 July 1994)

This interdependence can be seen as an artefact of the news production process, since headlines are written not by the reporter but, at a later stage, by a subeditor who typically seeks a headline which sums up the lead.[9]

This opening nucleus of headline plus lead acts to launch the reader immediately into the heart of the social-order disruption about which the report is organized. Unlike many other genres which offer introductory backgrounding and context setting, the hard news report provides nothing by way of textual preliminaries, no gearing-up of the textual process. The opening Headline/lead nucleus casts the reader abruptly into the core subject matter of the report, the threat to the social order. And perhaps most tellingly, the opening nucleus goes directly to those aspects of the event or state of affairs which are assessed as constituting the peak or climax of social-order disruption. That is, it singles out those aspects of the event or issue at hand which pose the greatest threat to the material, power-relational or normative *status quo*, extracting them from their original chronological or logical context and thus compelling the reader to engage immediately with some crisis point of social-order disequilibrium.

This process can be exemplified by reference to the news items already cited. In the 'Hurricane Andrew' report, for example, the Headline/lead nucleus does not set the scene by means of a general overview, nor by an account of first storm warnings or the first signs of the storm's arrival. Rather, it moves directly to a carefully selected subset of incidents, the thirteen deaths and the million evacuations, elements which represent what was maximally damaging and catastrophic for human material order. Similarly, the opening nucleus of the 'Tahiti Riot' report does not describe the geographical setting nor the political background of the French nuclear tests, nor does it set out the first step in a chronologically organized account of the events following the nuclear test. Rather, it takes the reader immediately to a description of those incidents which constitute maximal material and moral-order disruption – a *bomb rage* in which *rioters carve a blazing trail of destruction* through the island of Tahiti.

The Headline/lead nucleus of the issue report acts in a similar way although the climax of social-order disruption is, as discussed above, metaphenomenal rather than phenomenal. That is, rather than describing some actual catastrophic action or actions, the Headline/lead nucleus of the issues report presents statements which claim to identify points of social-order disruption. And just as the Headline/lead of the event story singles out the incidents representing maximal societal disequilibrium from their original position in an unfolding sequence of events, so too the Headline/lead of the issues report extracts the most 'newsworthy' statements from their position in the original sequence of the speech, interview, press release, etc. upon which the report is based.

This process of selection can be illustrated briefly by analysing the connection between a press release from the international aid organization, World Vision, and the news report based on that press release by the radio news department of Australia's SBS.[10] Figure 4.1 places the press release beside the news report in order to show how the SBS reporter ignored the press release's original ordering of information and the informational emphases which followed from it – the two boxes illustrate where similar information is presented within the two texts. The structure of the press release – displayed in the left column – begins with, and thereby foregrounds comments about the 'inspiring' resolve of the people of Bosnia and the role of World Vision in supporting them. The SBS reporter, however, selects what was essentially a footnote in the ori-

| [Word Vision Press Release] | [SBS news report] |
|---|---|
| AUSTRALIAN AID WORKER RETURNS FROM BOSNIA<br>World Vision Australian worker Margaret Jephson has returned from Bosnia where she spent the last five weeks as part of World Vision's Bosnia Relief Team.<br>Margaret travelled through central Bosnia, visiting World Vision relief projects and speaking with dozens of refugees including many from the former UN Safe Haven of Srebrenica and Zepa.<br>She witnessed the extreme condition which people have had to endure over the last three years and the resolve of Bosnia's people to go on living despite incredible hardship.<br>'The total destruction of life and property throughout Bosnia is quite staggering. The way the people have gotten used to living under the shadow of the gun and can still go on planning for the future is quite inspiring.'<br>World Vision's relief efforts are coordinated from the central Bosnian town of Zenica. From here, fresh fruit and vegetables are distributed to refugees and locals affected by war.<br>'The people have been living on canned and dried food for so long and they were overjoyed to have fresh vegetables suppled to them by World Vision.<br>'Apart from the obvious improvement to their diet, the positive psychological effect of having fresh fruit was great.'<br>However, the long term needs of Bosnia's refugees are looked after from Zenica also, with the provision of trauma counselling and the promotion of reconciliation between the different ethnic groups.<br>'World Vision has started training local teachers to take children through trauma and grief session. Some of these teachers have children who have seen family members hacked to pieces before them. They don't know how to deal with children in this situation and are extremely grateful for any help they can get.' | An AUSTRALIAN aid worker just returned from BOSNIA says the latest NATO bombing campaign has brought new hope for SARAJEVO residents hoping the action may finally free their embattled city. |
| At the end of August when NATO began retaliatory attacks against the Bosnia Serb Army, Margaret experienced the relief of Bosnia's war-weary refugees: 'When the news came through the first strikes had started, everybody was very happy. They were a little apprehensive that the Serbs may try to take some retaliatory activity, but that didn't eventuate.<br>'They are happy that there is action being taken at last and that the prospect of peace is finally starting to become a reality.' | MARGARET JEPHSON, from WORLD-VISION says spirits have been very low especially since the bloody mortar attack on the city's market place.<br>She says that in the first hours after the attacks there were fears the Serbs might strike back in retaliation.<br>But when this did not occur, there was great relief and a genuine hope that peace for the war-torn nation could finally be achieved. Ms. JEPHSON says the most important challenge for any aid organisation at the moment is to try and help the younger generation overcome their grief and trauma with the aim of preventing a continuation of the violence.<br>GRAB M#392 MARGARET JEPHSON [taped material from interview with Jephson]<br>If these young people especially carry these great hurts and traumas with them as they grow then the ground for further conflict is more fertile but if at this stage we can intervene when there's time for them to get over the events and to process them properly, to move on with their lives, I think that's a really important intervention that an aid organisation can make in a situation like that. |

**Figure 4.1** Informational organization of World Vision press release and SBS issues report compared

ginal release for maximum emphasis in the lead – descriptions relating to
the adversative rearrangements of power represented by NATO's aggres-
sive intervention in the war in Bosnia. Thus, just as the event story
extracts from its temporal context those aspects of the material activity
sequence (see Martin 1992: 321–5) which are construed as most disruptive of the social order, the issues report extracts that aspect of the verbal
sequence which the reporter construes as having the greatest impact on
social order and stability. In so doing, it may well ignore, or at least de-
emphasize, the primary message of the original source material.

### Headline/lead: interpersonal role

The Headline/lead nucleus is most typically the primary site within the text
for the intensifying interpersonal meanings discussed above. That is, while
such meanings may be found at any point in the text, they typically occur in
the highest concentration and with the greatest rhetorical affect in the
headline and lead. This concentration can be illustrated by reference to the
'Tahiti Riot' report. In the analysis set out in Figure 4.2, the points of intensification have been underlined and then their number totalled, in the left-
most column, as a rough guide to rhetorical impact. There are nine points
in the Headline/lead, no more than two points in any of the subsequent
sentences and no points in the final three sentences.

| 9 | BOMB RAGE<br>Riots sweep Tahiti<br>RIOTERS carved a blazing trail of destruction through the paradise island of Tahiti yesterday in a wave of fury sparked by French nuclear bomb tests. |
|---|---|
| 1 | Tahiti airport was left a smouldering wreck after more than 1000 protesters attacked riot police, drove a mechanical digger through the terminal and set the building alight. |
| 1 | France sent in tough Foreign Legion troops as riots spread to the nearby capital, Papeete. |
| 2 | Protesters looted shops, set a perfume store on fire and stoned an office building and the Territorial Assembly building. |
| 1 | Opposition to nuclear testing swept around the globe just a day after France exploded the first of up to eight bombs at Mururoa atoll, also in French controlled Polynesia. |
| 0 | Demonstrations included one by more than 10,000 people in Chile. |
| 0 | The riots in Tahiti are believed to have involved independence activists and trade unions. |
| 0 | Foreign Affairs Minister Gareth Evans said yesterday: 'France has really reaped what it has sown.' |

**Figure 4.2** Intensification analysis: distribution of points of intensification in
'Tahiti Riot' report (points totalled in left-hand column)

From this perspective, therefore, the Headline/lead can be seen as representing an interpersonal peak, as providing a burst of interpersonal meanings at the beginning of the text which then subsides as the remainder of the text unfolds. Accordingly, the Headline/lead acts to single out some point of maximal social-order disruption while simultaneously employing interpersonal values to characterize that point as dramatic, highly significant and/or emotionally charged.

### The body of the news story: satellite structure

The second phase of the hard news story – the body which follows the Headline/lead nucleus – acts to specify the meanings presented in the opening Headline/lead nucleus through elaboration, contextualization, explanation, appraisal and, in the case of the issues report, justification. That is to say, the primary role of the second phase is not to develop new meanings nor to introduce entirely new information but, rather, to refer back to the Headline/lead through a series of specifications.

The second phase can be further broken down into subcomponents according to the nature of the relationship or relationships of specification which the subcomponent enters into with the Headline/lead nucleus.

Analysis of a large number of news stories has revealed the following five broad modes or relationships of specification:[11]

- Elaboration: one sentence or a group of sentences provides more detailed description or exemplification of information presented in the Headline/lead, or acts to restate it or describe the material in the Headline/lead in different terms.
- Cause-and-effect: one or more sentences describe the causes, the reasons for, the consequences or the purpose of the 'crisis point' presented in the Headline/lead.
- Justification (issues reports): one or more sentences provide the evidence or reasoning which supports the newsworthy claim presented in the Headline/lead nucleus. This justification could be seen as a text internal cause-and-effect in that it explains why a particular claim has been made and hence could be included within a single broader 'Cause-and-effect category.[12]
- Contextualization: one or more sentences place the events or statements of the Headline/lead in a temporal, spatial or social context. The geographical setting will be described in some detail or the 'crisis point' will be located in the context of preceding, simultaneous or subsequent events. Prior events of a similar nature may be described for the purpose of comparison.
- Appraisal: elements of the Headline/lead nucleus are appraised, typically by some expert external source, in terms of their significance, their emotional impact, or by reference to some system of value judgement.

The operation of the second-phase subcomponents in specifying the Headline/lead nucleus via these relationships is illustrated in the analyses set out in Figures 4.3 and 4.4, the first of the 'Tahiti Riot' event story (Figure 4.3) and the second of the 'Knives Ban' issues report (Figure 4.4). The key feature of this specification of the Headline/lead by the second-phase subcomponents is that it is organized 'orbitally' rather than linearly. That is to say, the subcomponents do not link together to build a linear semantic pathway by which meaning is accumulated sequentially. Rather than building on what comes immediately before or preparing the way for what is to follow immediately after, each subcomponent reaches back to specify the Headline/lead nucleus, which acts as the text's anchor point or textual centre of gravity.

| |
|---|
| **[Nucleus – headline/lead]** |
| BOMB RAGE |
| Riots sweep Tahiti |
| RIOTERS carved a blazing trail of destruction through the paradise island of Tahiti yesterday in a wave of fury sparked by French nuclear bomb tests. |
| **[Specification 1: Cause-and-effect + Elaboration** – *consequences of the riot + details of 'trail of destruction'*] |
| Tahiti airport was left a smouldering wreck after more than 1000 protesters attacked riot police, drove a mechanical digger through the terminal and set the building alight. |
| **[Specification 2: Cause-and-effect** – *consequence of riot*] |
| France sent in tough Foreign Legion troops as riots spread to the nearby capital, Papeete. |
| **[Specification 3: Elaboration** – *details of 'trail of destruction'*] |
| Protesters looted shops, set a perfume store on fire and stoned an office building and the Territorial Assembly building. |
| **[Specification 4: Contextualization** – *protests simultaneous with riot*] |
| Opposition to nuclear testing swept around the globe just a day after France exploded the first of up to eight bombs at Mururoa atoll, also in French controlled Polynesia. Demonstrations included one by more than 10,000 people in Chile. |
| **[Specification 5: Elaboration** – *specifies 'rioters'*] |
| The riots in Tahiti are believed to have involved independence activists and trade unions. |
| **[Specification 6: Appraisal** – *riots appraised by Evans as France's 'just deserts', thereby implying some moral breach on the part of France*] |
| Foreign Affairs Minister Gareth Evans said yesterday: 'France has really reaped what it has sown.' |

**Figure 4.3** Tahiti Riot (event story): specification of Headline/lead analysis

This pattern of orbital textual development – in which the Headline/lead acts as nucleus and the second-phase subcomponents act as its satellites – can be strikingly demonstrated by exploring what I term the 'radical editability' of the second phase: the freedom with which the order of second-phase subcomponents can be changed without damaging the functionality of the text. In the first column of Figure 4.5, the 'Tahiti Riot' report is presented in its original, published form, with radically

[Nucleus: *proposition that knives should be confiscated because violent juvenile crime is increasing*]

Ban teens' knives

Juvenile violence 'rising sharply'

POLICE should have the power to confiscate knives from teenagers after an increase in violent offences, the State's most senior children's magistrate told a parliamentary inquiry yesterday.

[Specification 1: <u>Elaboration</u> – *restates, exemplifies 'an increase in violent offences' among teenagers*]

Rod Blackmore, senior children's magistrate for 17 years said violent offences had risen while others, such as car stealing and general theft, had fallen.

Mr Blackmore said violent matters accounted for 41 per cent of offences listed before him at Bidura Children's Court Glebe, for the next two months. They included malicious wounding, armed robbery, assault with bodily harm, assault on police, personal violence and assault with intent to rob.

[Specification 2: <u>Justification (Cause-and-Effect)</u> – *reason why confiscation of knives is proposed*]

Offences involving knives made up 30 per cent of all violent matters before him.

Mr Blackmore said knives had become the most popular weapon used by young criminals.

[Specification 3: <u>Elaboration</u> – *restatement of primary thesis as presented in headline/lead, restates 'police should have the power to confiscate knives . . .'*]

He said police should be given the power to confiscate pocket knives, butterfly and flick knives.

[Specification 4: <u>Contextualization</u> – *the prior situation*]

Mr Blackmore told the all party Standing Committee on Social Issues inquiry into youth violence that five years ago car theft was the big problem.

It made up more than half of his workload but a clampdown on car theft had reduced the number, Mr Blackmore said, to less than 20 per cent.

[Specification 5: <u>Elaboration</u> – *specifies, exemplifies 'an increase in violent offences' among teenagers*]

He said there were about 17 youths charged with murder going through the court system.

[Specification 6: <u>Justification (Cause-and-Effect)</u> – *reason why knives must be confiscated*]

'The real worry is the carrying of knives by juveniles which is very frequent in the community and schools,' he said.

Outside the inquiry, Mr Blackmore said he felt the proportion of violent offences involving knives had increased six-fold over the past five years.

'The use of knives, certainly in robberies, is a fairly frequent feature.'

[Specification 7: <u>Contextualization</u> – *legal context in which the call for confiscation is made*]

Mr Blackmore said the law says a person is not entitled to carry a weapon for personal protection.

[Specification 8: <u>Cause-and-Effect</u> – *tates purpose/consequence of primary proposal*]

Allowing police to confiscate a knife would mean teenagers could be cautioned, rather than charged for the offence.

It may be possible children could get their knife back from police if they proved they had a proper use for the weapon or their parents knew of it, Mr Blackmore said.

[Specification 8: <u>Cause-and-Effect</u> – *reasons for increase in violent crime*]

Mr Blackmore also raised the possibility the anti-car stealing push may have led to the increase in violent crime. 'If people are doing things for kicks, do they now go out and wander round streets at night looking for someone to mug rather than taking someone's car?' he said.

**Figure 4.4** Knives Ban (issues report): specification of Headline/lead analysis

| [Original, unedited version] | [Edited version 1] | [Edited version 2] |
|---|---|---|
| BOMB RAGE | BOMB RAGE | BOMB RAGE |
| Riots sweep Tahiti | Riots sweep Tahiti | Riots sweep Tahiti |
| RIOTERS carved a blazing trail of destruction through the paradise island of Tahiti yesterday in a wave of fury sparked by French nuclear bomb tests. | RIOTERS carved a blazing trail of destruction through the paradise island of Tahiti yesterday in a wave of fury sparked by French nuclear bomb tests. | RIOTERS carved a blazing trail of destruction through the paradise island of Tahiti yesterday in a wave of fury sparked by French nuclear bomb tests. |
| (1) Tahiti airport was left a smouldering wreck after more than 1000 protesters attacked riot police, drove a mechanical digger through the terminal and set the building alight. | France sent in tough Foreign Legion troops as riots spread to the capital, Papeete. (2) | [But the outrage was not confined to Tahiti as] Opposition to nuclear testing swept around the globe just a day after France exploded the first of up to eight bombs at Mururoa atoll, also in French controlled Polynesia. Demonstrations included one by more than 10,000 people in Chile. (4) |
| (2) France sent in tough Foreign Legion troops as riots spread to the nearby capital, Papeete. | Tahiti airport was left a smouldering wreck after more than 1000 protesters attacked riot police, drove a mechanical digger through the terminal and set the building alight. (1) | Foreign Affairs Minister Gareth Evans said: 'France has really reaped what it has sown.' (5) |
| (3) Protesters looted shops, set a perfume store on fire and stoned an office building and the Territorial Assembly building. | Protesters looted shops, set a perfume store on fire and stoned an office building and the Territorial Assembly building (3) | Protesters looted shops, set a perfume store on fire and stoned an office building and the Territorial Assembly building. (3) |
| (4) Opposition to nuclear testing swept around the globe just a day after France exploded the first of up to eight bombs at Mururoa atoll, also in French controlled Polynesia. Demonstrations included one by more than 10,000 people in Chile. | Foreign Affairs Minister Gareth Evans said yesterday: 'France has really reaped what it has sown.' (5) | France sent in tough Foreign Legion troops as riots spread to the capital, Papeete. (2) |
| (5) Foreign Affairs Minister Gareth Evans said yesterday: 'France has really reaped what it has sown.' | Opposition to nuclear testing swept around the globe just a day after France exploded the first of up to eight bombs at Mururoa atoll, also in French controlled Polynesia. Demonstrations included one by more than 10,000 people in Chile. (4) | Tahiti airport was left a smouldering wreck after more than 1000 protesters attacked riot police, drove a mechanical digger through the terminal and set the building alight. (1) |

**Figure 4.5** Three versions of the 'Tahiti Riot' report demonstrating 'radical editability'

edited versions in subsequent columns. In column 2, the sequence of adjacent subcomponents has been reversed with what was originally element (2) becoming element (1) and element (5) becoming element (4). Column 3 represents an even more radical rearrangement. After the addition of a short phrase (in square brackets) to smooth the transition, element (4), previously the penultimate sentence, has been moved into position immediately after the Headline/lead. What was the final element – element (5) – has been moved into second position and then the order of the remaining elements has been reversed with (3) remaining in place, (2) becoming (4) and (1) becoming (5). (The original position of elements is shown in curved brackets.) The point at stake here is that, despite the radical editing, both new versions function effectively as news reports. The rearrangement of the report's internal structure has not rendered the text communicatively dysfunctional or aberrant, nor has it produced some new subgenre of news report.

This feature is demonstrated further when the *Telegraph Mirror* 'Tahiti Riot' story is compared with reports of the same event from other newspapers. The variable ordering of information, achieved above by editing, is apparent when the internal structures of the alternative reports are examined. This is demonstrated by the comparison set out in Figure 4.6 of the *Telegraph Mirror* report and one from *The Age* of Melbourne. The same information is found in both reports but in a significantly different order.

This is not, of course, to suggest that the relative ordering of information within the body of news stories is without meaning, that it is possible to freely reorder this information without changing the text's overall meaning or that there are no constraints at all on the reordering of the subcomponents of the second phase. Van Dijk (1988), for example, has demonstrated how the promoting or demoting of information within news reports is one mechanism by which the author actively construes certain information, that presented at the earlier position, as having greater significance. But the point here is not that order is unimportant but that radical editing of the sort demonstrated in Figure 4.5 is possible without rendering the text incoherent or generically aberrant.

This freedom of movement is possible because, as an orbitally organized text, the key logical and lexical interactions in the hard news report are not between adjacent subcomponents in the body of the text but between each individual subcomponent and the Headline/lead nucleus. Accordingly, relationships of elaboration, causality, contextuality, etc. – which are more generally seen as linking adjacent clauses or clause complexes – operate between the Headline/lead nucleus and its satellites in the second phase regardless of the intervening textual distances. It is possible to move a satellite within the second phase because its action in specifying the nucleus is unaffected by its relative position in the unfolding text. This pattern of orbital relationships is illustrated diagrammatically in Figure 4.7.

The discussion to this point has demonstrated radical editability with

| [*Telegraph Mirror* 8/9/95] | [*The Age* 8/9/95] |
|---|---|
| BOMB RAGE<br>Riots sweep Tahiti<br>RIOTERS carved a blazing trail of destruction through the paradise island of Tahiti yesterday in a wave of fury sparked by French nuclear bomb tests. | Fallout – Tahiti burns.<br>French fly in the Legion<br>Billowing clouds of thick black smoke clung in the humid air over Papeete last night, after a day in which Tahitian anger over the French nuclear blast at Mururoa Atoll erupted into violent protests, arson and clashes with security forces. |
| [*Airport ablaze after attack*]<br>(1) Tahiti airport was left a smouldering wreck after more than 1000 protesters attacked riot police, drove a mechanical digger through the terminal and set the building alight. | [*France sends in reinforcements*]<br>France sent Foreign legion reinforcements to Tahiti to quell the worst civil violence ever seen there. |
| [*France sends in reinforcements*]<br>(2) France sent in tough Foreign Legion troops as riots spread to the nearby capital, Papeete. | [*Protests staged around the world*]<br>But it was not isolated violence, as opposition to the nuclear test continued to sweep the globe. A massive anti-nuclear demonstration was staged by more than 10,000 people in Santiago, Chile, today. Protests were also held in other capitals, while Japanese newspapers took up calls for a boycott of French goods in response to Tuesday's nuclear blast at Mururoa Atoll. |
| [*Details of rioting in Papeete*]<br>(3) Protesters looted shops, set a perfume store on fire and stoned an office building and the Territorial Assembly building. | [*Airport ablaze after attack*]<br>At Tahiti-Faaa airport outside Papeete, capital of French Polynesia, riot police fought a daylong battle with more than 1000 demonstrators who invaded the runway and blocked three jets, including one just about to take off for Los Angeles and Paris . . .<br>[sentences elaborating on the destruction at the airport omitted] |
| [*Protests staged around the world*]<br>(4) Opposition to nuclear testing swept around the globe just a day after France exploded the first of up to eight bombs at Mururoa atoll, also in French controlled Polynesia.<br>Demonstrations included one by more than 10,000 people in Chile. | [*Australian government reaction*]<br>The Australian Government yesterday appealed for calm in the Tahitian capital, but blamed France and its nuclear testing for the riots. The Foreign Minister, Senator Evans, said the violence was a measure of the depth of feeling aroused by the French test and reflected 'the frustration felt by many people – not just in Papeete but throughout the world – at the French Government's disdain for the views of the peoples of the South Pacific'. |
| [*Australian government reaction*]<br>(5) Foreign Affairs Minister Gareth Evans said yesterday: 'France has really reaped what it has sown.' | But France rebuffed the tide of global protests against the first of its tests . . . [sentences omitted covering French reaction] |
|  | [*Details of rioting in Papeete*]<br>As darkness fell on Tahiti, the rioters abandoned the airport and turned their attention to Papeete. A burning garbage bin was hurled through the window of the High Commissioner's residence, and burning bottles were directed at the French-controlled Territorial Assembly building. The protesters also set fire to nearby shops and cars before being forced out of the central Tarahoi square by security forces . . . [story continues] |

**Figure 4.6** Two 'Tahiti Riot' reports compared

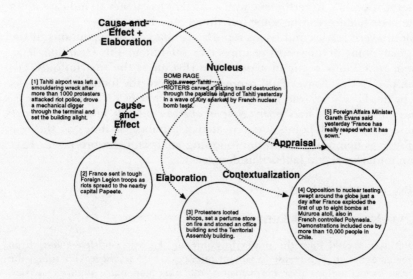

**Figure 4.7** Orbital structure of *Telegraph Mirror* 'Tahiti Riot' report

reference to event reports but it is similarly a feature of issues reports of the type exemplified by the 'Knives Ban' story cited above. As demonstrated above, issues reports have the same orbital structure of dependent satellites specifying an opening nucleus, and the radical editability of these satellites follows logically from this orbital mode of textual development.

*An informational pulse: repeating the 'point of impact'*

The hard news item, therefore, divides into two phases. The first phase or nucleus provides the core informational meanings relating to social-order disruption and, simultaneously, a burst or peak of interpersonal meanings which inscribe the informational content with a sense of drama, significance and heightened intensity. The second phase – where typically the concentration of intensifying interpersonal meanings falls away – is made up of individual subcomponents which depend on the opening nucleus and which act to elaborate, elucidate and to appraise its informational content. Thus, interpersonally, the hard news story is organized as a wave with a crest in the Headline/lead falling away to a trough as the story comes to a conclusion. Informationally the news story is organized according to a pattern of logical dependency with the primary or major component in the Headline/lead nucleus, and a set of dependent, qualifying elements provided by the subcomponents of the second phase.

There is, however, one further feature of textual organization within
the hard news story which operates in parallel with, or as a counterpoint
to, these two patterns. Although not found in all event and issues
reports, it occurs, nevertheless, with sufficient frequency to indicate it is a
systematic feature serving some functional objective.

Both event stories and issues reports are marked by repetitions of the
original point of newsworthy impact as set out in the Headline/lead.
These repetitions occur in a pulse-like rhythm as the text unfolds. For
example, in the 'Knives Ban' report, the newsworthy focus or 'angle' set
up by the Headline/lead nucleus is the claim that *POLICE should have the
power to confiscate knives from teenagers after an increase in violent offences.*
These two related points are repeated a number of times as the text
unfolds, as demonstrated in the following analysis. (The two points have
been underlined and labelled as they recur.)

**Ban Teens' Knives** [ *confiscate knives* ]

**Juvenile violence 'rising sharply'** [ *knife related violence rising* ]

POLICE should have <u>the power to confiscate knives</u> [ *confiscate knives* ] from
teenagers after <u>an increase in violent offences,</u> [ *knife related violence rising* ] the
State's most senior children's magistrate told a parliamentary inquiry yesterday.
Rod Blackmore, senior children's magistrate for 17 years said <u>violent offences
had risen</u> [ *knife related violence rising* ] while others, such as car stealing and general theft, had fallen.

Mr Blackmore said violent matters accounted for 41 per cent of offences
listed before him at Bidura Children's Court, Glebe, for the next two months.
They included malicious wounding, armed robbery, assault with bodily harm,
assault on police, personal violence and assault with intent to rob.

Offences involving knives made up 30 per cent of all violent matters before
him.

Mr Blackmore said <u>knives had become the most popular weapon used by
young criminals.</u> [ *knife related violence rising* ]

He said <u>police should be given the power to confiscate pocket knives, butterfly and flick knives.</u> [ *confiscate knives* ]

Mr Blackmore told the all party Standing Committee on Social Issues inquiry
into youth violence that five years ago car theft was the big problem.

It made up more than half of his workload but a clampdown on car theft had
reduced the number, Mr Blackmore said, to less than 20 per cent.

He said there were about 17 youths charged with murder going through the
court system.

'The real worry is <u>the carrying of knives by juveniles which is very frequent
in the community and schools,</u>' he said. [ *knife related violence rising* ]

Outside the inquiry, Mr Blackmore said he felt the proportion of violent
offences involving knives had increased six-fold over the past five years.

'<u>The use of knives, certainly in robberies, is a fairly frequent feature.</u>' [ *knife
related violence rising* ]

Mr Blackmore said the law says a person is not entitled to carry a weapon for
personal protection.

Allowing police to confiscate a knife [*confiscate knives*] would mean teenagers could be cautioned, rather than charged for the offence.

It may be possible children could get their knife back from police if they proved they had a proper use for the weapon or their parents knew of it, Mr Blackmore said.

Mr Blackmore also raised the possibility the anti-car stealing push may have led to the increase in violent crime. 'If people are doing things for kicks, do they now go out and wander round streets at night looking for someone to mug rather than taking someone's car?' he said.

The following analysis illustrates this pattern within an event story report of a fatal car crash. Here, most notably the description of the car crashing into a tree is repeated at roughly equal intervals as the text unfolds.

SCHOOL JAUNT ENDS IN DEATH CRASH [*boy killed*]

A 17-year-old boy was killed [*boy killed*] instantly when a car carrying eight school friends – two in the boot – skidded on a bend and slammed into a tree yesterday. [*car crashes into tree*]

A 16-year-old girl passenger was in a critical condition last night – police said she might need to have her leg amputated – and a 17-year-old boy was in a serious but stable condition after the tree embedded itself in the car. [*car crashes into tree*]

Incredibly, the two girls in the boot of the V8 Holden Statesman and another girl escaped with only cuts and bruises.

The eight friends, two boys and six girls from years 11 and 12, had left Trinity Senior High School in Wagga yesterday at lunchtime, cramming into one car to go to an interschool sports carnival.

But a few kilometres later the car ploughed into a tree in Captain Cook Drive. [*car crashes into tree*]

Police believe the driver lost control on a bend, skidded on a gravel shoulder and slammed into a tree on a nearby reserve. [*car crashes into tree*]

Emergency crews said that when they arrived, the uprooted tree was embedded in the car.

It had been raining heavily and police believe the car might have been going too fast.

The driver, 17-year-old Nicholas Sampson, was killed instantly. [*boy killed*]

Deanne McCaig, 16, from Ganmain, had massive leg injuries and was trapped for more than 90 minutes. She was in a critical condition last night at Wagga Base hospital, where police say she is in danger of having her leg amputated. Peter Morris, 17, from Coolamon, suffered multiple injuries and was in a serious but stable condition. Among the other students Paulette Scamell and Anita McRae were also in a stable condition, while Shannon Dunn, Catherine Galvin and Rochelle Little, all 16, suffered minor injuries.

Police believe the friends from the Catholic high school were on their way to one of the students' homes before heading to the carnival.

(*Sydney Morning Herald*, 14 August 1992. Used by permission of Shelli-Anne Couch)

Perhaps the most salient consequence of this pattern of repetition for the event story is an orientation to temporal sequence in which the actual chronological ordering of events is afforded little importance. As is demonstrated with the 'Car Crash' report, the unfolding structure of the event story does not map chronological sequence – in contrast to many of the text types seen traditionally as narrative or story telling – but is organized around this repeated return to the original point of maximal social-order disruption. Consequently the unfolding of the text in the event story will typically take the reader backwards and forwards in time as it moves in a zigzag pattern around the time of the point of maximal disruption.

### Rhetorical outcomes: the narrative impulse and the communicative function of the news story's generic structure

#### News and narrative

At its very broadest level of operation, the notion of narrative has been applied to account for the way human discourses act to construct social reality. The narrative impulse is said to be at work when some text is organized so as to transmit key social values, cultural assumptions and culturally or ideologically determined themes and patterns of thought. It is through the operation of this narrative impulse that the text is inflected in such a way that its categories, relationships and orderings reflect culturally meaningful, rather than natural, entities and arrangements. (See, for example, Barthes 1966; Bremond 1964, 1966, 1973; Todorov 1966; Propp 1968; Greimas 1971; Bakhtin 1973; Adam 1985, 1992; Bird and Dardenne 1988; Mumby 1993.)

In its strongest formulation, this notion of narrative is part of a theoretical framework which holds that all human discourse has a narrative element in that texts necessarily act to construct and maintain social realities. Accordingly, the human species has been relabelled 'homo narrans' (Mumby 1993: 1). From this perspective, the notion of narrative is part of a theoretical challenge to the rationalist or realist epistemology which holds that at least part of human experience is made up of a fixed, external and objective reality which can be accurately and truthfully mirrored or mapped by at least certain types of texts.

In what might be thought of as a weaker or less extreme theoretical framework, the notion of narrative operates in a context where a distinction is made between objective texts which are held to directly reflect some external, non-socially determined reality and those texts in which the narrative impulse is at work constructing the contingent categories of culture and society. That is, this weaker position sees the narrative impulse at work in some, but not all, texts. (See, for example, Bird and Dardenne 1988.)

The identification of such a distinction is part of a long tradition, underlying, as it does, Aristotle's celebrated views on the differences between history and literature outlined in the *Poetics*:

> The difference between the historian and the poet is not in their utterance being in verse or prose ... the difference lies in the fact that the historian speaks what has happened, the poet the kind of thing that *can* happen. Hence also poetry is a more philosophical and serious business than history; poetry speaks more of universals, history of particulars. (Aristotle, 1977: 33)

The distinction is found today in textual categorizations which distinguish between what is sometimes termed the 'chronicle' – a supposedly objective genre which simply recounts a sequence of events as it happened – and the narrativizing genres where the sorts of shaping and construing of events outlined above can be observed. Thus, in 'Myth, chronicle and story', Bird and Dardenne set up an opposition between objective news reports and those that involve genuine story telling. They state:

> [Journalists] face a paradox; the more 'objective' they are, the more unreadable they become; while the better storytellers they are, the more readers will respond, and the more they fear they are betraying their ideals [of objective reporting]. So journalists do some chronicling, some story-tellings and a lot that is something of both. (Bird and Dardenne 1988: 78)

In the current context, it is not necessary to evaluate the relative merits of the two positions, nor to rule on whether it is, in fact, possible for those texts described as chronicles to transparently and objectively represent some external reality. Event stories and issues reports are clearly not chronicles in that they do not set out simple chronological sequences of happenings. And the discussion to this point has provided compelling evidence that hard news reports are thoroughly informed by the narrative impulse, evidence which applies regardless of whether we hold a strong or weak view of narrative. The precise mode of expression that this narrativizing impulse finds in hard news reporting will be examined in detail below.[13]

### News and the narrative of a social order at risk

It was demonstrated above that the key purpose of news reporting as a social practice was the identification of points of maximal disruption of the *status quo*. Of key relevance here is the ideologically informed nature of these processes of identification and selection. Clearly these selections will be conditioned by the cultural experiences, the social identity and the political and economic objectives of those in a position to dictate their terms. In particular, they will rely on value-laden assumptions about which behaviours, actions, relationships and roles are normal parts of the social order, and which are disruptive or deviant. They will depend on assumptions about which parts of the social order are crucial and hence must be monitored for signs of change, damage or instability, and on assumptions about which forces have the potential to disrupt or reorganize these core social entities. This point can be demonstrated briefly by an examination of the following two news stories.

In the report of the Athens flood cited above (p. 109), the reporter/subeditor chose for his/her 'point of maximum impact' details of the deaths, the damage and, interestingly, the disruption to traffic which resulted from the flooding. The report began: *Nine people died in and around the Greek capital as torrential rains lashed the region at the weekend, causing damage of 'biblical' proportions and bringing a nation-wide halt to rail traffic.* But contained in international wire copy available at the time was information that large-scale and poorly regulated new land developments in and around Athens were believed responsible for much of the damage and possibly even some of the deaths. The new construction had been allowed to proceed without adequate drainage or floodwater controls. Thus, rather than giving primary focus to the *nine dead* and the *nation-wide halt to rail traffic*, the report might just as easily have begun with: *Rapid and unregulated land development in the Athens region is believed responsible for large scale flooding and millions of dollars of damage following torrential rains in the area.* Such an opening would have construed the greatest threat to the social order in this case as having a human rather than a natural origin and thereby would have construed the events according to a different ideological perspective.

At first glance, the following report of a proposed increase in water rates in New South Wales in 1993 seems as neutral as is possible for a news story.

> Households in NSW will pay more for water under plans announced by the Water Board. The Board has proposed a flat rate of 65-cents-a-kilolitre for all water.
> Under the proposal the average household would pay an extra 39 cents a week – about 20 dollars a year.
> The board has also proposed the abolition of the 80-dollar a year environment levy as well as cuts in charges to business and safety measures for pensioners and low income families. (SBS Central Newsroom)

But the action of a set of ideologically informed value judgements is revealed by a closer examination of the text's structure and in particular of the way the lead gives priority to certain information. We can provide a rather different ideological spin on the events described if, for example, a new point of impact for the lead is developed by taking information from what was the final sentence and by adopting a more active grammatical structure. Thus we would begin:

> The Water Board wants to increase the amount ordinary households pay for water while cutting water rate charges to business.
> Proposals currently before the government would see the average household pay $20 more a year [etc.].

An even more marked shift can be achieved by a reworking which sees the abolishing of the environmental levy (a charge to fund an urgently required upgrading of the New South Wales water system) as representing a significant threat to the social and moral order and hence worthy of being made part of the lead's point of maximum impact.

> The Water Board wants to scrap the environmental levy, a charge introduced to help the government tackle the continued degradation of the State's water-ways, while at the same time lowering the cost of water to big business [etc.].

Clearly ideological perspective is reflected in these alternative judgements about which aspects of the event represent the greatest disruption of the *status quo*. The original version construes the proposed changes as representing just a minor inconvenience – as a largely uncontroversial, routine part of the bureaucratic process and hence as providing only a minor disruption of the *status quo*. In contrast, both alternative versions suggest that the proposed increase is not entirely routine, not so obviously a normal part of the administrative process and hence construe it as representing more of a threat to the *status quo*. They both indicate that the changes may represent at least a minor threat to the moral order in that they raise questions of fairness and/or the government's concern for the environment.

A similar process was at work in the selection of the point of impact for the issues report about Bosnia discussed above. Clearly a complex system of values underlay the reporter's decision to ignore the angle provided by World Vision – a claim about the inspiring resolve of the people of Bosnia and the role of World Vision in supporting them – and to choose, instead, an angle which turned on the shift in power relations represented by NATO's violent intervention in the war.

From this perspective, then, we see that the generic structure of the hard news requires that the reporter construes events and statements in terms of the purported risk they pose for the social order and that this construal is an act of ideologically and culturally determined interpretation. In this sense, then, both event stories and issues reports are conditioned by the narrative impulse in that they inflect events and statements with a highly significant social value. They act to categorize events and issues as more or less disruptive, transformative, transgressive or destructive of the social order.

But there is more to the hard news story than this narrative of social-order disruption. The structure of news reports of this type provides a powerful rhetorical device for representing these ideologically determined choices about *status-quo* disruption as natural, necessary and value-free. The structure operates on multiple levels to achieve this outcome.

The organization of the Headline/lead provides the textual platform for some incident or statement – the one being construed as maximally disruptive of the *status quo* – to be plucked from its context in a temporal or verbal sequence. This act of extraction of itself constructs the incident or statement as notable, as possessed of informational features which warrant its removal from its original context. But the incident or claim is not just extracted. It is also presented at the very beginning of the story, as the story's inception point. In this way the element chosen for this lead is cast into sharp textual relief. It is represented as not just informationally noteworthy but as so noteworthy that it requires that the introductory, orienting steps normally associated with so many other text types be abandoned. Thus the lead's abruptness, its offering of only the most limited and reduced textual gearing up or preamble, turns out to be highly functional.

As discussed above, not all Headline/leads contain the intensifying elements discussed previously. These do, however, occur with high frequency and when present obviously serve to reinforce the sense that there is something innately remarkable about the events or statements therein described. The evaluative intensification characterizes the element selected for the lead as innately dramatic, heightened and full of impact and thus supports the journalist's act of extracting this element from its temporal or verbal context and giving it such textual prominence and informational priority.

Thus, individually and together, these features represent the incident or statement selected for the reader's attention as inherently newsworthy, as having compelled itself upon the reporter as obvious subject matter for a report and an unavoidably appropriate starting point. The features conspire to naturalize, to represent as necessary and as based in some external reality, the thoroughly ideological selection process by which that crisis point of social-order disruption was selected in the first place.

The orbital structure of the body of the hard news story supports this representation of the reporter's selections as objective and inevitable. The orientation set up by the pulse-like return to the Headline/lead's crisis point serves to keep that point in focus, to construct the crisis point as pivotal and a natural point of informational prominence. Similarly, the way the satellites of the unfolding text reach back to interact lexically and logically with the lead serves to construct the lead as constantly in focus, as textually and informationally pre-eminent. Thus the text throughout its length remains *about* the lead, as each satellite, regardless of distance, elaborates, contextualizes, explains, justifies or appraises some element of that opening burst of informational and interpersonal impact. The structure of the body acts to represent that initial judgement about a threat to the social order as commonsensical, consensual and unavoidable.

There is one claim sometimes made about the structure of the hard news report which needs to be addressed briefly at this point, namely that it can be explained by reference to the news story's suitability for skim reading. While the concentration of information in the Headline/lead nucleus does make such an abbreviated reading possible, to explain the structure entirely in these terms is to underestimate the rhetorical potential of these texts. As demonstrated above, there is nothing neutral or necessary about the choices which underline the angle presented in the Headline/lead. In fact, the Headline/lead does not so much summarize the action or set of statements at issue as provide a particular interpretation of their significance for the social order. Similarly, the function of the Headline/lead's supporting satellites cannot be satisfactorily explained in terms of brevity or communicative efficiency. As demonstrated above, the need for each satellite to establish a direct link back to the Headline/lead nucleus means there is significant redundancy or repetition in the body of the news story as the original point of impact is elaborated or restated by individual satellites. A structure for news reporting better suited simply for skim reading might be devised in which a brief, but more thorough synopsis is provided upfront for readers who want only the essentials, with an extended recount coming afterwards for those who want all the details without the repetition typical of the nucleus/satellite mode of development.[14]

## Conclusion

In both the event story and issues report, therefore, the action of the narrative impulse can be observed in the way the reporting of events or statements is organized so as to construct a model of the social order. Both types construct that model by identifying the points at which society is at risk, by constructing a narrative in which the world is construed primarily as a site for disequilibrium, disorder, damage and transgression.

The model at issue here is not, of course, an explicit, consistent and monolithic social construct. The term model is, in fact, a metaphor for the assemblage of beliefs, assumptions, value judgements, social objectives and desires which mass-media power-brokers – and presumably some proportion of their audience – hold more or less in common. And the model is always subject to change as the various groups which exercise power in society contest and negotiate the parameters of what constitutes social normality and acceptability.

Most tellingly this modelling of a social order is carried out by means of a text type which is organized so as to naturalize and to portray as commonsensical the ideology which informs it. The naturalization is achieved through the simultaneous operation of a distinctive pattern of textual development and a distinctive tone or mode of authorial address – by the interaction between the news story's lead-dominated, orbitally organized generic structure and an impersonalized authorial voice in which a wide range of interpersonal meanings are severely circumscribed. In this way, the subjective presence of the journalist–author in the text is obscured, thereby representing the text as neutral and anonymous and thus as directly and mechanically determined by the events it portrays.

It is in this context that we can understand the claims of objectivity,

impartiality and neutrality so often made by the media about hard news
reporting texts. The claims do have a genuine basis in the lexicogrammar
and the textual organization of the news story. The canonical hard news
circumscribes a key set of interpersonal values. When compared, therefore, with journalistic commentary and many other types of texts, it
appears to put significantly fewer interpersonal values at risk and hence is
not felt to position the reader emotionally or attitudinally. The lead-dominated orbital structure has similar consequences, enabling an ideologically informed process of interpretation to be portrayed as a
commonsensical presentation of the facts.

   In the final analysis, of course, the claims cannot be sustained. To
accept them is to take the rhetoric at face value, to fail to deconstruct that
rhetoric in order to discover the social and ideological purposes by which
it is motivated. It is to ignore the fact that the news story's circumscription
of interpersonal values is a rhetorical stratagem, a ploy by which the role
of the author's social subjecthood in the text's construction can be
hidden but never, of course, actually reduced or eliminated. It is to overlook the fact that a complex, highly wrought textual structure is required
to portray tendentious, value-laden judgements about maximal social-
order disruption as the facts of the matter. And coming from journalists
themselves, the claim of objectivity is, in fact, a polemical one, a crucial
part of the media's perpetual campaign to acquire for its texts positions of
high social standing and epistemological supremacy. Event stories and
issues reports are indubitably informed by the narrative impulse and, as
such, must be seen as complex rhetorical devices which, rather than
mirroring social realities, construct them.

## Notes

1  It is noteworthy that many journalistic training texts fail to note the difference
   between the two types, perhaps a reflection of their commonality of textual
   structure, although Harold Evans in his highly influential (but unfortunately
   titled) training journalistic training text, *Newsman's English*, does make the distinction, applying the label statement/opinion story to the communicatively
   based report.
2  Numerous attempts have been made in media studies to provide a systematic
   account of the informational themes involved in the media's assessments of
   newsworthiness. Perhaps the most influential of these is by Galtung and Ruge
   (1965).
3  For an extended analysis of news values and the social order in the context of
   crime reporting see Ericson *et al.* (1991). For a discussion of journalists'
   understanding of the subject matter of hard news see Tiffen (1989).
4  Australia's Special Broadcasting Service (SBS) is a government-funded, independent broadcaster with a commitment to reflecting Australia's multicultural
   diversity. Its radio arm, which broadcasts nationally, provides locally produced
   news, current affairs, community affairs and cultural programming in 68 languages and employs some 250 journalists.

5   The British tabloids are an egregious exception to this rule.
6   For various analyses of the interpersonal semantics at issue here see, for exam-
    ple, Biber and Finegan (1988, 1989), Labov (1972, 1982, 1984) and Martin
    (in press).
7   See Carter (1987) for an analysis of these meanings by reference to a notion
    of core vocabulary.
8   The term 'lead' is used by Australian and, I believe, North American journal-
    ists while, if *Newsman's English* is a reliable guide, UK journalists use 'intro' to
    refer to this opening sentence.
9   This style of headline is typical in British and Australian newspapers while
    more extended headlines which go beyond the content of the lead are found
    within the North American journalistic tradition.
10  The example is taken from a broadcast rather than a print media organization
    but the principles illustrated here apply across the media.
11  Although not based on the mode of analysis developed by van Dijk in his
    extended analysis of news reporting texts in *News as Discourse* (1988), this
    approach would appear to be entirely compatible with his and seems to lead
    to similar conclusions about the structure of this type of text.
12  Thompson and Mann (1987) argue for a textual relation of justification in
    their theory of Rhetorical Structure, though it is not identical with that pro-
    posed here. The approach to analysing textual organization set out in this
    chapter is strongly influenced by that of Rhetorical Structure Theory.
13  Within the field known as narratology and elsewhere in this book, the term
    narrative is used in a more specific sense as a label for a particular subtype of
    story-telling text, the one frequently associated with fairy stories and other fic-
    tional texts, and consisting typically of the stages of Orientation, Complica-
    tion, Evaluation, Resolution and Coda. Hard news reports are clearly not
    narratives in this sense.
14  In the past, many English-language newspapers adopted an approach in which
    up to five or even six headlines and subheadlines provided a much more
    extended, less interpretive synopsis than is provided by the Headline/lead of
    modern British and Australian newspapers. It could be argued that this older,
    now largely abandoned approach provides more effectively for skim reading
    than that adopted today since the reader is provided more quickly with a clear
    synopsis of the socially disruptive action.

## References

Adam, J. (1985) *Le Text narratif.* Paris: Nathan.
Adam, J. (1992) *Les Textes: types et prototypes: récit, description, argumentation, explica-
    tion et dialogue.* Paris: Nathan.
Aristotle, trans. Else, G. (1977) *Poetics.* Ann Arbor, MI: Ann Arbor Paperbacks.
Bagnall, N. (1993) *Newspaper Language.* Oxford: Focal Press.
Bakhtin, M. (1973) *Problems of Dostoevsky's Poetics.* Ann Arbor, MI: Ann Arbor.
Barthes, R. (1966) 'Introduction à l'analyse structurale des récits'. *Communications*
    8, 1–27.
Bell, A. (1991) *The Language of News Media.* Oxford: Basil Blackwell.
Biber, D. and Finegan, E. (1988) 'Adverbial stance types in English'. *Discourse
    Processes* 11(1), 1–34.
Biber, D. and Finegan, E. (1989) 'Styles of stance in English: lexical and grammat-

ical marking of evidentiality and affect', *Text* 9(1) (Special Issues on the Pragmatics of Effect), 93–124.

Bird, E. and Dardenne, R. (1988) 'Myth, chronicle, and story – exploring the narrative quality of news'. In J. W. Carey (ed.) *Media, Myths, and Narratives: Television and the Press*. Newbury Park, CA: Sage Publications.

Bremond, C. (1964) 'Le message narratif', *Communications* 4, 4–32.

Bremond, C. (1966) 'La logique des possible narratifs'. *Communications* 8, 60–76.

Bremond, C. (1973) *Logique du récit*. Paris: Seuil.

Carter, R. (1987) *Vocabulary: An Applied Linguistics Guide*. London: Allen & Unwin.

Ericson, R., Baranek, P. and Chan, J. (1991) *Representing Order*. Milton Keynes: Open University Press.

Evans, H. (1972) *Newsman's English*. Oxford: Heinemann.

Galtung, J. and Ruge, M. (1965) 'The structure of foreign news'. *Journal of Peace Research* 1, 64–90.

Granato, L. (1991) *Reporting and Writing News*. New York: Prentice Hall.

Greimas, A. (1971) 'Narrative grammar: units and levels'. *Modern Language Notes* 86, 793–806.

Halliday, M. A. K. (1994) *An Introduction to Functional Grammar*. London: Edward Arnold.

Herman, S. and Chomsky, N. (1988) *Manufacturing Consent: The Political Economy of the Mass Media*. New York: Pantheon Books.

Husson, D. and Robert, O. (1991) *Profession journaliste: source d'information, typologie d'article, styles d'écriture*. Paris: Eyrolles.

Iedema, R., Feez, S. and White, P. (1994) *Media Literacy*. Sydney: New South Wales Department of School Education.

Inglis, F. (1990) *Media Theory*. London: Basil Blackwell.

Labov, W. (1972) 'The transformation of experience in narrative syntax'. In *Language in the Inner City*. Philadelphia: Pennsylvania University Press, 354–96.

Labov, W. (1982) 'Speech actions and reactions in personal narrative'. In D. Tannen (ed.) *Analysing Discourse: Text and Talk* (Georgetown University Round Table on Language and Linguistics 1981). Washington: Georgetown University Press.

Labov, W. (1984) 'Intensity'. In D. Schiffen (ed.) *Meaning, Form and Use in Context: Linguistic Applications* (Georgetown University Round Table on Language and Linguistics). Washington: Georgetown University Press, 43–70.

McQuail, D. (1987) *Mass Communication Theory: An Introduction*. London: Sage Publications.

Martin, J. (1992) *English Text: System and Structure*. Philadelphia/Amsterdam: John Benjamins.

Martin, J. (in press) 'Beyond exchange: appraisal systems in English'. In S. Hunston and G. Thompson (eds) *Evaluation in Text*. Oxford: Oxford University Press (under review).

Mumby, D. (ed.) (1993) *Narrative and Social Control: Critical Perspectives*. Newbury Park, CA: Sage Publications.

Plum, G. (1988) 'Textual and contextual conditioning in spoken English: a genre-based approach'. PhD thesis, Department. of Linguistics, University of Sydney.

Propp, V. (1968) *Morphology of the Folktale*. Austin: University of Texas Press.

Rothery, J. (1990), 'Story writing in primary schools: assessing narrative type genre'. Unpublished PhD thesis, Department. of Linguistics, University of Sydney.

Thompson, W. and Mann, S. (1987) 'Rhetorical structure theory: a theory of text organisation'. In L. Polany (ed.) *The Structure of Discourse*. Norwood, NJ: Ablex.

Tiffen, R. (1989) *News and Power*. Sydney: Allen & Unwin.

Todorov, T. (1966) 'Les catégories du récit littéraire'. *Communications* 8, 125–51.

van Dijk, T. (1988) *News as Discourse*. Hillsdale, NJ: Lawrence Erlbaum.

White, S. A. (1991) *Reporting in Australia*. Melbourne: Macmillian.

# 5 Curriculum macrogenres as forms of initiation into a culture

*Frances Christie*

## Introduction

It is a commonplace to observe that while many of the practices associated with education in the Western sense are now several centuries old, the particular significance attaching to state-directed schooling is historically much more recent. State-directed schooling, with all its elaborate apparatus involving policies for the organization and maintenance of schools, design and implementation of curricula, evaluation and assessment of students' learning, and programmes for the preparation of teachers, had its origins in the nineteenth century. But state-directed schooling has achieved a particular significance in the twentieth century, and such a development needs to be understood both as a measure of the growth of modern nations and as itself a mechanism critical in the maintenance and perpetuation of such nations. In contemporary Western countries such as the UK or Australia, significant proportions of the national budgets are annually devoted to provision of school programmes, while since the Second World War so-called 'Third World' countries have also devoted increasing proportions of their budgets to provision of school programmes.

The contemporary interest of modern states in the provision of education is part of a wider enterprise intended to regulate and manage what have become complex sociopolitical systems. This enterprise is a necessary feature of modern life. In a recent analysis of the emergence of contemporary schools, at least in the Anglo-Australian tradition, Hunter (1994) has argued that the nineteenth century witnessed the emergence of the modern elementary school, and that its character very early reflected the social purposes for which it came into being. Such a school was created in response to two quite different sources of social pressure or need: the need to achieve a degree of social order and economic stability and the need to produce morally responsible subjects, capable of acting in independent, if disciplined ways. The two themes, in Hunter's analysis, have run like motifs through the history of the development of schooling well into the twentieth century, and remain relevant to this day.

Hunter's analysis is an important one. It offers a useful corrective to the tendency, not uncommon in twentieth-century professional theorizing about education, to see modern schools as agencies that have failed,

or at best only partly succeeded, because they have not achieved programmes that develop reflective, self-actualizing individuals, operating
instead as servants of the state to oppress and subjugate subjects (Hunter
1994: 27–31). As Hunter shows, the model of the reflective, self-actualizing
individual implicit in many such critiques is very questionable, an artefact
more of the particular liberal, sometimes neo-Marxist, speculations of the
educational critics involved than of the social processes that made the
institution of schooling necessary.

Yet a satisfactory analysis of the contemporary school will need to take
us further and to more delicate levels of explanation than Hunter's, in
order to examine both how the agencies of schools work and what it is
they transmit to their subjects. Schools, so Bernstein (1990) has claimed,
are agencies of 'symbolic control', and he defines the latter thus:

> symbolic control is the means whereby consciousness is given a specialized
> form and distributed through forms of communication which relay a given dis-
> tribution of power and dominant cultural categories. Symbolic control trans-
> lates power relations into discourse and discourse into power relations.
> (Bernstein 1990: 134)

In Bernstein's terms it is of the utmost importance to examine and
explain how the pedagogic discourses of schooling (but of other pedagogic agencies as well) achieve symbolic control, how access to forms of
knowledge is achieved, what forms of knowledge are made available to
which groups, and how all these matters create the forms of consciousness found in a culture. This chapter seeks to offer at least a partial
answer to some of these questions, by developing analyses of two primary
school texts, selected for their status, in the first case, as an instance of an
early childhood curriculum genre, and, in the second case, as an instance
of an upper primary school curriculum macrogenre (Christie, 1989,
1990, 1991a, b, 1994, 1995a, b) in which certain pedagogic discourses
are in operation. These pedagogic discourses, it is hoped to show, help to
shape certain pedagogic subject positions, and these in turn create
particular forms of consciousness.

## Curriculum genres and curriculum macrogenres

Teacher education programmes generally recognize that lessons, ideally
at least, have purpose and structure, and necessarily a sequence of steps
in which these are realized. The notion of a lesson as a structured
sequence of activities is thus not in itself entirely foreign to those who
work in education. Why then describe lessons as instances of curriculum
genres? What is gained by adopting such terminology, and how does it
encourage us to view differently the activities of teaching and learning? At
least two broad but ultimately related answers can be offered to these
questions, one to do with the linguistic theory being developed in this

book, the other to do with issues of pedagogy as an area urgently requiring further investigation. To take the former first, the adoption of the term 'curriculum genre' has the important theoretical merit that it draws attention to the claim made here that social activities generally are realized in genres: staged, purposive activities in which significant goals of various kinds are realized. School activities are thus in this sense, importantly, consistent in character with other social activities and, as such, subject to the same sorts of linguistic scrutiny in order to analyse and explain how they work. Curriculum genres, incidentally, are temporally sequenced and serial in character, reflecting those requirements of pedagogic activities to do with pacing and ordering the steps in which teaching and learning are done. In this they contrast with some other genres, whose ordering is other than serial, especially many written ones. One such genre is the news story whose manner of setting out and ordering events follows other than the temporal sequence of events in which they occurred in real life (Iedema *et al.* 1994).

To turn to the second of the answers offered in response to the questions about adoption of the term 'curriculum genre', our answer here relates to the need to achieve much better understandings of the nature of pedagogic discourses: the notion of a curriculum genre, and associated notions to do with curriculum macrogenres and the registers that operate within them (to be explained below) are seen as important tools in developing the needed understandings. This is of concern not only to such relatively specialist areas as teacher education, but to other areas of social research in which an effort is made to explore and explain the nature of social processes. Pedagogic practice is itself an important site in which to examine so much else about social life.

Operating within an instance of a curriculum genre will be two registers, a regulative and an instructional (e.g. Christie 1989, 1994), where the two terms are adapted from Bernstein's work on pedagogic discourse (e.g. Bernstein 1986, 1990).[1] The first order or regulative register refers to sets of language choices which are principally involved in establishing goals for teaching–learning activities, and with fostering and maintaining the direction of the activities until the achievement of the goals. The second order or instructional register refers to language choices in which the knowledge and associated skills being taught are realized. As will be shown below, the two registers operate in such a way that the former fundamentally determines the introduction, pacing and ordering of the other.

In fact, the relationship of the two is so intimate, it is argued that the regulative register 'projects' the instructional register, where the term is used metaphorically from the functional grammar, following Halliday's advice (1979, 1981, 1982) about the value of thinking grammatically about a text, modelling its organization on that of the clause. Where a relationship of projection applies, a secondary clause is said to be projected through the primary one (Halliday 1994: 219), so that something either said or thought hitherto is in this sense 'reinstated'. The metaphor of projection is a useful one to employ for the relationship of the two registers, as we shall see. It accords with Bernstein's general view about the manner in which a pedagogic discourse takes a discourse from sites elsewhere, and reinstates or even 'relocates' it for the purposes of the pedagogic activity (Bernstein 1990: 183–5).

## A genre of early childhood

The early years of schooling are very important for a number of reasons, not least that it is here that children are expected to learn some significant lessons in what it is to be a pedagogic subject for the purposes of formal school teaching and learning. Hence it is that early childhood teachers tend to focus on directing children towards desirable behaviours, including, for example: moving in groups in and out of the school building; taking lunch and any other meals at particular times and in particular places; using the school toilets at appropriate times, often with the associated requirement to wash one's hands afterwards; moving about the classroom in acceptable ways, sitting on chairs for some parts of the day, and often sitting on the floor for other parts of the day; learning to listen to others in group situations; learning to take turns in responding to teacher questions, where this often involves learning to put up a hand in order to signal to the teacher preparedness to answer questions. In an ethnographic study of the primary school Mehan (1979) showed how much the routines of the school day were defined in terms of movements from one set of physical dispositions to another. Such moves, always orchestrated by the teacher, serve to construct a great deal of what it is to adopt the desired pedagogic subject position, where this is expressed both in physical dispositions and in linguistic behaviours, for the two are intimately related, both involved in the semiotic processes of the classroom. As Lemke (1995: 8) has suggested, movement, gesture and speech 'share important underlying unities', and any theory of the role of language in meaning making will need to acknowledge this.

Over time, much of the language associated with teaching and learning the acceptable classroom behavioural patterns becomes lost, as students acquire those patterns. That is to say, they develop regular routines so that the explicit expression of teacher advice and/or direction concerning a great deal of what is to be done simply disappears. However, the injunction to behave in particular ways still applies, and its increasingly tacit recognition is one measure of the success of its earlier explicit expression, as both Green and Kantor-Smith (1988) and Christie (1989) have shown. Christie followed the same population of 50 to 55 early childhood students for three years, where a particular curriculum genre applied for the purposes of teaching and learning how to write. Observing several teachers working with the same children over the time, Christie noted firstly that the children were always grouped on the floor in front of the teacher for the early stages of the curriculum genre, when the nature of the writing task and the 'content' or field for writing were established, and secondly that an important stage was finished, and the commencement of another was heralded when the children were to get up off the floor, return to their desks, and commence their writing. The latter steps, to do with the need to get up, physically collect writing books and sit on designated chairs to write, achieved more and more minimal realizations in the classroom texts over time, and indeed on occasion they found no linguistic expression at all, the children obediently getting up and performing the necessary steps without overt teacher direction.

What of the language behaviours the children are required to learn as part of the processes of achieving appropriate subject positions? How are these learned, and what capacities in dealing with experience appear to be involved? We have already alluded above to the school practices of teacher questioning and student answering. The very fact that it is much more commonly the teacher's role to ask questions than it is the children's in itself indicates the asymmetry of their relationship, revealing a great deal of the pedagogic subject position in construction in the talk.[2] But what of those activities in the school day when children are required to use language for reasonably sustained periods of time? What is their purpose? In contemporary English-speaking countries one of the activities much favoured by early childhood teachers is that which is sometimes called 'sharing time', sometimes 'morning news', and even sometimes 'show and tell'. The two former terms suggest the activity of talking about experience of some kind, where this may involve narrating some event or it may involve display of a toy or some other object and talking about it. The latter term, 'show and tell', necessarily implies display of such an item and associated talk. The two activities of narrating and of showing and telling are in fact linguistically very different (Christie 1989), though space will not permit pursuit of this point here. Suffice it to note that the activity of what we will term 'morning news' would appear to enjoy a status of some importance in early childhood education, and it is worth noting also that it is not uncommon for primary schoolteachers to retain the custom of holding such an activity, often on a weekly rather than a daily basis, as students move right up the primary school.

It will be argued here that morning news actually has an important role in establishing some desired linguistic behaviours of a kind that schooling appears to reward. Some of these behaviours are to do with offering narration or description of events or phenomena in a reasonably sustained and public way; others are to do with behaving in a 'well-mannered' way, addressing and listening to others politely; others still are to do with selecting and developing upon fields of experience for talking, chosen because of their relevance to a model of childhood as a time for being cheerful and for celebrating happy things. There is in fact a very strong moral imperative in the activity of morning news to talk politely at some length about happy things. All these matters have very strong consequences for the pedagogic subject position in construction. The point can be demonstrated by reference to one reasonably representative early childroom text, selected from a longer text constituting an instance of a morning news curriculum genre, taken from Christie (1989). Before displaying this, it will be necessary to provide a sense of the schematic structure of the morning news genre.

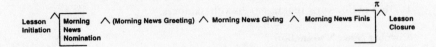

**Figure 5.1** The schematic structure of the morning news genre

As Figure 5.1 is intended to suggest, the opening element of schematic structure, the Lesson Initiation, is an initiating one, normally realized in teacher talk. A subsequent recursive sequence of steps follows, here suggested by use of the brackets [ ], while π indicates recursion. A final element, again normally realized in teacher talk, termed Lesson Closure, signals the end of the genre preparatory to moving on to something else. Within the zone of recursion, the element referred to as Morning News Nomination indicates the obligatory step by which a morning news giver is determined. Typically, the teacher nominates the first morning news giver, and she will often name subsequent class members for this role, though teachers sometimes allow the finishing morning news giver to name the person to follow him or her. The Morning News Greeting, in which morning news giver and other class members exchange greetings is optional, though many early childhood teachers require its observance. The subsequent Morning News Giving element is of course obligatory, and within this element will be found one of several possible embedded genres: in fact, on some occasions, really successful morning news givers will produce several embedded genres, although one is the norm. The genre or genres found embedded within the Morning News Giving element will always realize the second order or instructional field, chosen by the child, but none the less selected in accordance with the requirements of the regulative register.

Text 1 is set out, the various elements of structure labelled, including the elements of the genre embedded within the Morning News Giving element, which is an example of an anecdote (Plum 1988).

**Lesson Initiation**
(Teacher sits on a chair, some 25 children grouped in a semicircle on the carpeted floor at her feet.)
T: Okay. Sh. Simone, can you please shut the door? (Simone is addressed because she has just returned to the classroom after running an errand for the teacher, and she has overlooked to close the door, so she attends to this as the teacher goes on speaking.) I'm going to let you have your show and tell now

(ahs of excitement greet this).[3] Please remember your manners. Miss M was talking about manners this morning. (This is a reference to the weekly school assembly held that morning before the start of the school day, at which the principal, Miss M, had addressed the children.) Unfortunately, some people didn't even have the manners to listen to her, and I was a little bit cross with them. Manners in school and out of school are very very important, so make sure you can show each other how good your manners are.
Child: Mrs S. I seen some yellow sawdust this morning.
T: I don't know what that has to do with manners.

## Morning News Nomination
T: Yes, Aaron, you can start off please.
(Aaron has been sitting painstakingly well behaved and in a manner intended to attract the teacher's favourable attention. He comes and sit in the teacher's seat at the front, and the teacher stands well back on the side. He looks very pleased with himself.)

## Morning News Greeting
Aaron: Good morning boys and girls.
Chorus: Good morning Aaron.

## Morning News Giving
## Embedded genre: an anecdote

### Orientation
Aaron: When Brian was getting the rubbish bins, he found this box of old stuff, and he saw this racing car, and he gave it to me. He gave it to me, and the wheel's broken,

### Events
and Stephen came over to my house on Saturday and he saw it.
Stephen: So did Mirko (the latter is another class member, who sits listening).
Aaron: And Mirko. And the car –
Stephen: We got toys down at the creek, and um we was taking it up the hill and rolling it down –
Aaron: Rolling it down –
Stephen: And then we jumped on it,

### Crisis
and then it came down and rrm splash! It had gone down to the river (laughter).

### Reaction
Stephen: I didn't even get in trouble when I was soaking wet (more laughter).

### Coda
Aaron: And it's up at Ross's place, 'cause I was going to bring it, except Ross said he might try and fix it.
Child: Ross?
Aaron: Yes, Jodie's dad. My brother's friend.

**Morning News Finis**
Aaron: Finished. (Called out on a high rising note)

**Morning News Nomination**
(Aaron looks around the group, determining his choice for the next morning news giver.)
Aaron: Susy. (Said on a low tone)
(Susy comes to the front of the group to start a new sequence, while Aaron sits down.)
(Several more instances of morning news giving ensue.)

**Lesson Closure**
T: Right have you finished Sam? It's time to do some maths today.

In considering the above text, we will make selective use of Halliday's (1994) functional grammar in order to determine how the elements of structure are constructed and how the two registers are realized.

In a manner characteristic of opening elements in any curriculum genre the Lesson Initiation foregrounds the first order or regulative register, and this is apparent in the language choices made with respect to all three metafunctions. Thus, from the point of view of the textual meta-function, the element starts with a textual theme choice 'okay', one of a number of available continuatives that feature in teacher discourse at points where an element is being either initiated or sometimes closed, and more sparingly in their talk elsewhere in a curriculum genre. Such a choice, while sometimes appearing also in children's talk, appears more rarely than in teacher talk, and only at functionally relevant points, such as those where students work together in collaborative activity, directing each other as they go (Christie 1994). Continuatives did not appear at all in the classroom talk of the early childhood students sampled here, though they were quite commonly found in their talk outside the class-room. The other major linguistic choice in which the textual metafunc-tion is realized is that of teacher monologue. Just how strong is the teacher's commitment to her opening monologue can be gauged by her manner of dealing with the child who offers the contribution 'Mrs S. I seen some yellow sawdust this morning'. The latter is regarded as an unacceptable interruption, and hence the child is not simply ignored (as can sometimes happen), but actively checked when the teacher says 'I don't know what that has to do with manners'. It is probable that the child's contribution was a premature and hence unacceptable attempt at some morning news giving. There is a sequence of steps to be followed here, in the manner of other pedagogic genres, and any student who attempts to flout that sequence receives short shrift.

Experientially, the text is notable for the quite overt manner in which the issue of acceptable behaviour is dealt with. In fact, the principal lexical item in the teacher talk is 'manners', which appears six times, twice in association with the possessive pronoun 'your' as in 'your manners',

reminding the children of their personal investment in having acceptable
manners. A relational process of attribution is selected to make a very
strong observation about manners, made the stronger both in the two
qualifiers ('in school and out of school') found in the nominal group in
which the carrier is realized, and in the intensity that is a feature of the
way the attribute is realized ('very very important'):

| manners in school and out of school | are | very very important |
|---|---|---|
| Carrier | Pro: int | Attribute |

Interpersonally and hence in terms of the relationship at issue, the regulative register is apparent in several language choices. It is apparent, for
example, in the largely declarative mood choice, signalling that some
information is being given, and it is the children's obligation to listen.
Another choice building the interpersonal is one use of the imperative,
softened a little by the modal adjunct ('please') in:

please remember your manners.

Two other modal adjuncts ('unfortunately' and 'even') appear in yet
another clause, where the former is placed in interpersonal theme position, and the latter is used in association with a negative polarity
('didn't'):

unfortunately some people didn't even have the manners to listen to her.

Finally, the teacher makes clear her own judgement about the behaviour
of children who don't have acceptable manners, when she selects a relational process of attribution to create a sense of her state of mind about
them:

| I | was | a little bit cross | with them. |
|---|---|---|---|
| Carrier | Pro: int | Attribute | Circumstance: Matter. |

Overall, the linguisic resources for foregrounding the regulative register
and hence also for building the opening element of the genre are both
rich and varied. A very strong sense of what constitutes pedagogically
acceptable behaviour for the ensuing activity has been established.

The Morning News Greeting is the most completely fixed, quite ritual-
ized element of the genre, and its linguistic analysis need not detain us,
but it is worth noting the value of the ritual. Children who experience difficulties in adopting the morning news giving role often appear to enjoy
the Morning News Greeting element because, confident of what is
involved here, they can talk up quite loudly, even though they then frequently relapse into whispered remarks to the teacher, or even silence,
while the teacher tries, not always with success, to elicit louder, more sus-

tained talk. Most, but not all children, are eager to participate as morning news givers, but not all are successful. Indeed, the continuing failure over months of some children to perform well in the morning news giving task is remarkable evidence for the very differential ways in which, it seems, children are prepared by prior life experience for participation in the activities schooling prizes. Williams (1995) has recently shown compelling evidence for the ways in which children of different social classes operate with different meaning orientations in the activities of joint book reading. An important consequence is that children arrive at school very differentially prepared for literacy activities that schooling appears to prize. At issue in the activity of morning news, as already noted, is the ability to talk in some sustained way about an aspect of experience in the relatively public forum of the classroom. Children operate very differently in their ability to talk in this way. It seems likely that they are very differentially prepared to handle language in this sense, and that the differences reflect the operation of different meaning orientations in children.

Turning to the Morning News Giving element, as earlier noted, it is at this point that the second order or instructional register is foregrounded, and since it was also noted that certain constraints apply upon the choice of the instructional field, themselves a feature of the regulative field, the matter merits some brief attention for the light it throws upon the pedagogic subject position in construction. Figure 5.2 displays a representative range of instructional field choices found in early childhood morning

**Figure 5.2** Choices of instructional fields for morning news giving

news. Each of them represents some field of personal experience or events drawn from the sites of family or community activities, and 'relocated' for the purposes of the pedagogic activity.

All of the choices deal with enjoyable or happy events or items. They are selected in part because they are 'nice', or at least acceptable and hence calculated to be approved by the teacher, whose authority as ultimate arbiter of what constitutes 'good manners' is always present. In practice, children select topics that are happy, often celebratory, thus building and constantly reaffirming a particular view of the pedagogic subject as happy and engaging in 'good' or perhaps 'wholesome' activities. Teachers regularly reward children who make happy selections for morning news giving, while on occasion discouraging others who do not make such selections. In the study cited here (Christie 1989), for example, one teacher with unconscious if startling cruelty, told a boy student that he 'never had anything nice or interesting happen to him' because he never offered to participate in the morning news giving, though he always listened politely to those who did. Reflection on the instructional fields sought for the purposes of the activity, as well as some knowledge of the child's family, made it clear that he must have engaged in a number of them, but it seemed he was unwilling or unable to make similar choices from his life and reconstruct them, and he therefore was criticized. Thus are the rewards of schooling differentially offered to children in activities as apparently simple as morning news.

The genre selected for the morning news giving is an instance of an oral story genre first identified by Plum (1988) in adult Australian native speakers of English but also found by Christie in the language of primary and junior secondary school students (Christie 1995b). The anecdote is one of a number of story genres identified by Plum having an opening (the Orientation), some happenings (the Events) and a subsequent Crisis, where the success of the latter depends not on any explicit resolution, but rather upon a shared understanding of what is involved (apparent in laughter or a gasp of surprise or shock). The Reaction draws attention to the critical nature of the events, often in a manner that invites a sympathetic or amused response.

Oral stories, including anecdotes, are very typically told by two or more participants, and the fact that the anecdote here is jointly constructed by two boys, Aaron and Stephen, both of whom participated in the events reconstructed, may in one sense cause no surprise. But for the purposes of the morning news genre in which this anecdote is embedded, the joint construction is unusual. Normally, the teacher would not have permitted joint construction in the morning news giving element of the genre, on the grounds that this was one opportunity when the morning news giver told his or her events or news in an independent and singular way. But on this occasion, she did permit a joint construction. The probable explanation for this was that Aaron was an accomplished story-teller, so that his 'right' to construct his tale did not need to be defended by the teacher, as did sometimes happen with less successful story-tellers, for whom she would intervene to prevent other children taking over. In any case, the anecdote was patently judged a great success by all who heard it, students and teacher, and it produced considerable laughter.

We will comment only selectively on the linguistic choices in which the instructional register and the elements of structure are realized.

In the familiar pattern of many a story genre, the Orientation starts with a hypotactic clause of time, placed in marked theme position:

<u>When Brian was getting the rubbish bins</u> he found this box of old stuff . . .

while the transitivity choices, mainly involving material processes, in this and the subsequent five clauses, build the critical experiential information upon which the rest of the story depends:

when Brian <u>was getting</u> the rubbish bins (material process)
he <u>found</u> this box of old stuff (material process)
and he <u>saw</u> this racing car (process of perception)
and he <u>gave</u> it to me (material process) (uttered twice)
and the wheel<u>'s broken</u> (material process).

The sequence of jointly constructed clauses in which the Events are realized is linked either additively ('<u>and</u> Stephen came over to my house') or in terms of time ('<u>and then</u> we jumped on it'), while the critical transitivity choices are again mainly material, constructing the activities in which the children engaged (e.g. 'we <u>got</u> toys'; 'and then we <u>jumped</u> on it').

The Crisis marks a new and unexpected turn to the story, once more realized primarily in the transitivity choices, both material, where the second makes clear the fate of the toy car:

it <u>had gone</u> down to the river.

The Reaction is signalled through the choices of a negative polarity (the first in a story otherwise marked by positive polarity) and the use of a modal adjunct helping to give emphasis:

I <u>didn't even</u> get in trouble when I was soaking wet.

The success of the Reaction depends very much upon the success of the previous element, and its success has been ensured by the ready laughter of teacher and class. An implicit but shared knowledge of the subculture of early childhood is at issue here: children are not supposed to do naughty things like getting wet, especially near potentially dangerous places such as creeks or rivers, and it normally incurs parental displeasure. Part of the point of the Reaction element is that this is recognized: the two boys did something mildly naughty, and they got away with it.

The Coda element brings the anecdote to a conclusion by rounding it off and bringing the events back to the present. This is signalled in part by the shift in tense from the past to the present tense in the clause that opens the element:

and it's up at Ross's place,

and in part by the experiential information that is exchanged concerning 'Ross', his identity and his role with respect to the car.

The closing recursive elements of structure may be dealt with quickly. They are of interest both in that it is in these that the first order or regulative register is again in construction, and in that this register now finds very elliptical expression, this time in the talk of a child rather than that of the teacher. But their successful elliptical expression is an important measure of the fact that there have been earlier non-elliptical expressions of what is involved, no doubt initially at least in the teacher's talk. That is to say, in much earlier instances of this genre, the teacher no doubt directed the child in the morning news giving role to nominate a successor, and it may even be that in earlier expressions the child offered a less elliptical expression than is given here, when only a child's name is stated. As it is, the Morning News Finis is realized in the one item 'finished', where the choice of a high rising tone (very characteristic in morning news givers at this point, and in no sense idiosyncratic to this child) seems to signal a degree of pleasure in a task well done. The Morning News Nomination ('Susy'), which is equally elliptical, is said on a lower tone (again characteristic at this point), and this seems to suggest some acknowledgement by Aaron that the time for his public performance is over, as he prepares to rejoin the other students on the floor.

The final element of structure, the Lesson Closure, as one would expect, is one realized in teacher talk, where the regulative register is again foregrounded. Here the teacher both determines the end of one pedagogic activity and heralds the start of another.

To summarize the major claims of this discussion thus far, it has been argued that at work in the morning news genre, as in other instances of pedagogic discourse in schools, are certain important choices in the language that help construct a particular pedagogic subject position. The language choices realize two registers, a regulative one to do with pedagogic goals and directions, and an instructional register, to do with the skills and 'content' to be dealt with. The operation of the former determines or projects the operation of the latter. As we have seen, the regulative register is foregrounded in the opening element of the genre, where, in the instance examined in particular, the teacher talk is entirely devoted to establishment of pedagogically acceptable modes of behaviour for the coming activity of morning news giving; but the regulative register is also foregrounded in the closing stages of what is a recursive element in the genre, preparatory to introducing a new morning news giving phase. It is also foregrounded in the final element of structure, the Lesson Closure. The two registers are realized very differently, providing important evidence for the claim that the two are at work in a pedagogic discourse. The particular pedagogic subject position in construction in the discourse is that of one who can build sustained narration or description of event or phenomena in an acceptably well mannered way. While the example examined was unusual in that two boys constructed the genre embedded within the Morning News Giving element, it was in other ways representative of successful narration about personal experience, where that experience had been chosen for its amusement and pleasure, and because it met the general criteria of what was acceptable to the teacher.

The pedagogic subject positions of early childhood education are of importance for many reasons, not least because they help to build in children certain habits of working, certain predispositions towards the teacher and peers, and certain abilities in using language that are intended to be foundational for participation in later pedagogic activity. In this sense, certain forms of consciousness are in construction, to return to Bernstein's observations noted earlier, about the 'symbolic control' that functions in a pedagogic discourse. It does not follow that all students adopt the desired habits or achieve the desired forms of consciousness in the same ways, or with equal degrees of success. Indeed, as was earlier suggested, this is not the case. Not all children readily choose to take up the role of morning news giver, while others, eager to take the role, none the less experience great difficulties in fulfilling it, either because they have trouble selecting an appropriate instructional field of 'outside school' activity and relocating it for school purposes, or because they have trouble building sustained narration or description about it. As already noted, schooling differentially rewards students, and we have suggested that this reflects the presence of different meaning orientations in children.

## A curriculum macrogenre of the upper primary school

A curriculum macrogenre is so called because it constitutes a sustained sequence of curriculum genres (a curriculum cycle, to use less technical language) occurring over several days, sometimes over several weeks, in which new understandings are taught and new kinds of consciousness are formed. An increasing body of research (see Green and Dixon 1993 for a representative example) has recognized that if we are to understand the complexities of any one instance of a lesson, then we actually need to study the ways classroom participants interact over time, following the ways in which the discursive and social practices develop and 'how these practices contribute to the construction of knowledge in classrooms' (Green and Dixon 1993: 234). The argument proposed here is that the notion of a curriculum macrogenre offers a particularly powerful tool for analysis of the practices involved. But, as already suggested, it enables us to go further, and to pursue the pedagogic subject position in construction in the discourse.

Two theoretical matters need to be dealt with briefly before proceeding to offer some analysis of our selected macrogenre from the upper primary school. One concerns what constitutes a macrogenre, since it is not the case that any sequence of lessons necessarily creates a macrogenre. The other concerns the manner of operation of the two registers in the macrogenre for, as we shall see, this differs from their manner of operation in the morning news genre examined above.

As already noted, a curriculum macrogenre constitutes a sequence of curriculum genres in which new understandings and new forms of consciousness are taught and learned. A series of genres unfolds, each with its own elements of schematic structure, and the genres constitute important elements, in turn, of the macrogeneric structure, such that the genres stand in relation to each other, much as clauses relate to each other in a clause complex (see Martin 1994, 1995 for some discussion of this). That is to say, they will be in states of interdependency, in terms, metaphorically at least, either of expansion or projection (Halliday 1994), and this will have important consequences for the successful completion of the pedagogic tasks. As the macrogenre unfolds, there will ,be some growth in the *logos* – some changes logogenetically (Halliday in Halliday and Martin 1993: 18) – as the classroom text gains momentum, moving forward across its 'beginning, middle, end' progression, opening up possibilities in using language, closing others, and hence building forms of consciousness. On occasion, in the hands of less successful teachers, a set of lessons can occur in which very little is taught and learned. At best, some set of lessons can emerge that are loosely thematically linked, but they lack strong connectedness in the sense that a relationship of real interdependency would require, and they also lack logogenesis (Christie 1995a).

To turn to the issue of the two registers, the success with which these operate will necessarily vary, for it is upon their successful operation that the logogenesis will occur, and as we have just noted, logogenesis is not a necessary feature of any set of lessons, though it is of a macrogenre. But, that noted, it is also important to observe that the two registers function very differently, in an instance of a macrogenre of the kind we are to examine shortly, from the way in which we saw them operate in the morning news genre examined above. In fact, the morning news genre is unique in the manner in which the two registers operate within it, because the two do not converge. As we saw, the first order or regulative register is foregrounded in the Lesson Initiation and Lesson Closure and in the Morning News Nomination, the Morning News Greeting and the Morning News Finis. But in the critically important element that is Morning News Giving it is the second order or instructional register that is foregrounded. There is, however, no element in which the two converge, and we may conclude that this is a condition of a curriculum genre in which, subject to the pedagogic constraints discussed above, the children select the instructional field for narration or description.

In any other curriculum genre and/or macrogenre, however, the two registers will converge, as the teacher selects the instructional field to be used and guides its introduction and development, encouraging the students to use the field information in particular ways. Thus, the teacher paces the students as they learn, on the one hand, how to go about their tasks (the regulative register), and, on the other hand, the 'content', topics or information (the instructional field) they are to use in order to complete their tasks. Typically, but the matter is subject to considerable variation, depending on the teacher and the age of the students, the opening stage(s) of a curriculum genre and of a curriculum macrogenre will foreground the regulative register, a subsequent element or elements will involve a convergence of the two registers as a task or tasks are specified, yet another will involve a foregrounding of the instructional register as students research and explore it, some convergence of the two registers will often then occur in a subsequent element, while, in a final element, the regulative register will disappear, though it will continue to operate tacitly as the instructional register comes to the fore. The function of the regulative register is to guide and direct the behaviour of the pedagogic subjects: its functions will have been achieved, when at the end of a curriculum macrogenre, the subjects are enabled to do certain new things, where these are realized in instructional register choices.

The curriculum macrogenre of the upper primary school to be briefly examined here is drawn from a unit of work in the social science programme. The macrogeneric structure is set out in Figure 5.3. There are three genres involved: the Curriculum Initiation, the Curriculum Negotiation and the Curriculum Closure. The figure allows us to see how the macrogenre is built up in a layered way through its various genres and the elements of structure within these. The Curriculum Initia-

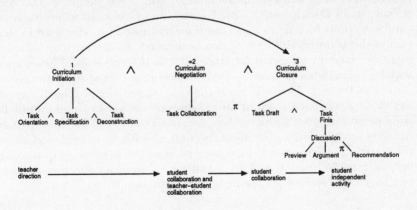

**Figure 5.3** A macrogenre of the upper primary school social science programme

tion consists of only genre, and its elements are a Task Orientation, a Task Specification and a Task Deconstruction. It is in the Task Orientation that the teacher points directions for the whole sequence. The Task Specification defines the pedagogic task, in this case involving the writing of a target text type, and the Task Deconstruction in turn involves an analysis or a 'deconstruction' of the target text type. As we shall see, the regulative register is foregrounded in the Task Orientation while in the Task Specification the two registers converge, and in the Task Deconstruction again it is the regulative register that is foregrounded. The middle genre, called Curriculum Negotiation, stands in a relationship of elaboration (indicated with the notation =) to the Curriculum Initiation and it involves several constituent genres, operating recursively (indicated with $\pi$), called Task Collaborations, in which students and teacher work collaboratively, researching the field for writing, and also preparing notes for their ultimate writing task. Here it is the instructional register that is foregrounded for the most part. The concluding genre, the Curriculum Closure, stands in a relationship of projection to the Curriculum Initiation (indicated with the notation"), for it has been projected very early in the Curriculum Initiation (in fact in the Task Specification). This also has several constituent genres, operating recursively, called Task Draft and a Task Finis. As the names suggest, the Task Draft involves writing a sample of the target text type, and this is recursive because all the students produce their sample texts, discussing them with class peers. Here, both registers are involved. In the Task Finis, however, when the target texts are finished, the instructional register is foregrounded. Interpersonally, there is a shift from overt teacher direction, which is a feature of the Curriculum Initiation, to student collaboration and teacher–student collaboration in the Curriculum Negotiation, towards further student colaboration and eventually student independent activity in the Curriculum Closure.

The unit of work developed as part of the upper primary social science programme focused on uranium mining, and it was taught in the Australian city of Darwin with a Year 6 class. Darwin is a city where such an issue is a controversial one, because uranium mining is permitted in that part of the country, and its propriety is debated. The immediate issue for focus involved an imagined advertisement in the major local newspaper, seeking expressions of opinion about the construction of a nuclear power station in Darwin. The object was that the students read this, discuss its significance, research relevant information on the subject, and eventually write persuasive texts about it. Over a three-week period, five lessons, constituting most but not quite all of the unit of work, were recorded. Since the resulting classroom text is substantial, it will be possible to quote only very selectively from it, and to identify only some of the more salient language choices in which the meanings are realized.

*Curriculum initiation: Task Orientation*

A great deal of the talk for the first few minutes concerns arrangements for the physical dispositions of the students, and talk about the needed equipment to get on with the pedagogic tasks. There is a relationship between the teacher's concerns here and those of the early childhood teacher examined above, with her focus on 'manners', and all that implied about acceptable pedagogic behaviour. The teacher's concern is very much with establishing desired patterns of behaviour for working, and the very high incidence of modality in her talk is one important measure of her effort to direct the students towards these patterns. The uses of modality in her talk are much more frequent than was true in the talk of the early childhood teacher examined above, although the latter teacher, like the one here, enjoyed very good relations with her students. The greater use of modality here perhaps reflects the fact that the teacher is dealing with older students (they are aged 10–11 years), and she finds it more appropriate to direct by persuasion and suggestion than by overt command. Incidences of modality are marked in bold in the text.

> T: The way to work **might** be to sit around this group. All right? Because **perhaps** people will be (inaudible) and less wriggling if they're seated. Now a lot of work [[that you **may have** to do]] **may** be with a partner. Some you'll do by yourself. So you're **probably best** to sit next to somebody [[that you will work with]]. OK? Now, two, four, six, eight ... there's one person away today so **maybe** it **might** be a group of three. All right? It's up to you. But **could** you find yourself a seat around the desks and be sitting next to someone that you will identify to work with **please**? If you two are going to work together ... there'll have to be one odd person sitting there ... OK? So move down one **please**.

A few seconds later, physical dispositions having been dealt with, the teacher goes on to establish some other aspects of desired behaviours:

> T: You really do need something to write with so if you don't have your own pens and pencils would you collect those please? And there are a couple of other organizational things to do before we get started.
> Philip: Will we need a ruler?
> T: I don't think you'll need a ruler. I'd like you each to ... and I want these back ... this might support in some of the work as well (a reference to some handouts held but not yet distributed by the teacher). I'd like you each to have a highlighter as well on the desk in front of you.
> Ashley: What if you don't have a highlighter?
> Renee: I bags yellow. (This is a reference to the colour of the highlighter.)
> (There is much noise as the students move about fetching writing materials and highlighters before they settle back in their places to proceed.)

To this point, and indeed for a few minutes more, it is only the regulative register that is realized in the text. Some important issues, to do with the values of working 'with a partner', and hence cooperatively, are of

concern here, as well as practical issues to do with adoption of the desirable tools for working (rulers and highlighters). Both sets of issues have
significance in building particular predispositions for working here.

Later, as the teacher moves the students towards their reading of the
advertisement and hence their initial exposure to the instructional field,
the two registers converge, in such a manner that it is the regulative register that is paramount, while the instructional field finds some expression,
typically in one participant role in transitivity. One example will suffice to
illustrate the point. Distributing copies of the mock newspaper advertisement, the teacher says:

Now I want to point your attention to <u>one of the articles</u>.

Here, in transitivity terms, the instructional field is realized in the participant role of Phenomenon ('one of the articles'), while the other participant role of Senser ('I') and the mental process itself ('want to point your
attention') realize aspects of the regulative register. Subsequent talk about
the details of the advertisement leads to the Task Specification, where the
two registers continue to converge as students and teacher talk about
what they will do (regulative register) with respect to the advertisement
and its contents (the instructional field).

### Curriculum initiation: Task Specification

The following text is drawn from the Task Specification, although at
points marked with a row of dots, some of the talk has been removed in
the interests of conserving space:

T: Well what are we going to do?
Marcus: We're going to write and tell them that we don't want the power plant.
T: All right. What are we going to write?
Richard: Personal opinion.
T: How are we going to write it?
..................................
Layla: Well a petition might help. If there are people who don't actually have
the time to write they could just sign their names so they know actually how
many people.
..................................
Richard: Maybe we could write like an argument or something that shows both
points of view and putting your own personal opinion at the end.
T: Great. Now is it actually called an argument when you put both points of
view across? Is it?
Marcus: Mrs W, a discussion
T: It's a discussion. All right. Now what does a discussion show? What does a
discussion show Ashley?
Ashley: Two sides of a story and it sort of like depends on which side wins.
T: OK. And how do you decide which side wins? When you give a discussion
how do you know what side wins?

Marcus: By the one that goes last. Like you put the one that you think is wrong before.
T: But how do you decide that? What gives you . . . how do you know which one to decide? Richard?
Richard: Because after listening to all the information you found out you can make up your own mind if it benefits you or if it benefits other people.
T: Good. So you're saying that it's the information that tells you?
Richard: Yeah.

The reference to writing a 'discussion', it should be noted, comes from earlier work done in this class, using discussion genres as they have been contrasted with argumentative genres in Australian work on written genres (Metropolitan East Disadvantaged Schools Program 1989). In a discussion, a writer previews an issue, outlines arguments for and against the issue, and concludes with an expression of the writer's own opinion.

Apart from the reference to 'the power plant' in one participant role ('we don't want the power plant'), the language on the whole realizes the regulative register, as teacher and students together construct a sense of what they might do. Several processes realize aspects of the students' behaviours, all of them directed towards the goals of the teaching–learning activity:

We're going to write and tell them that we don't want the power plant.
Maybe we could write like an argument or something . . .
Because after listening to all the information you found out you can make up your own mind . . .

Operating in participant roles in several key points is a developing language for handling the writing task:

Richard: Maybe we could write like an argument or something [[that shows both points of view]]* and putting your own personal opinion at the end.
T: Now is it actually called an argument when you put both points of view across? Is it?
Marcus: Mrs W, a discussion
T: It's a discussion. All right. Now what does a discussion show?

Interpersonally, the text is of interest for the modality in the children's talk, indicating that they are aware they are engaged in some exploratory activity. Once again, modality is marked in bold:

Well a petition **might** help.
**Maybe** we **could** write like an argument . . .

Textually, the teacher's role remains important in helping to build the connectedness in the construction of the information here:

---

* The notations [[ ]] indicate an embedded or down-ranked clause.

<u>Well</u> what are we going to do?
<u>Now</u> is it actually called an argument when you put both points of view across?
Is it?
<u>Now</u> what does a discussion show?
<u>And</u> how do you decide which side wins?
<u>When</u> you give a discussion how do you know what side wins?
<u>But</u> how do you decide that?
<u>So</u> you're saying that it's the information that tells you?

Looking in particular at the operation of the conjunctions here ('and', 'when', 'but' and 'so'), we can see that the teacher's role helps shape the logic that the discourse takes as well.

Overall, a primary object of the Task Specification is to establish what is to be done, and some of the technical language with which to handle it. A particular set of values about the nature of evidence and research is also at issue, as is apparent when, a little later in the discourse, the teacher makes use of strong attitudinal expression, here marked in bold:

T: Do you make up your mind now?
Several students: No.
T: See, when we first started talking that's what I felt you had done. All right, because maybe of that story we read. I felt that maybe you'd made your mind up and it's **really good** to see that people **actually haven't made their mind up** and that they're **prepared** to look at both sides. And it's that evidence that'll tell us. And I **think** writing a discussion is **an excellent idea**. It's **probably the best idea**. Because when we send that in it means we've been **fair**. We've looked at it **properly**, we've looked at both sides and we've **thought** about it before we've made the decision.

Thus is the pedagogic subject position also constructed in the text with a particular set of values concerning recourse to evidence being appealed to. That set of values is fundamental to a great deal of effort in English-speaking cultures, of interest in part to the scholarly pursuits of academe, but also to many other areas of life, for example in legal and commercial activities of many kinds. There is in this sense a relationship between the values and pedagogic subject positions of schooling and those of the wider community.

*Curriculum initiation: Text Deconstruction*

In the Text Deconstruction stage, the object is that the students identify the elements of the target discussion genre they are to write by reference to an example. Here again it is the regulative register that is fore-grounded. Interpersonally, the teacher overtly invites joint participation with her in the task with an inclusive imperative:

Now <u>let's have a look</u> . . .

while processes and participant roles and in one case a circumstance ('in a discussion') realize aspects of the metalanguage for talking about discussion genres:

> T: Now let's have a look and see if we can work out how <u>a discussion is structured</u>. OK? We've <u>identified the issue</u>. What other things are there that you're aware of in <u>a discussion</u>? Layla?
> Layla: They have <u>an introduction</u>.
> T: Right. Yes they have <u>an introduction</u>. It has <u>a special name</u>,
> ....................................
> Richard: It's <u>a preview, kind of preview</u>.
> Asked what this means, the students go on:
> Marcus: I was going to say <u>previews are [[like telling you [[what it's going to be about]] ]]</u>

Subsequent elements in the discussion genre are established in a passage too long to show here: arguments for a point of view; arguments against a point of view; and a final recommendation.

### Curriculum Negotiation

Space will not permit any detailed examination of those aspects of the text that constitute the Curriculum Negotiation. We can note, however, that within this overall genre, discussion focuses sometimes on the language of the genre for writing, foregrounding the regulative register, and sometimes on the field for investigation and for writing about. Later on, extensive amounts of time are devoted to collection and reading of materials on the uses, advantages and disadvantages of nuclear power.

### Curriculum Closure: task draft

The Curriculum Closure involves a review of the draft discussion genres that the students have written individually, and comparing them with the models used to analyse and deconstruct. After some group discussion, they are to edit their own texts before typing them up.

Discussion of the introductory preview and its function leads to talk of ways to introduce the different points of view. Here too the regulative field is foregrounded, as the students talk of appropriate expressions to signal the start of a new point of view:

> Richard: I thought it would be <u>on the other side</u>.
> Layla: <u>On the other side of the argument</u> many people believe . . .
> Penny: <u>On the other hand</u> . . .

Later discussion turns to how a decision is made on the nature of the recommendation, and again the regulative field is foregrounded. Here students articulate appropriate behaviours, realized in particular in the transitivity choices:

T: Now how <u>do you decide on your recommendation</u>? Marcus?
Marcus: By <u>reading through the argument</u>
........................................
Penny: <u>By what's stronger</u>.
T: <u>How you know it's stronger? How will you decide it's stronger?</u>
Penny: Well <u>the benefits should outweigh the effects or the effects should out-
weigh the benefits</u>.

### Curriculum Closure: the discussion genres

One example only of a text written by students in the class will be examined here, illustrating the type of discussion genre produced. It will be
noted that in this text it is the instructional register that is foregrounded.
The regulative register has literally disappeared in the discourse though,
as we earlier suggested, it continues to operate tacitly, having shaped the
manner of selection and organization of instructional field information
in order to produce the written text.

It will be apparent that the young writer has made successful use of a
significant body of technical language relevant to the instructional field,
much of it identified initially with assistance from the teacher. Such items
include: 'nuclear fuelled power station' or 'fossil fired power stations';
'the environment'; 'nuclear waste'; 'pollution'; 'radiation'; 'electricity'. It
will also be apparent that the text is successfuly organized as an instance
of a discussion genre. The elements of schematic structure are marked,
though no detailed grammatical analysis of these will be offered.

**Preview**
There are some people who believe we should have a nuclear power station
because it's cheaper and does not pollute the environment as much as fossil-
fuelled power stations.

However, other people do not want a nuclear-fuelled power station. They
feel it is unsafe due to accidents and problems with disposal of radioactive
waste materials that are harmful to the environment.

**Argument 1**
Some people say that nuclear power is better than fossil fuels because it is safer,
cleaner and cheaper. In Western countries nuclear power reactors have three
main barriers to prevent leakage of radiation. At Chernobyl where a major
accident occurred they had no third barrier to prevent radiation leaking into
the environment. Maybe they had no third barrier because of money and
technology.

Nuclear power plants are cleaner than fossil-fired plants. Nuclear power stations do not release as much pollution and that means it is not as damaging to
humans and environments.

In France two-thirds of their electricity is cheaper than most Western countries that use fossil-fired power stations because uranium is cheaper than fossil
fuels, e.g. oil, coal and gas.

**Argument 2**

On the other side, some people say that nuclear power is not safe, cheap and clean. Nuclear waste will remain radioactive for thousands of years. The safest methods of deep burial cannot be 100 per cent guaranteed against natural events in the future, e.g. earthquakes.

Building and running a nuclear power station is not cheap. Solar power stations in the United States cost half a billion dollars to build and electricity costs $500 per kilowatt.

Nuclear power is not clean because of the danger of radioactive waste and materials. The radioactive waste is very dangerous to humans and the environment. With humans it can cause cancer and deformities in unborn babies and large amounts of radiation can be deadly.

**Recommendation**

Thus, in summary, both sides put forward convincing arguments.

Nuclear power is an alternative to fossil fuel because our supply is running out but at the moment Darwin does not need a nuclear power station. Therefore I believe a power station is not needed in Darwin because of the danger involved with nuclear power.

What can we say of the pedagogic subject position in construction in the discourse in the social science curriculum macrogenre? Such a position involves a capacity to work with a partner in discussion and research, a capacity to read and research evidence to do with a particular instructional field, weighing up the evidence in favour of particular judgements about it, a capacity to identify a particular target genre appropriate to dealing with the instructional field, and a capacity finally to constuct an instance of such a genre.

## Conclusion

In this chapter we have examined two instances of classroom texts, one selected as an instance of an early childhood curriculum genre, the other as an example of a curriculum macrogenre of the upper primary school. The two were selected in part because, drawn as they were from two very different age groups within the primary school, they offered contrasting yet complementary means of observing the operation of pedagogic discourses at work in schools. A principle is involved in the operation of a pedagogic discourse, so Bernstein has claimed, such that a regulative discourse takes or 'delocates' an instructional discourse from elsewhere and relocates it for the purposes of its selective transmission. The manner of its transmission, involving certain pacing and sequencing principles, helps to build a particular pedagogic subject position, and this in turn involves adoption of a form, or forms, of consciousness. In this sense, the agency responsible for the initiation and maintenance of a pedagogic discourse may be seen as an agent of 'symbolic control'.

In the classroom texts examined here, we have argued, firstly, that the regulative discourse is a *regulative register*, involving sets of language choices designed to regulate, direct and maintain the pedagogic activity of schooling, and, secondly, that the instructional discourse is an *instructional register*, involving sets of choices that realize the instructional field that has been selected from elsewhere for educational purposes. The operation of the two registers, and their different realizations across a classroom text, may be accounted for in terms of a theory of genre. A genre is a staged, purposive activity in which certain significant goals are achieved; its various stages or elements of structure are built through changing sets of register choices, each fundamentally involved in the eventual achievement of the pedagogic goals. The regulative register is always dominant, at least in the opening stages of a curriculum genre or macrogenre, shaping the manner of engagement with the instructional register. Yet as the curriculum macrogenre in particular unfolds, the regulative register is no longer expressed in the discourse, while the instructional register is foregrounded. Nonetheless, the operation of the regulative register remains tacit in the discourse, and this is an important measure of its success. That is to say, once pedagogic subjects are enabled, or apprenticed, to do new things, the regulative register that constrained and directed their abilities no longer needs explicit expression.

As was indicated much earlier in this discussion, it does not follow that all students in schools adopt the same pedagogic subject position, or that they adopt it in the same ways. Students bring to the pedagogic activity of schooling very different meaning orientations, shaped by the wider experiences of family and community life, and they perform variously for the purposes of schooling. That point acknowledged, however, this discussion has sought both to demonstrate some linguistic evidence for the operation of the two registers and their role in building curriculum genres and macrogenres, and to indicate, in the cases of the two classroom texts sampled, something of the 'ideal' pedagogic subject positions apparently in construction in each.

In a deep and profound sense the pedagogic practices of schooling merit serious scholarly attention for the light they throw on the manner in which subjectivities more generally are constructed. Bernstein has commented (1990: 169) on the remarkable, even 'overwhelming' similarity of the operation of educational systems round the world, regardless of the predominant ideology found in them. We must conclude that, so enduring and apparently stable is the operation of pedagogic practices, they are fundamentally involved in the construction of social reality.

## Notes

1 Bernstein has argued of pedagogic discourse (e.g. Bernstein, 1986, 1990) that the discourse consists of a regulative discourse and an instructional discourse, where the latter is 'embedded' in the former. This general characterization of the pedagogic discourse is accepted here, though it is cast differently. Thus,

using terms taken from systemic functional linguistic theory it is argued that the two are to be thought of as 'registers', regulative and instructional, and that the former 'projects' the latter.

2 The general observation, supported by much research this century, that teachers talk more than students, and in particular that they ask more questions than the latter, while certainly true, none the less needs to be treated with some caution. It is only when we subject classroom discourse to sustained scrutiny over the course of a whole successful curriculum cycle or curriculum macrogenre that we can demonstrate how selective can be a teacher's use of questioning, and also how useful it can be in the total scheme. Thus, in the whole macrogenre, there will be particular curriculum genres or lessons in which intensive teacher questioning and student answering are of critical importance to the activity of building a shared knowledge base. However, in other curriculum genres in the same macrogenre, other linguistic patterns can apply, involving, for example, student questioning of the teacher and other students, or on other occasions, a great deal of collaborative building of the discourse, where questioning has only a minor role in the total pattern. These matters are discussed in Christie (1994).

3 The teacher involved always used the term 'show and tell', though in fact she was quite indifferent to whether the students physically displayed an object to describe and 'tell about', or whether, as in this case, they simply narrated some experiences.

## References

Bernstein, B. (1986) 'On pedagogic discourse'. In J. Richardson (ed.) *Handbook of Theory and Research in the Sociology of Education*. New York: Greenwood Press, 205–39.

Bernstein, B. (1990) *The Structuring of Pedagogic Discourse: Class, Codes and Control*, Vol. IV. London: Routledge.

Christie, F. (1989) 'Curriculum genres in early childhood education: a case study in writing development'. Unpublished PhD thesis, University of Sydney.

Christie, F. (1990) 'The morning news genre'. *Language and Education* 4(3), 161–80.

Christie, F. (1991a) 'First and second order registers in education'. In E. Ventola (ed.) *Functional and Systemic Linguistics: Approaches and Uses* (Trends in Linguistics Studies and Monographs 55). Berlin: Walter de Gruyter & Co., 235–56.

Christie, F. (1991b) 'Pedagogical and content registers in a writing lesson'. *Linguistics and Education* 3, 203–24.

Christie, F. (1994) 'On pedagogic discourse'. Final Report of a research activity funded by the Australian Research Council 1990–92. University of Melbourne.

Christie, F. (1995a) 'The teaching of literature in the secondary English class'. Report 1 of a Research Study into the Pedagogic Discourse of Secondary School English. A study funded by the Australian Research Council. University of Melbourne.

Christie, F. (1995b) 'The teaching of story writing in the junior secondary school'. Report 2 of a Research Study into the Pedagogic Discourse of Secondary School English. A study funded by the Australian Research Council. University of Melbourne.

Green, J. and Dixon, C. (eds) (1993) 'Special Issue: Santa Barbara classroom discourse group'. *Linguistics and Education* 5(3) and (4).

Green, J. and Kantor-Smith, R. (1988) 'Exploring the complexity of language and learning in the life of the classroom'. Paper given at the Post World Reading Congress Symposium on Language in Learning, University of Queensland, Brisbane, 10–15 July 1988.

Halliday, M. A. K. (1979) 'Modes of meaning and modes of expression: types of grammatical structure, and their determination by different semantic functions'. In D. J. Allerton, E. Cartney and D. Holdcroft (eds) *Function and Context in Linguistic Analysis: Essays Offered to William Haas*. Cambridge: Cambridge University Press, 57–79.

Halliday, M. A. K. (1981) 'Types of structure'. In M. A. K. Halliday and J. R. Martin (eds) *Readings in Systemic Linguistics*. London: Batsford, 29–41.

Halliday, M. A. K. (1982) 'How is a text like a clause?' In S. Allen (ed.) *Text Processing: Text Analysis and Generation, Text Typology and Attribution* (Proceedings of Nobel Symposium 51). Stockholm: Almqvist & Wiksell, 209–47.

Halliday, M. A. K. (1994) *An Introduction to Functional Grammar*. 2nd edition. London: Edward Arnold.

Halliday, M. A. K. and Martin, J. R. (1993) *Writing Science: Literacy and Discursive Power* (Critical Perspectives on Literacy and Education. Series Editor: Allan Luke). London: Falmer Press.

Hunter, I. (1994) *Rethinking the School: Subjectivity, Bureaucracy, Criticism*. Sydney: Allen & Unwin.

Iedema, R., Feez, S. and White, P. (1994) *Media Literacy*. (Write It Right Industry Research Monograph No. 2). Sydney: Disadvantaged Schools Program, Metropolitan East.

Lemke, J. L. (1995) *Textual Politics: Discourse and Social Dynamics* (Critical Perspectives on Literacy and Education. Series Editor: A. Luke). London: Taylor & Francis.

Martin, J. R. (1994) 'Macro-genres: the ecology of the page'. *Network* 21, 29–52.

Martin, J. R. (1995) 'Text and clause: fractal resonance'. *Text* 15(1), 5–42.

Mehan, H. (1979) *Learning Lessons: Social Organization in the Classroom*. Cambridge, MA: Harvard University Press.

Metropolitan East Disadvantaged Schools Program (1989) *A Brief Introduction to Genre: Examples of Six Factual Genres and their Generic Structure*. Sydney: Language and Social Power Project, Metropolitan East DSP.

Plum, G. (1988) 'Text and contextual conditioning in spoken English: a genre-based approach'. Unpublished PhD thesis, University of Sydney.

Williams, G. (1995) 'Joint book-reading and literacy pedagogy: a socio-semantic examination'. Unpublished PhD thesis, Macquarie University, Australia.

# 6 Learning how to mean – scientifically speaking: apprenticeship into scientific discourse in the secondary school

*Robert Veel*

> Adults may choose to deny it, but children in school know very well that there is a 'language of science'.
>
> Halliday in Halliday and Martin (1993: 2)

## Introduction

This chapter explores the role played by written language in school science. In particular it deals with how written language construes for students distinctive and favoured ways of thinking about the world; ways which we recognize as 'scientific', 'logical' and 'rational'. It will analyse the purpose, structure and grammatical features of some of the prevalent types of written text (genres[1]) in school science and consider how these texts work to construe and privilege certain kinds of meanings and to construct certain kinds of 'ideal' pedagogic subjects in the science class-room. The chapter closes by reflecting upon the adequacy of this process in scientific, educational and ideological terms.

Most of the example texts and some of the discussion in this chapter derive from research conducted in Australian secondary science class-rooms between 1990 and 1993 by the Disadvantaged Schools Program (Veel to appear). Like earlier work on writing in Australian schools (Cope and Kalantzis 1993; Martin 1993a), the text description and discussion is based on the model of language and context developed through systemic functional linguistic (SFL) theory (Halliday and Hasan 1985; Halliday 1994; Matthiessen 1995) and register genre theory (Martin 1992). There also exists a good deal of published research outside of SFL which deals with the relationship between context and language in research science, particularly on the link between investigation in the lab-oratory and published scientific research (Bazerman 1988; Lynch and Woolgar 1990; Latour and Woolgar 1986; Myers 1990). Both this linguis-tic and non-linguistic research share a common view of language and meaning: language is *constitutive* of meaning and social context, not simply a conduit or tool to transmit thought or reality. The language of school science may thus be considered as actively constructing a particu-lar realm of scientific reality, and constructing roles for students within this realm. The kind of language encountered and used by students in school science makes possible some ways of thinking about the world and simultaneously prevents, or at least marginalizes, other ways of thinking. From this point of view, literacy in school science is not just a matter of acquiring certain mechanical skills, but an apprenticeship into a whole world view. In examining the language of school science, then, we need also to think of broader issues. Do the ways of making meanings offered in school science make for good science in a general sense? Do they (should they) reflect what happens in 'adult science'? What kinds of social subjects does the language of school science produce?

An account of the language of school science must therefore do more than document genres and their grammatical features. Many institutional factors affect the types of meanings that can be made and the value accorded to these meanings. In secondary school science, for example, discourses of child development, school administration, scientific method, social class, gender, ethnicity, technology and economics all influence the language used in the classroom and individual students' orientation to that language.[2] To make sense of the way particular texts and particular grammatical patterns occur in school science, and why they occur in a particular order, it is essential to consider what is distinctive about texts *within their particular institutional context*. In order to make links between text and institutional context and between language and broader questions of educational practice this chapter will examine:

- some institutional contexts for scientific language;
- the range of written genres in school science;
- the location and ordering of written genres in secondary science;
- the encoding of different meanings through different grammatical resources in different genres.

The emphasis in this chapter is very much on *written* text. Through textbooks, practical 'worksheets', written tests and exams, students in school science are apprenticed into meanings which are recognizably different both from 'everyday' meanings and from the meanings produced in other disciplines, such as history, English and mathematics. Although spoken language, images and physical activity all play an important part in producing meanings in school science, historically it has been written language which has played a central role in the construction, production, reproduction and dissemination of scientific meaning (Halliday and Martin 1993). This continues to be the case today, even though the physical appearance of written texts has altered radically in recent years and the teaching of science exclusively through written textbooks has become unfashionable classroom practice.

## Laboratory, industry and school: institutional contexts for scientific language

Before considering the nature of the relationship between context and language in school science, it is worth pausing briefly to consider how this relationship differs from that found in research science in the laboratory and applied science in industry. The issue of how one discourse, here scientific discourse, is reformulated in different institutional contexts has been usefully discussed by Bernstein and others under the rubric of **recontextualization** (Bernstein 1990).

As researchers such as Bazerman (1988), Latour (1986) and Myers (1990) note, the final form of written texts in research science, particularly the experimental report, needs to be interpreted in light of the historical tradition of scientific writing, and the very real need to create a sense of progress and to justify ongoing research activity, and even ongoing research funding. Bazerman expresses this succinctly:

> Experimental reports tell a special kind of story, of an event created so that it might be told. The story creates pictures of the immediate laboratory world in which the experiment takes place, of the happenings of the experiment, and of the larger, structured world of which the experimental events are exemplary. The story must wend its way through the existing knowledge and critical attitude of its readers in order to say something new and persuasive, yet can excite imaginations to see new possibilities in the smaller world of the laboratory and the larger world of nature. And these stories are avidly sought by every research scientist who must avidly keep up with the literature. (Bazerman 1988: 59)

The result of such contextual pressures is that experimental reports are very often both persuasive and informative in function. This persuasive function is demonstrated clearly in the following passage, the opening paragraph of a paper in *Electronics Letters*. I have italicized those words in the text which have a clear persuasive function (cf. Hunston 1993, 1994).[3]

> Single-mode fibre lasers (SMFL) possess *a number of advantages* over their bulk counterparts. *By virtue* of their small cores, *very-low* thresholds and high gains can be achieved. Since the typical fibre diameter is about 100 μm, thermal effects which plague glass lasers are *minimal*. The fabrication process is *economical* in dopant, since a typical device uses *only* 0.1 μg of rare-earth oxide. Devices can be packaged *compactly* – a coiled 1 m-long laser readily fits into a 1 cm³ enclosure. Silica, the laser medium, has *good* power handling characteristics; *moreover*, it broadens the rare-earth transitions, enabling tunable lasers and broad-band amplifiers to be constructed. It is this aspect, the tunability of fibre lasers, that is considered in this paper. (Mears *et al.* 1985: 738)

In discussing this text with its authors, I learned that the principal function of the text, and indeed of the whole journal, in their opinion, was not to report research findings, which were only very sketchily presented, but to associate the names of the authors with a technical innovation. In this way the authors can assert ownership of the innovation and lay claim to any patent arising from the innovation! The context in which this text arises is a very long way removed from that of 'objectively' reporting research findings, and one can only make sense of the text's persuasive grammatical organization in light of this specific context. Such a context does not occur in school science, and so it is very unlikely that an experimental report in school science will be worded like the one above.

Summarizing the work on context and text in research science, we can say that the language of scientific laboratory activity cannot be understood without also understanding the need of researchers to challenge and innovate scientific understandings and practice continually. In research science, the rhetoric of persuasion and innovation spills over into the 'objective' reporting of laboratory activity. Conversely, the language of laboratory activity spills over into the persuasive language of scientists; this is what makes their arguments 'scientific'. Laboratory activity is recontextualized as scientific argument and scientific argument is recontextualized as laboratory activity. Figure 6.1 models this.

In the area of applied science, it is the relationship between scientific activity and the application of this activity in military/industrial technology which characterizes the context and influences choices in language. The recontextualization of scientific discourse within industrial contexts has been explored in detail by Rose *et al.* (1992). In their work they identified many genres which also occur within schooling. The following

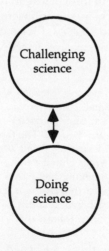

**Figure 6.1** 'Doing' and 'challenging' science in laboratory research

text, for example, is a **procedure**, similar in organization and linguistic features to procedures found in the science classroom.

5.1 ISOLATE PRECIPITATOR ELECTRICALLY
1 Move the main isolator switch (CFS) in the precipitator switch room to the OFF position and tag, 'OUT OF SERVICE'.
2 Lock the main isolator switch switching arm using 'Castell Key 2'.
3 Remove the 'Castell Key 2' and attach an 'OUT OF SERVICE' tag to the key identifying No. 12 Tar Precipitator.
4 Place the 'Castell Key 2' in the shift supervisor's office. (Rose *et al.* 1992)

Whilst the organization and linguistic features of this procedure are identical to those found in procedures in school science, the purpose of the text and its context of use are not. In the industrial context the scientific procedure is recontextualized as a way of organizing work, in this case a safety protocol. For the purposes of industrial application laboratory activity (doing science) is recontextualized as scientific innovation (challenging science) and is then recontextualized further as the design, construction, maintenance and operation of technology (applying science). In the industrial context science becomes an important agent in the creation of products and wealth. Figure 6.2 models the recontextualization of science in military/industrial technology.

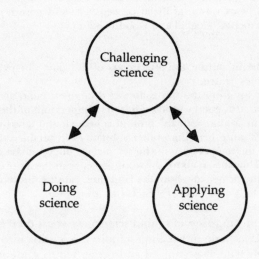

**Figure 6.2** 'Doing', 'challenging' and 'applying' science in military/industrial technology

Turning our attention now to school science, many educators have observed that the process of *reproducing* scientific knowledge in the school science classroom is often very different to the process of *creating* scientific knowledge in the laboratory or *applying* it in industry. One of the most remarked-upon differences is the tendency of school science to present students with 'bodies of facts' to be learned. The following two texts, one a **descriptive report** and the other a **causal explanation**, exemplify this phenomenon. Both texts construe information as general, well-established and timeless facts. There is no evidence of human activity in the creation of the knowledge that lies behind these texts and there is no scope for questioning or challenging the information presented.

### Silicones

Silicones are similar to hydrocarbons, but the 'backbones' of the molecules consist of silicon and oxygen atoms, instead of carbon atoms. Attached to the silicon atoms are side-chains of carbon and hydrogen.

Silicones have exceptional resistance to heat. They repel water, and are not affected by most chemicals.

Silicones with small molecules are oils and greases. They are used as hydraulic fluids, water repellants and release agents for moulds.

Silicones with large molecules are resins or rubbers. In the rubbers, the silicon-oxygen chains are cross-linked by hydrocarbon chains. Silicon rubbers remain inert and pliable over a wide temperature range. They are used for seals in oven and freezer doors, heat resistant seals in engines, surgical spare parts such as heart valves, artificial corneas, ear and nose replacements and breast enlargements. (Coghill and Wood 1989: 117)

### Sea Breezes

Sea breezes begin during the afternoons of hot days when the air over the ground becomes heated.

Radiant energy from the sun is absorbed by the ground and this energy is converted into heat energy which raises the temperature of the rocks and soil. Thus the air in contact with the ground is heated, and tends to rise. Because water requires more heat than other substances to produce the same rise in temperature, the temperature of the sea surface does not rise as much as that on the land. Thus the air above the sea is cooler than the air over the land. The result is that the heated air above the land rises, causing the cooler air from the sea to flow in to take its place. (Messel *et al.* 1965: 7-2)

In modelling the language of school science we must therefore introduce an additional layer, one in which generalized scientific information, held to be objectively true, is organized and presented to students. A model of language in school science might look something like Figure 6.3. The hierarchical organization of this model is deliberate and will be discussed later in the chapter.

**Doing science** refers to the teaching and learning of science through classroom activity. It often commences with fairly open-ended 'observa-

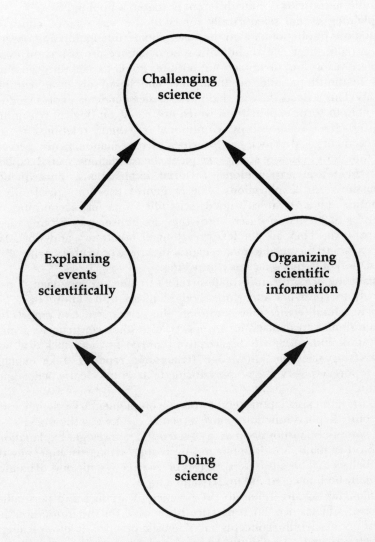

**Figure 6.3** Domains of language use in school science

tions' and 'activities', but usually leads to more formally organized experiments, designed to test hypotheses. The language most closely associated with 'doing science' is that which enables particular kinds of activity to take place and that which serves to record observations and methods accurately. The two written genres which achieve these functions are **pro-**

**cedures** and **procedural recounts.** Whilst these genres appear in both laboratory and workplace contexts, it is important to remember that their role in these contexts is quite different to that in schooling.

**Explaining events scientifically** refers to the way science constructs explanations of phenomena on the basis of experimentation and observation. Initially, most explanations in school science are based on events which are visible and unambiguous, but they go on to deal with cause and effect relationships, and eventually become based on quite complex theories. This reflects the fact that most science curricula expect students to be able to form explanations which are based on 'logical reasoning': cause-and-effect relationships, conditional (if/then) relationships and abstract/theoretical principles. Six types of explanation genre perform these functions in school science: **sequential explanations, causal explanations, theoretical explanations, factorial explanations, consequential explanations** and **explorations.** Theses genres function specifically to apprentice students into valued scientific ways of accounting for sequences of events; in other words they are genres specific to pedagogical contexts. They are far less prevalent in laboratory and workplace contexts, where the need to model logical processes or to give a generalized explanation of events is far less compelling.

**Organizing scientific information** refers to the way language is used explicitly to construct and store 'bodies' of scientific knowledge. This occurs in school science mainly through the written genre of **report**. In a manner similar to explanations, reports are either constructed around observation and/or activity (**descriptive reports**) or more technical ways of classifying scientific knowledge (**taxonomic reports**). Like explanations, reports are very much apprenticing texts with a clearly pedagogical function.

Reports and explanations tend to play a complementary role in exploring a topic. Reports function to give a picture of 'the way the world is' – a static, synoptic snapshot of an area of scientific knowledge. Explanations, on the other hand, are dynamic and unfolding, telling us 'how/why the world behaves'. These two perspectives on science – static and dynamic – are usually both necessary to understand a topic.

**Challenging science** refers to the practice of arguing and persuading about issues in science. Such practice is essential for the innovation and renovation of scientific concepts and scientific practice. It allows students to develop a 'critical scientific literacy' and to use science-based arguments to advocate for change in the way we live and think. Scientific arguments may also be turned on science itself, to question existing theories and practices. The main written genres involved in challenging science are **exposition** and **discussion**, both of which aim to persuade readers to act or to think in a particular way.

So why is the language of school science different from that of laboratory or industrial science? There are at least two reasons why school science recontextualizes scientific knowledge. The first has to do with the process of 'gatekeeping' – selecting those people who can gain access to a discourse and exercise power through that discourse, and those who cannot. For Bernstein this is the chief purpose of pedagogic discourse:

> Pedagogic discourse is a principle for appropriating other discourses and bringing them into special relations with each other for the purposes of their selective transmission and acquisition. Pedagogic discourse then is a principle which removes (delocates) a discourse from its substantive practice and context, and relocates that discourse according to its own principle of selective reordering and focussing. (Bernstein 1990: 183–4)

The 'selective transmission and acquisition' of scientific discourse occurs at all levels of education systems. Through overt and covert forms of assessment, usually based on written language, ideal pedagogical subjects are constructed and ideal forms of scientific knowledge are construed, against which less-than-ideal subjects can be assessed and thus denied access to further study. As Rose *et al.* have shown (1992), this process now extends also into the field of industrial production, where grades and promotions depend heavily upon formal training.

Taking a more benevolent view of schooling, however, it can also be argued that without pedagogical recontextualization of science, it would not be learnable. School science reduces, simplifies, generalizes and idealizes centuries of scientific activity, in order for students to assimilate important understandings and to move on to 'real science', i.e. empirical research and dispute. This requires science educators to organize knowledge into taxonomies, to create axioms, laws and principles to explain phenomena. Each of these taxonomies, axioms, laws and principles is, of course, open to examination and dispute. Without them, however, the science might become unlearnable.

The pedagogic recontextualization of scientific discourse has been an issue of concern to science educators for some time. In particular, the way in which school science tends to present scientific knowledge as an abstract, impersonal, body of facts, divorced from the socio-historical processes which led to its formation, is seen as problematic.[4] Progressive science educators often emphasize the need to 'rehumanize' school science, advocating, for example, the reintroduction of the active voice in discussing laboratory work to show the human agency at work and even designing entire curricula which examine competing scientific theories and explanations. One consequence of this critique is that the reliance on traditional science textbooks of the 1950s and 1960s is seen as poor teaching practice. This has led to radical changes in the appearance of many textbooks, though not of the written language they contain. Feminist and poststructuralist critiques of the way scientific knowledge is presented in schools have also led to calls for the redesign of curricula and teaching materials (Harding 1983; Kelly 1987).

## The range of written genres in secondary science: an overview

Before proceeding to a detailed discussion of specific texts, it is helpful to have an overview of the range of written texts used in school science. Register genre theory has already described a number of written genres used in teaching and learning. Procedures, reports and explanations are the principal factual genres that have been explored in this work (Christie *et al.* 1990a, b, 1992). Importantly, science textbooks were amongst the materials analysed by these researchers. Martin, for example, describes reports as 'the major genre in science textbooks' (1990: 100) and explanations as 'for many students . . . the main form of extended writing' in science (1990: 104). Shea's research (Shea 1988) confirms that reports and explanations are the most recognizable genres in school science textbooks.

Further research and classroom trialling during the 1990s has developed this work further by linking the analysis of texts to the specific disciplinary fields in which these texts are deployed. Research in English (Rothery 1994), history (Veel and Coffin 1996), geography, mathematics and science revealed, not surprisingly, that each of these disciplines organizes and deploys language in quite different ways. It became clear that one could not comprehend the use of language in a specific discipline without also having a sense of the way that discipline organizes knowledge. Moreover, as the research became more sensitive to disciplinary variations, the description of texts also had to become more sensitive. In secondary science, for example, it became useful to describe a number of different kinds of related explanation genres (sequential, causal, theoretical, etc.), rather than the notion of a single explanation genre found in earlier work.

Figure 6.4 sets out a taxonomy of the range of written genres used in secondary science. The terms 'story' and 'factual' on the left represent the broadest choice in written school genres. The terms 'enable', 'explain', 'document' and 'persuade' cover a range of functions and purposes for language in secondary science, and can be linked to the broad domains of language use which are described in Figure 6.3. The binomial naming system used for many of the genres on the right of the taxonomy is designed to show both the relationship of the various genres to the broader system in the centre and their relationship to similar but different (i.e. **agnate**) genres in the same branch of the taxonomy. Hence a 'sequential explanation' is a type of explanation – a text that explains something but is different from other types of explanation because of its focus on sequence (rather than cause, theory, etc.).

For each of these genres we can identify distinct social purposes, different generic structures and linguistic features. Although the detailed discussion of texts in this chapter will be limited to explanations, there are examples of procedures and reports earlier in this chapter, and an appendix at the end of the chapter which contains an example of a procedural

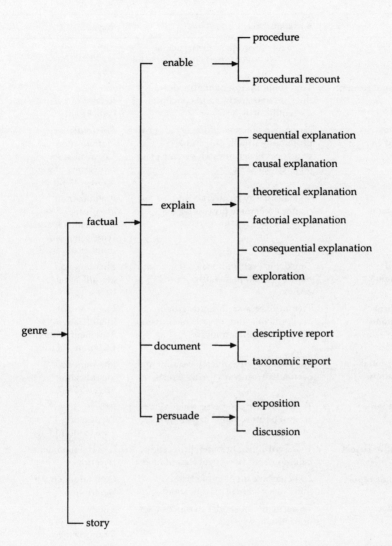

**Figure 6.4** Genres in secondary school science

recount and an exposition. Reports are described in detail in Christie *et al.* (1990a) and Veel (1992) gives an account of the language of 'doing science'. Veel (to appear) gives a detailed account of all of these texts.

Table 6.1 summarizes the purpose and generic structure of these texts.

**Table 6.1** Social purpose and generic structure of genres in school science

| Genre | Social purpose | Stages |
|---|---|---|
| **procedure** | To enable scientific activity, such as experiments and observations, to occur | Aim^ Materials needed^ Steps |
| **procedural recount** | To recount in order and with accuracy the aim, steps, results and conclusion of a scientific activity | Aim^ Record of Events^ Conclusion |
| **sequential explanation** | To explain how something occurs or is produced – usually observable sequences of activities which take place on a regular basis | Phenomenon identification^ Explanation sequence (consisting of a number of phases) |
| **causal explanation** | To explain why an abstract and/or not readily observable process occurs | Phenomenon identification^ Explanation sequence (consisting of a number of phases) |
| **factorial explanation** | To explain events for which there are a number of simultaneously occurring causes | Phenomenon identification^ Factor [1–n] |
| **theoretical explanation** | To introduce and illustrate a theoretical principle and/or to explain events which are counter-intuitive | Phenomenon identification/ Statement of theory^ Elaboration [1–n] |
| **consequential explanation** | To explain events which have a number of simultaneously occurring effects | Phenomenon identification^ Effects [1–n] |
| **exploration** | To account for events for which there are two or more viable explanations | Issue^ Explanation 1^ Explanation [2–n] |
| **descriptive report** | To describe the attributes, properties, behaviour, etc. of a single class of object | General statement^ Description |
| **taxonomic report** | To describe a number of classes of thing in a system of classification | General statement^ Description |
| **exposition** | To persuade the reader to think or act in particular ways | Thesis^ Arguments 1–n^ Reinforcement of Thesis |
| **discussion** | To persuade the reader to accept a particular position on an issue by considering more than one perspective | (for example) Issue^ Dismissal of opponent's position^ Arguments for own position^ Recommendation |

Whilst synoptic overviews, such as those given in the taxonomy in Figure 6.4 and in Table 6.1, are useful starting points for investigating the role of language in a specific context, several caveats need to be placed on their use. The first is that they do not account for *all* written language used in school science. There are many other types of text to be found in materials written for students: linking passages, captions, cartoons, narratives, even jokes! The genres that are accounted for here are those which recur in a range of published materials[5] and those which students are asked to produce in examinations and classroom writing – in other words, those texts which seem to play a key role in construing scientific knowledge in the school context.

A second point is that the exact form, or realization, of a genre will vary from instance to instance and will change over time. It is impossible to state conclusively what all the language features of every instance of a genre will be, or in what configuration genres will occur in a textbook or school programme. The description of generic structure and language features given here must necessarily be general, whereas the examples are necessarily specific. Only through an examination of hundreds of texts does one gain a feel for the possible range of realizations of a genre. Such limitations do not invalidate the use of genre as a descriptive tool, however. Over fifteen years of experience in Australia has shown that genre is a very useful concept for both teachers and students in coming to grips with the language demands of schooling. Nor is it the case that descriptions of genres are 'conservative', applying only to older, traditional textbooks and not to more recent materials or approaches to teaching. Although the physical appearance, role of images, 'reading path'[6] and interactive role of the reader have changed greatly, the written language of science teaching materials is much the same as it has been for most of this century.

Finally, neither the taxonomy nor the table accounts for how the texts are actually used in the classroom. Which texts are for students to read and understand, and which are for them to produce in writing? Which do they have to read *and* write? Which texts receive more emphasis in the form of assessment, and which less? At what point in schooling do certain texts become pre-eminent? At what point do some texts become less important? Some of these issues are addressed in general terms below, but one needs a more detailed description of classroom interaction to appreciate how the texts function. Christie (1994) has investigated this in relation to primary school science.

## The location of written genres within the discourse of secondary science

Written genres rarely occur independently of each other in secondary school science. Certain configurations, or sequences, of texts occur and recur. These configurations set up particular kinds of 'knowledge paths' for students, in which one kind of knowing about a topic leads to another kind and then to another. The investigation of a topic in the classroom, for example, will frequently commence with physical activities such as experiments and observations, proceed to more generalized 'bookish' study of the topic and conclude with an investigation of how the topic in question affects people's lives. In terms of written genres, this will involve a shift from procedures and procedural recounts to explanations and reports and then to expositions and discussions.

The shift from one genre to another is highly significant. In moving from procedural recounts (doing science) to explanations, for example, students are required to move from the recount of specific events and specific objects in specific places and times, all of which are assumed to lie within students' own experience, to a generalized account of objects and events in non-specific place and time which is often outside students' experience. Such a move is essential for the construction of scientific knowledge, but it is not always an easy one for students to make. Many teachers have reported that students are able to write accurate recounts of experiments and observations, but have great difficulty in making generalized conclusions on the basis of what they have done and observed.

Depending on the aims and objectives of the unit of work, different types of meanings will be valued more highly than others. Thus, if the focus of a unit is on developing practical laboratory skills, then the type of scientific meaning constructed through procedures and procedural recounts will become important, and students' ability to read and write these genres will most likely be an important assessment strategy. Conversely, if the focus of a unit is on the social issues surrounding a topic, then the type of meaning constructed by expositions and discussions will become important and students' understanding of the topic will be based on their ability to negotiate these genres. Figure 6.5 attempts to model the way 'semiotic emphasis' can be given to one genre or another in a unit of work.

This shift in emphasis, which can be seen occurring across a unit of work, also takes place on a larger scale. As students progress through secondary school science there is a gradual shift away from the types of meanings built up through practical, physical activity towards more bookish, fact-oriented knowledge. This is not to say that students stop doing experiments and observations – they are a fundamental part of the scientific method. It simply means that the path to scientific meanings through experimentation and observation becomes a 'given' and that privilege is given to that generalized body of knowledge which we call science. Such a move is inevitable if students are to gain even a minimal understanding of the field of contemporary science. Martin, in criticizing the notion of a syllabus based entirely on physical activities, warns against

> the denial of the use of scientific language to accumulate and document the results of previous research in such a way that it can be taken as the starting point for new investigations. Learning scientific method is obviously important; but it is not necessary for every student to rediscover every wheel. (Martin 1990: 98)

(i) focus on practical skills

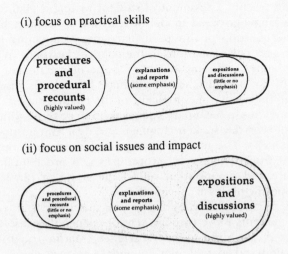

(ii) focus on social issues and impact

**Figure 6.5** Focus of teaching unit and value placed on certain types of meaning

Evidence for the gradual change in emphasis from 'knowing by doing' to 'knowing by reading' can be found in the language of syllabus documents, school programmes and textbooks. In many textbooks written for junior secondary students (Years 7 and 8), for example, there are a great number of written procedures and activities requiring students to write procedural recounts, some reports, comparatively few explanations (mainly sequential) and almost no expositions or discussions. Some textbooks even contain explicit instructions on how to write procedures and procedural recounts. In texts written for middle school students (Years 9 and 10) there are many more sequential and causal explanations and some expositions and discussions. In senior secondary textbooks the explanations are mainly causal and theoretical, and expositions and discussions deal with disputed or controversial scientific issues.

The shift in the way different types of scientific meaning are valued can also be seen in the way teachers assess students' work. Many science teachers with whom this writer has worked, for instance, report that they expect students to develop their ability to read and write scientific texts as they progress through school. The term 'develop' appeared to have a remarkably consistent meaning for these teachers. When presented with a range of explanations written by students and asked to rank them, all valued causal explanations more highly than sequential explanations, claiming they showed greater evidence of students' development. Terms such as 'logical', 'rational', 'clear cause-and-effect sequence', 'knowledge of concepts', 'ability to generalize', 'knowledge of the facts' were used to describe the greater development displayed in causal explanations.

Where does this system of values originate and how is it perpetuated? The evidence gained by examining the language of textbooks, syllabus

documents and teacher assessment of student writing is vital to the construction of a language-based model of learning in science, but it does
not answer the question of why particular types of meaning have privileged status in particular situations in the science classroom. What makes
one type of scientific meaning valuable in a particular unit of work, but
less valuable in the overall scheme of things? Part of the answer to this
question lies in the nature of complexity of the language used. The more
valued written genres in secondary science tend to be those which are further away from everyday spoken language and deal with abstract properties and phenomena. The generic structure and grammar of these texts is
quite different from that of, say, procedures and procedural recounts,
whose structure and organization reflect the world of physical activity
occurring in specific places at specific times.

The valuing of particular types of meaning in science is also a product
of history. As students move through school science they also take a linguistic journey through the history of science (Martin 1993b). Many of
the activities undertaken in junior secondary science aim to replicate
scientific discoveries that are, in some cases, hundreds of years old. The
replication of Newton's experiments in the reflection and refraction of
light, for instance, is almost ubiquitous in Australian science classrooms.
The language required to describe and explain such activities, although
modern English, uses genres and grammar that have been established
in science for a long time. More advanced school science tends to focus
on more recent scientific knowledge, and thus uses more recent, and
often more complex and more abstract, language. Science education
has thus established a kind of historical 'canon', which leads to greater
value being placed on more recent, and linguistically different, types of
meanings.

A third reason for the valuing of certain scientific meanings over others
lies in the interface between science and technology. Certain types of scientific meaning allow us to intervene in our environment and control it.
The ability to appropriate and exploit these types of meanings is an economically valuable commodity and this is reflected in science education.
For example, if a doctor understands what *causes* digestion to occur, s/he
can take steps to intervene at the right point when a problem occurs in
the digestive system. A knowledge of how and where digestion occurs,
although necessary, is not sufficient to intervene. Thus the ability to construct a **causal explanation** (what causes digestion to occur) is more
socially valuable than a **sequential explanation** (how/where digestion
occurs).

The preference for one type of meaning over another in educational
contexts has been studied in the field of educational sociology. Bernstein,
in writing about students' orientations to meanings, uses the concept of
'privileged' meanings and the 'privileging' of individuals to account for
the way certain types of meanings are favoured over others in educational
settings. Bernstein's concepts are a useful way of thinking about not only

what causes meanings to be hierarchically organized in education, but also the social and economic consequences (i.e. 'privileging') of being able to use the more highly valued meanings.

> It may be useful first to put a gloss on 'orientations to meanings'. The latter refer to privileged and privileging referential relations. 'Privileged' refers to the priority of meanings *within* a context. 'Privileging' refers to the power conferred upon the speaker as a consequence of the selected meanings. Now the source of power and its legitimisation does not arise out of the social relationships *within* the context but out of a social base external to that context. That is privileging refers to relationships between contexts, whereas 'privileged' refers to relationships within a context. (Bernstein 1990: 16)

Using Bernstein's argument, we can say that processes of education (i.e. practices within the context of education), especially written resources, teaching practices and assessment, make certain types of meaning privileged, whilst the social and economic order (i.e. the social base external to the context of education) is privileging for those members of society who can appropriate and exploit privileged meanings. These influences combine to create a distinct hierarchy of meanings within the discipline of school science. Figure 6.3 above models this hierarchy.

## Some examples of explanation genres

Having discussed in very broad terms the distinctive context for written language in school science and having given an overview of genres in school science, it is now necessary to illustrate in more detail the link between written genres used in school science and the recontextualization of scientific knowledge for pedagogical purposes. In order to do so we will focus on four different kinds of explanation: sequential, causal, factorial and theoretical. Through an examination of the different purpose, organization and linguistic features of these explanations it is hoped to build up a picture of how language creates a kind of 'knowledge path' along which ideal pedagogical subjects travel as they move into scientific ways of making meaning.

### Sequential explanations

Sequential explanations explain *how* something occurs. They describe observable sequences of activities which take place on a regular basis and are either naturally occurring phenomena such as volcanoes, earthquakes, reproduction in plants and animals, etc. or human-made processes such as the *modus operandi* of machinery and technology. Sequential explanations usually comprise a Phenomenon Identification stage, in which the thing to be explained is introduced to the reader, followed by an Explanation Sequence, in which the reader is taken through a sequence of events describing the phenomenon.

Sequential explanations explain not through invoking the logic of cause and effect but by describing a chain or sequence of events which lead to a phenomenon. This emphasis on sequence can be seen clearly in the language features of sequential explanations.

Sequential explanations also tend to be limited in the 'depth' with which they treat a topic. For example, in describing the behaviour of single living organisms, sequential explanations will deal only with observable characteristics of that organism. They will rarely go into detail about the chemistry or physiology of the organism, or the way it interacts with its environment. To do so entails reasoning about cause and effect and is thus beyond the scope and purpose of this type of explanation.

Sequential explanations usually deal with localized phenomena. The sequences of events described in sequential explanations generally cover a relatively short time scale and a small area of space. In other words, they cover events which are visible to humans both over time and space and therefore open to our immediate scrutiny. Events which are beyond our immediate scrutiny – too large, too small, too slow or too fast – tend to be explained by causal or theoretical explanations.

Because the processes described are open to physical verification, sequential explanations they lie towards the empirical end of scientific discourse. They collate the information obtained in 'doing science' and generalize upon it. Linguistically and epistemologically they also form the building blocks for more complex kinds of explanations.

| Text 1 | **Sequential explanation** |
|---|---|
|  | **Making sugar** |
| **Phenomenon identification** | In some cooler parts of the world such as Europe, sugar is obtained from a plant called sugarbeet. In Australia and other warmer areas, sugar cane is used. The process that removes sugar from sugar cane uses many types of separation. |
| **Explanation sequence** | **Making raw sugar** |
|  | As the sugar cane comes from the farms it is washed of dirt and shredded into many small pieces. The juice can then be squeezed out with many large rollers. More modern factories use hot solutions to dissolve the sugar present. |
|  | The next step is to remove some impurities. Limewater and other chemicals are added to make these impurities form particles. These are allowed to settle out by **sedimentation**. The juice is then concentrated by **evaporation** and boiling in special vacuum chamber so that the raw sugar crystallizes out. The crystals and left over solution are then **centrifuged** to remove the liquid. |

**Refining of sugar**

Raw sugar is refined to produce the white crystals available in the shops. The raw sugar is dissolved in warm water and the colouring removed. This is first done with special chemicals, and the impurities that form are filtered. The final traces of colour are removed by adsorption using charcoal.

The solution is then concentrated by evaporation and boiling in a special vacuum chamber. This causes crystallization of the white crystals of sugar. These crystals are then centrifuged to drive off most of the liquid. Finally, the crystals are dried in a long rotating drier by using hot air.

(from Heffernan and Learmonth 1988a: 227)

*Causal explanations*

Like sequential explanations, the purpose of causal explanations is to describe a sequence of events which is of particular significance to science. Their generic structure is identical to that of sequential explanations: a Phenomenon Identification stage followed by an Explanation Sequence. However, causal explanations function not only to describe *how* a particular sequence of events occurs, but also *why* it occurs. For this reason, causal explanations link events together *both* as a sequence and as a set of cause-and-effect relationships. Although sequential and causal explanations are essentially variations of the one genre, and many explanation texts contain a fairly equal distribution of temporal and causal links, there is a distinct group of text where causal links predominate in both number and position (see Figure 6.8). It is these texts which we may define as causal explanations. The fact that students need to extend their control of grammatical resources in order to comprehend and construct causal explanations also justifies their status as a distinct text type. There are a variety of linguistic resources which are used to construct cause and effect relationships in these texts.

Causal explanations generally deal with either abstract entities and properties, or they describe events that are generally not accessible to immediate observation or experience. Because the entities and processes being described are not directly accessible to the senses, the cause and effect relationships between events need to be made explicit and emphasized in order to construe a logical and credible explanation.

| Text 2 | Causal explanation |
|---|---|
|  | **Sea Breezes** |
| **Phenomenon identification** | Sea breezes begin during the afternoons of hot days when the air over the ground becomes heated. |
| **Explanation sequence** | Radiant energy from the sun is absorbed by the ground and this energy is converted into heat energy which raises the temperature of the rocks and soil. Thus the air in contact |

with the ground is heated, and tends to rise. Because water requires more heat than other substances to produce the same rise in temperature, the temperature of the sea surface does not rise as much as that on the land. Thus the air above the sea is cooler than the air over the land. The result is that the heated air above the land rises, causing the cooler air from the sea to flow in to take its place.

(adapted from Messel *et al.* 1965: 7–2)

### Factorial explanations

Factorial explanations explain phenomena which arise from the *combination of a number of factors*, rather than from a single, linear sequence of events. These phenomena are usually naturally occurring events, where it may be impossible to pin down a single event or chain of events which leads to the phenomenon occurring. Factorial explanations often seek to contextualize the events they explain within a physical environment, rather than treat them as isolated or abstract phenomena. With an increasing emphasis on the environment in science education in recent years, factorial explanations have increased in frequency and prominence.

The generic structure of factorial explanations is that of a Phenomenon Identification, followed by a non-temporal listing of different Factors which may cause the phenomenon to occur.

| | |
|---|---|
| Text 3 | **Factorial explanation** |
| | **Physical weathering** |
| **Phenomenon identification** | This process is the cause of the breaking-up of large rocks into smaller pieces. Physical processes can cause changes in rocks. The two most important methods are changes in *temperature* and the *freeze–thaw changes* of water. |
| **Factor 1** | Changes in temperature cause the rock to expand and shrink. Different parts of the rock expand and shrink by different amounts and so the rock is made weaker. You have probably seen the effect of freeze–thaw changes of water: the size of ice cubes is always larger than the amount of water put into the ice cube trays to make them. If water is trapped in a crack in a rock and then freezes, it can force that crack to widen. |
| **Factor 2** | There are also four other processes that are important to the breakdown of rocks. Firstly, rocks may be shattered by *lightning* as it strikes high peaks during thunderstorms. Only very few people have been on hand to see how much change this action causes. |
| **Factor 3** | Secondly, *plants* assist the breakdown of rocks by their roots growing into cracks. These cracks may have first formed by temperature changes, then widened by ice freezing. The growing roots can widen cracks further. |

| | |
|---|---|
| **Factor 4** | Thirdly, *animals'* burrows often loosen and mix soil and rock pieces. This exposes fresh rock pieces to air, wind and water. |
| **Factor 5** | Finally, the actions of people cannot be forgotten. We can and do cause changes in rocks much more quickly than any of the natural forces. What natural forces can match bull-dozers and dynamite? |

(from Heffernan and Learmonth 1988b: 29)

## Theoretical explanations

Theoretical explanations are designed to introduce and illustrate an important theory. They are very much 'apprenticing' texts; that is, they are designed to teach novice readers about a theory. This is usually done by stating the theory and then explaining one or more observable events in terms of the theory. The structure of theoretical explanations consists of a Statement of Theory, in which the principle, law or axiom is enunciated, followed by a non-temporal listing of Elaborations, in which the theory is exemplified in various situations. These texts have been explored in detail by Unsworth (1995).

Theoretical explanations are often used to explain phenomena which *defy 'common-sense' explanations*. There can be no scientifically satisfactory common sense explanation of why, for example, things fall to the ground when unsupported. We need to invoke a theory involving forces and counter-forces to be able to explain it. Similarly, theoretical explanations are used to deal with phenomena which are *counter-intuitive*. Why, for example, does the shadow of an object have a different shape and size to the shape of the object which casts the shadow? Common sense would tell us that the shadow should be the same size and shape as the object. We need a theory of how light travels to explain this phenomenon.

Because of their reliance on an axiom, law or premise, theoretical explanations belong unequivocally to the world of scientific knowledge and are thus remote from everyday experience. Many people who have spent time with young children will know the frustration of trying to answer questions such as *Why is the sky blue?* in everyday terms. *It just is* is the answer many adults give, because the answers to questions like these cannot be expressed in terms of everyday experience. A theoretical understanding is necessary.

| | |
|---|---|
| **Text 4** | **Theoretical explanation** |
| | **Buoyancy and density** |
| **Statement of theory** | Now that we have considered the application of Archimedes' principle both to objects which sink and objects which float we should be able to understand that there is a relationship between buoyancy and the density of an object relative to the density of the fluid in which it is immersed. |
| **Elaboration 1** | If the object is completely submerged it displaces its own volume of fluid. The weight of displaced fluid, and there-fore the upthrust, will depend on the density of the fluid. |

| Elaboration 2 | If the density of the fluid is less than the average density of the object, the weight of displaced fluid will be less than the weight of the object, and the object will sink. |
| Elaboration 3 | If, on the other hand, the density of the fluid is greater than the average density of the object, the weight of the displaced fluid will then exceed the weight of the object. The net upward force will then cause it to rise to the surface where it will float. |
| Elaboration 4 | The volume of the object remaining submerged will be such that the weight of the fluid displaced just balances the weight of the floating object. |
| Elaboration 5 | Thus, an object whose average density exceeds that of a fluid will sink in that fluid, whereas an object whose average density is less than that of the fluid will float. |

(from Heading *et al.* 1982: 180–1)

## Order out of chaos: constructing a knowledge path through language

Throughout this chapter I have suggested that the written genres of school science are organized hierarchically, and that a path leading from the empirical towards the theoretical is constructed for students. Such suggestions will seem to many readers as out of step with much recent thinking about language and disciplinary knowledge, coming mainly from the diverse body of studies known as poststructuralism. Poststructuralist critiques of science have questioned notions of 'hierarchy' and 'progress' in scientific knowledge, stressing instead the fundamentally chaotic nature of human activity and the arbitrary way in which we impose order, mainly for the purposes of maintaining power relations in society (Foucault 1972). Many readers would also reject the notion of a single 'knowledge path' construed by the writer in favour of a range of 'reading positions' construed by readers (Barthes 1975). In this environment of reassessment and critique what is the meaning of terms like 'hierarchy' and 'knowledge path', and what is the evidence for their existence?

In looking at the grammatical organization of the language in school science, however, we see that the ordering and hierarchy of texts in school science functions not only by the 'top-down' privileging of particular texts but because the language itself moves from childlike forms to adult forms. In other words, the language of school science construes a developmental path which is remarkably similar to the way child language develops (Derewianka 1995; Halliday 1975, 1995; Painter 1987, 1993). This similarity between the ontogenetic path of language development and the 'logogenetic' path in school science should come as no surprise. Both derive at least to some extent from processes of socialization.

We will now compare a range of language features in the four explanation texts introduced earlier in order to show what this knowledge path looks like.

*Lexical density*

Halliday (1985: 63–7) suggests that the average number of lexical items (i.e. 'content words') per clause, or **lexical density**, of a text is a way of measuring the proximity of a text to the 'here-and-now'. The lower the lexical density, the more 'spoken-like' a text is and the closer to the here-and-now. Non-specialist spoken language typically has a lexical density of about two items per clause. The more abstract a text is, the more removed from here-and-now, the greater the lexical density. Written language, because it is inherently at some distance from the here-and-now will typically have a greater lexical density than spoken language.[7]

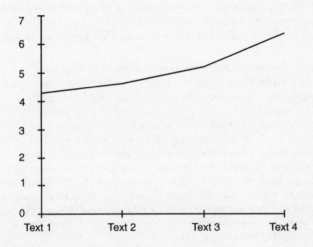

**Figure 6.6** Lexical density in Texts 1–4

Figure 6.6 compares lexical density in the four explanations. The gradual increase reflects a move in the texts away from the relatively everyday, visible world of sugar production in Text 1 to the abstract entities and principles involved in discussing Archimedes' principle in Text 4. Comparing extracts from the texts, one sees immediately how the level of abstraction affects the lexical density. The lexical items are in bold.

Text 1, nine lexical items over three clauses:
As the **sugar cane comes** from the **farms**‖ it is **washed** of **dirt**‖ and **shredded** into many **small pieces**.

Text 4, twelve lexical items over two clauses:
If, on the other hand, the **density** of the **fluid** is **greater** than the **average density** of the **object**,‖ the **weight** of the **displaced fluid** will then **exceed** the **weight** of the **object**.

A similar kind of movement, from lexically sparse 'spoken-like' structures to lexically dense written-like ones, occurs in child language development, when the child gains control of the written mode in learning to read and write (Hammond 1990).

### Virtual entities: nominalization and abstraction

**Nominalization** is the process by which events, qualities and relationships come to be represented not as verbs, adverbs or conjunctions but as things, nouns. Through the process of nominalization an event (e.g. *it moves*) or a property (e.g. *it is hard*) is construed as a noun (*motion, hardness*). Nominalized entities appear in scientific language for a number of reasons: to create technical terms, to create cause-and-effect relationships between disparate phenomena, to synthesize and systematize detailed information, to create measurable entities. Halliday and Martin (1993) have explored the role of nominalization in scientific language in considerable detail.

Nominalization, involving a transference from a 'congruent' form of expression to a 'metaphorical' one, is a kind of grammatical metaphor. In relation to language development, Halliday makes the following point:

> Metaphorical modes of expression are characteristic of all adult discourse. There is a great deal of variation among different registers in the degree and kind of metaphor that is encountered; but none will be found entirely without it. The only examples of discourse without metaphor that we normally meet with are in young children's speech, and in traditional children's rhymes and songs that seem to survive for that very reason: that they lack grammatical metaphors. Otherwise any text of more than minimal length is almost certain to present us with instances where some metaphorical element needs to be taken into account. (Halliday 1994: 342)

As scientific texts move away from the here-and-now, they also rely more on **abstractions**. Like nominalizations, abstractions construe 'virtual entities': concepts, notions, properties, facts, ideas, etc. which are not tangible in the way that physical objects are. Unlike nominalizations, however, abstractions do not involve a process of transference. Whereas it is possible to 'unpack' a nominalization into a more 'congruent' form (*motion* → *moves*), this is less easily done with abstractions. Abstractions do not have a semiotic 'history' in the way that grammatical metaphors do. What, for example, are the congruent versions of abstractions such as *force, energy* and *principle*? What are the more 'childlike' ways in which they can be presented to young learners?

Figure 6.7 shows the average number of 'virtual entities', nominalizations and abstractions, per clause for Texts 1–4. There is a significant increase across the texts, indicating a move from a more everyday, congruent picture of the world to one which relies upon the invocation of metaphorical entities. Like the shift in lexical density, the increasing reliance on grammatical metaphor in the texts removes the text from the

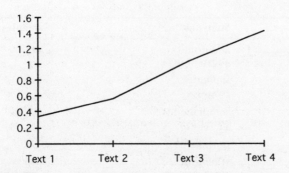

**Figure 6.7** Average 'virtual entities' per clause in Texts ·1–4

here-and-now. This can also be seen clearly in the two extracts from Texts 1 and 4.

Text 1, no nominalizations or abstractions over three clauses:
As the sugar cane comes from the farms‖ it is washed of dirt‖ and shredded into many small pieces.

Text 4, four nominalizations over two clauses:
If, on the other hand, the **density** of the fluid is greater than the average **density** of the object,‖ the **weight** of the displaced fluid will then exceed the **weight** of the object.

### Logical relations

An analysis of the kinds of logico-semantic links that are made between clauses can also provide us with an indication of the relative logical complexity of a text. Martin (1992: 179–83) identifies four main types and eleven subtypes of conjunction used in English to create logico-semantic links within texts. These are summarized in Table 6.2 below. We will concern ourselves here with two main types: Temporal and Consequential.

Figure 6.8 shows a drift in the four texts away from temporal relations in Text 1 (*as*, *then*, etc.) towards consequential relations in Texts 3 and 4 (*because*, *thus*, *if*, etc.). Again this can be seen in the two extracts we have been examining.

Text 1, temporal (simultaneous) conjunction:
**As** the sugar cane comes from the farms it is washed of dirt and shredded into many small pieces.

Text 4, consequential (conditional) conjunction:
**If**, on the other hand, the density of the fluid is greater than the average

**Table 6.2** Classification of logico-semantic relations

| Main type | Subtypes | Examples |
|-----------|----------|----------|
| **Additive** | addition | *and* |
| | alternation | *or* |
| **Comparative** | similarity | *likewise* |
| | contrast | *but* |
| **Temporal** | simultaneous | *while, as* |
| | successive | *then, after* |
| **Consequential** | purpose | *so that* |
| | condition | *if, unless* |
| | consequence | *because, since* |
| | concession | *although* |
| | manner | *thereby* |

density of the object, the weight of the displaced fluid will then exceed the weight of the object.

Like the shifts towards increased lexical density and towards increased deployment of nominalizations, the movement towards consequential conjunctions indicates a movement away from the here-and-now of everyday life and towards more abstract discourse. In describing temporal relations Martin, for example, notes:

> External temporal relations are strongly oriented to the activity sequences constituting fields

whereas for consequential conjunctions,

> the connections between events are 'modulated' in such a way that the one event is seen as *enabling* or *determining* the other rather than simply preceding it. (Martin 1992: 185–93)

The link between the language of school science texts and child language development, alluded to earlier, is quite noticeable in the area of logical relations. In her case study Painter, for example, notes that additive conjunctions are the first to appear in child language and consequential conjunctions the last (Painter 1993: 193–8)

*Internal/external conjunctions*

As well as analysing the type of logico-semantic relations deployed in a text, we may also analyse whether the point of reference of a conjunction is to the external world or part of the internal organization of the text.

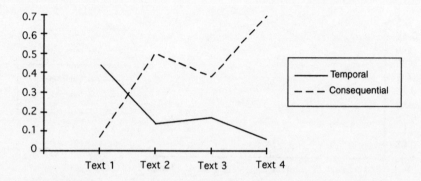

**Figure 6.8** Deployment of logical relations: (1) average number of temporal and consequential conjunctions per clause

Halliday and Hasan argue that there are

> two closely analogous sets of conjunctive relations: those which exist as relations between external phenomena, and those which are as it were internal to the communicative situation. (Halliday and Hasan 1976: 240)

As Martin (1992: 180) notes, internal conjunctions are primarily concerned with the organization of text. An increasing use of internal conjunction signifies, therefore, that a text itself is more overtly construing scientific knowledge. Rather than construing knowledge as if it were following a 'natural' sequence of physical happenings, as texts with predominantly external conjunction tend to do, internal conjunction foregrounds the primary role of the text in shaping knowledge. Martin's remarks about external and internal conjunction are expanded by Halliday, who argues that it is through language that fluid, undifferentiated experience is turned into knowledge (1995: 13).

Here are examples of internal and external conjunctions from Texts 1 and 3:

> Text 1, external conjunction:
> **As** the sugar cane comes from the farms it is washed of dirt and shredded into many small pieces.

> Text 3, internal conjunction:
> **Thirdly**, *animals'* burrows often loosen and mix soil and rock pieces. This exposes fresh rock pieces to air, wind and water.

Figure 6.9 graphs the movement away from external conjunctions towards internal conjunctions across Texts 1–4. The significance of this movement for student learners is similar to that we have noted for other

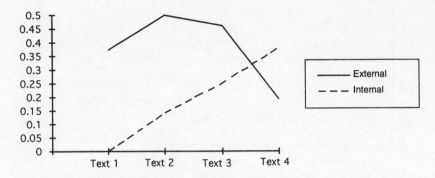

**Figure 6.9** Deployment of logical relations: (2) average number of internal and external conjunctions per clause

grammatical features; the kind of knowledge construed by the text is increasingly removed from the knowledge construed in the here-and-now of everyday life. We have moved into the world of specialist technical discourse. Again, this mirrors Painter's study of child language development in which 'field-oriented' external conjunction appeared before 'mode-oriented' internal conjunction (Painter 1993: 332–7).

### The 'syndrome' of features

Considering all of these changes in grammatical features across Texts 1–4 as a whole one begins to understand how different uses of language can construe different kinds of meaning. Halliday suggests that it is through the co-occurrence of these features that we recognize distinct registers in English:

> Any variety of language, whether functional or dialectal, occupies an extended space, a region whose boundaries are fuzzy and within which there can be considerable internal variation. But it can be defined, and recognized, by certain syndromes, patterns of co-occurrence among features at one or another linguistic level – typically features of the expression in the case of a dialect, features of the content in the case of a functional variety or 'register'. Such syndromes are what makes it plausible to talk of a 'language of science'. (Halliday 1993a: 4)

In this chapter Halliday's notion of a syndrome of features has been extended to look at how, in the pedagogical context, syndromes of features mutate in order to create new kinds of meanings. In school science, as in other disciplines, changing configurations of grammatical features lead students away from the kinds of meanings which are linked to the here-and-now towards the abstract, technical and 'transcendental' kinds of meaning we expect of adult, educated discourse. Like a child learning

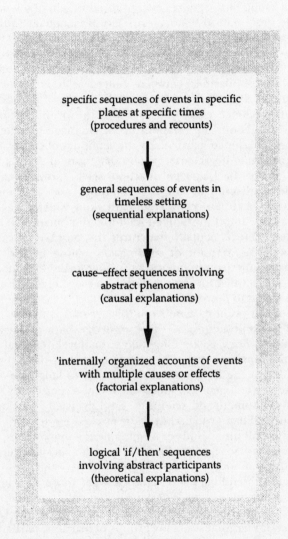

specific sequences of events in specific
places at specific times
(procedures and recounts)

general sequences of events in
timeless setting
(sequential explanations)

cause–effect sequences involving
abstract phenomena
(causal explanations)

'internally' organized accounts of events
with multiple causes or effects
(factorial explanations)

logical 'if/then' sequences
involving abstract participants
(theoretical explanations)

**Figure 6.10** Overview of changing syndromes of grammatical features in school
science

its mother tongue, the language of school science attempts to move students seamlessly into 'adult' forms of scientific meaning-making. Figure
6.10 summarizes this idealized knowledge path.

## Conclusion: reforming the language of school science

In this chapter an attempt has been made to give a language-based account of learning in school science. Such an account requires much more than a listing of the genres encountered in school science, or a catalogue of the grammatical features in scientific language, although these are important starting points. It requires the consideration of a number of simultaneously occurring aspects of language: institutional context, genre and lexico-grammar. Accounting for development and learning is as much about similarities between genres as it is about differences between genres, and as much about combinations of genres used in the context of the science classroom as about the properties of individual genres. It is also about the relationship of language to other systems of meaning used in science, particularly the semiotics of physical activity and of visual representations (charts, graphs, diagrams, etc.).

Our account of the language of school science reveals that there are recognizable syndromes of language features, and that these features work to produce a kind of knowledge path along which ideal pedagogical subjects will move into fully fledged scientific discourse. The organization and grammar of texts actually structures the possible types of learning that may occur as a result of reading or writing a text. Pedagogical processes, especially assessment and reporting, make this knowledge path a desirable one to tread for it gives students access to adult forms of scientific discourse and to power.

One important point to arise from this account is that, whatever one's view of the appropriateness of this knowledge path in social and ideological terms, it does make some sense in developmental terms. The path from the language of doing science to that of theoretical scientific knowledge (logogenesis) is remarkably similar to language development in the individual (ontogenesis). Moreover, it is also remarkably similar to the historical development of scientific English itself (phylogenesis), as described in Halliday (1993a). As we remarked earlier, this is not really surprising since all three kinds of development – logogenesis, ontogenesis and phylogenesis – are manifestations of broader social patterns.

This similarity amongst kinds of development – the personal, the historical and the disciplinary – is significant for those with an interest in reforming science education. The knowledge path outlined in this chapter has often been criticized for the way, in privileging one kind of pedagogic subject, it marginalizes many groups of learners, particularly female students. Indeed the whole notion of 'development', of moving to a higher or better state, has been called into question. The most obvious solution to this situation is to 'open up' science education, to value means of expression other than those narrowly defined as scientific, to remove the overwhelming sense of hierarchy in reading and writing practices. And this, of course, is exactly what science educators have been attempting in the last few decades. In terms of classroom practice reformers have succeeded in removing some of the most obvious impediments for marginalized students. There are more female students studying senior science subjects, for example, and more female teachers teaching it. Specialist materials have been developed for students from language backgrounds other than English, and teachers have been trained to better deal with these students. However, attempts to reorder the way scientific knowledge itself is construed for students, particularly through language, have been less successful.

Part of the reason is because the ordering of discourse in school science is not simply a localized product of the school system. The ordering of meanings is random only in a very general sense, in the way that all signifier/signified pairs are in the end random. Apprenticeship into scientific discourse redounds with many other types of apprenticeship into Western culture; and this means its established patterns and hierarchies are almost impossible to break, without reforming society itself. Like most other social processes it has evolved over time and is extraordinarily resistant to sudden change. This is not to say that we ought not attempt to reorder the way scientific knowledge is construed for school students if we feel it needs reordering, simply that we should not underestimate the task. Merely repeating the cry that it has to be changed will not achieve the task.

Perhaps the most viable strategy in the short term would be to try to change who gets to use scientific discourse rather than trying to change the discourse itself. Discourses become 'patriarchal', 'racist', 'classist', etc. not simply because of inherent patterns in the language (cryptogrammar), but also because of who gets access to them and who does not. If we consider scientific discourse to be patriarchal, for example, this is partly because it was developed and is practised largely by men. If there have been changes in scientific discourse and scientific language in recent years it is mainly because powerful people *within the discipline* have initiated change. Reforming who gets access to scientific discourse in schools may well be the best way of changing scientific discourse itself in the long term.

## Notes

1  Genres are described as 'staged, goal-oriented social process'. 'Staged' refers to the fact that genres usually consist of a number of distinct parts which work together to build the meaning of a text. 'Goal-oriented' refers to the fact that genres usually function to achieve some purpose – they get something done (e.g. action, learning, persuasion, entertaining, etc.). 'Social' refers to the fact that genres are dialogic, they evolve from social interaction. They are shared by two or more people in the process of exchanging goods and services or information.

2  Orientation to meaning in relationship to social class is described in detail in the work of Bernstein (1977, 1990). It is a significant alternative to the simplistic 'quantity' notion of meaning and language, which suggests that types of meaning and language are something students 'have' or do 'not have' in various

quantities, and that this affects their success in schooling. Rather, Bernstein argues, it is students' orientation to school meanings and school language that is a key criterion for success.

3 Many categories of linguistic features have been glossed over here. For the idea of internal conjunctions (e.g. *moreover*) serving a persuasive purpose, see Martin (1985). For a discussion of systems lexical items construing interpersonal meaning in text (Judgement, Affect, Appreciation, etc.), see Veel (1995) and Iedema *et al.* (1994).

4 Lemke (1990: 129 ff.) contains a thoughtful discussion of these issues in relation to language.

5 Over 1000 texts from all published materials in Australia were examined in the Write It Right research, as well as 1400 texts written by students.

6 Kress and van Leeuwen (1990: 97) describe a reading path as 'a particular trajectory of the movement of the hypothetical reader within and across the different elements'. Although they are describing visual images, the term can be equally applied to the arrangement of written texts in printed teaching materials.

7 These are, of course, generalizations. It is possible for written forms of communication (e.g. e-mail) to be quite spoken-like and spoken forms to be quite written-like (e.g. scripted speeches).

## References

Barthes, R. (1975) *The Pleasure of the Text* (trans. Richard Miller). New York: Hill and Wang.

Bazerman, C. (1988) *Shaping Written Knowledge: The Genre and Activity of the Experimental Article in Science.* Madison, WI: University of Wisconsin Press.

Bernstein, B. (1977) *Class, Codes and Control*, Vol. 3. London: Routledge and Kegan Paul.

Bernstein, B. (1990) *The Structure of Pedagogic Discourse.* London: Routledge.

Christie, F. (ed.) (1990) *Literacy for a Changing World.* Melbourne: Australian Council for Educational Research (ACER).

Christie, F. (1994) 'On pedagogic discourse'. Final Report of a Research Study funded by the Australian Research Council, University of Melbourne.

Christie, F., Gray, P., Martin, J., Macken, M., Gray, B. and Rothery, J. (1990a) *Exploring Reports.* Sydney: Harcourt, Brace, Jovanovich.

Christie, F., Gray, B., Martin, J., Macken, M., Gray, P. and Rothery, J. (1990b), *Exploring Reports: Teachers Manual.* Sydney: Harcourt, Brace, Jovanovich.

Christie, F., Gray, P., Martin, J., Macken, M., Gray, B. and Rothery, J. (1992) *Exploring Explanations.* Sydney: Harcourt, Brace, Jovanovich.

Coghill, G. and Wood, P. (1989) *Spectrum Science* 3. Melbourne: Heinemann.

Cope, B. and Kalantzis, M. (eds) (1993) *The Powers of Literacy: A Genre Based Approach to Teaching Writing.* London: Falmer Press.

Derewianka, B. (1995) 'Language development in the transition from childhood to adolescence: the role of grammatical metaphor'. PhD thesis, Macquarie University (Australia).

Foucault, M. (1972) *The Archaeology of Knowledge and the Discourse on Language* (trans. A. M. Sheridan Smith). New York: Pantheon Books.

Halliday, M. A. K. (1975) *Learning How to Mean.* London: Edward Arnold.

Halliday, M. A. K. (1985) *Spoken and Written Language.* Geelong, Vic.: Deakin University Press.

Halliday, M. A. K. (1993a) 'On the language of physical science'. In M. A. K. Halliday and J. R. Martin (1993) *Writing Science: Literacy and Discursive Power.* London: Falmer Press.

Halliday, M. A. K. (1993b) 'Some grammatical problems in scientific English'. In M. A. K. Halliday and J. R. Martin (1993) *Writing Science: Literacy and Discursive Power.* London: Falmer Press, 54–68.

Halliday, M. A. K. (1994) *An Introduction to Functional Grammar.* 2nd edition. London: Edward Arnold.

Halliday, M. A. K. (in press) 'The grammatical construction of scientific knowledge: the framing of the English clause'. In R. R. Favretti (ed.) *Proceedings of the International Conference 'Languages of Science',* University of Bologna, 25–27 October 1995.

Halliday, M. A. K. and Hasan, R. (1976) *Cohesion in English.* London: Longman.

Halliday, M. A. K. and Hasan, R. (1985) *Language, Context and Text: Aspects of Language in a Social-semiotic Perspective.* Geelong, Vic.: Deakin University Press.

Halliday, M. A. K. and Martin, J. R. (1993) *Writing Science: Literacy and Discursive Power.* London: Falmer Press.

Hammond, J. (1990) 'Is learning to read and write the same as learning to speak?' In F. Christie (ed.) *Literacy for a Changing World.* Melbourne: Australian Council for Educational Research (ACER), 26–53.

Harding, J. (1983) *Switched Off: The Science Education of Girls.* York: Longman for Schools Council.

Heading, K., Provis, D., Scott, T., Smith, J. and Smith, R. (1982) *Science for Secondary Schools,* Vol. 3. 3rd edition. Adelaide: Rigby.

Heffernan, D. A. and Learmonth, M. S. (1988a) *The World of Science,* Book 1. Melbourne: Longman Cheshire.

Heffernan, D. A. and Learmonth, M. S. (1988b) *The World of Science,* Book 3. Melbourne: Longman Cheshire.

Hunston, S. (1993) 'Evaluation and ideology in scientific writing'. In M. Ghadessy (ed.) *Register Analysis: Theory and Practice.* London: Pinter (Open Linguistics Series), 57–73.

Hunston, S. (1994) 'Evaluation and organisation in a sample of written academic discourse'. In M. Coulthard (ed.) *Advances in Written Text Analysis.* London: Routledge, 191–218.

Iedema, R., Feez, S. and White, P. (1994) *Media Literacy* (Write It Right Literacy in Industry Research Project, Stage Two). Sydney: Disadvantaged Schools Program, New South Wales Department of School Education, Metropolitan East Region.

Kelly, A. (ed.) (1987) *Science for Girls?* Milton Keynes/Philadelphia: Open University Press.

Kress, V. and van Leeuwen, T. (1990) *Reading Images.* Geelong, Vic.: Deakin University Press.

Latour, B. and Woolgar, S. (1986) *Laboratory Life: The Social Construction of Scientific Facts.* Princeton, NJ: Princeton University Press.

Lemke, J. (1990) *Talking Science.* Norwood, NJ: Ablex.

Lynch, M. and Woolgar, S. (1990) *Representation in Scientific Practice.* Cambridge, MA: MIT Press.

Martin, J. R. (1985) *Factual Writing: Exploring and Challenging the Experiential World.* Geelong, Vic.: Deakin University Press.

Martin, J. R. (1990) 'Literacy in science: learning to handle the text as technology'. In F. Christie (ed.) *Literacy for a Changing World*. Melbourne: Australian Council for Educational Research (ACER), 79–117 (republished in Halliday and Martin 1993, 166–202).

Martin, J. R. (1992) *English Text: System and Structure*. Amsterdam: Benjamins.

Martin, J. R. (1993a) 'Genre and literacy: modelling context in educational linguistics'. *Annual Review of Applied Linguistics* 13, 141–72.

Martin, J. R. (1993b) 'Technology, bureaucracy and schooling: discursive resources and control'. *Cultural Dynamics* 6(1), 84–130.

Mattheissen, C. (1995) *Lexicogrammatical Cartography: English Systems*. Tokyo: International Language Sciences Publishers.

Mears, R. J., Reekie, L., Poole, S. and Payne, D. (1985) 'Neodymium-doped silica single-mode fibre lasers'. *Electronics Letters* 21(17), 738–40.

Messel, H., Crocker, R. L. and Barker, E. N. (1965) *Science for High School Students*, Book One. Sydney: The Science Foundation for Physics, University of Sydney.

Myers, S. (1990) *Writing Biology: Texts in the Social Construction of Scientific Knowledge*. Madison, WI: University of Wisconsin Press.

Painter, C. (1987) *Learning the Mother Tongue*. Geelong, Vic.: Deakin University Press.

Painter, C. (1993) 'Learning through language: a case study in the development of language as a resource for learning from 2½ to 5 years'. PhD thesis, Department of Linguistics, University of Sydney.

Rose, D., Korner, H. and McInnes, D. (1992) *Scientific Literacy* (Write It Right Literacy in Industry Research Project, Stage One). Sydney: Disadvantaged Schools Program, New South Wales Department of School Education, Metropolitan East Region.

Rothery, J. (1994) *Exploring Literacy in School English* (Write It Right Resources for Literacy and Learning). Sydney: Metropolitan East Disadvantaged Schools Program.

Shea, N. (1988) 'The language of school science textbooks'. BA (Hons) thesis, Department of Linguistics, University of Sydney.

Unsworth, L. (1995) 'How and why: recontextualising science explanations in school science books'. PhD thesis, Department of Linguistics, University of Sydney.

Veel, R. (1992) 'Engaging with scientific language: a functional approach to the language of school science'. *Australian Science Teachers Journal* 38(4), 31–5

Veel, R. (1995) 'Making informed choices or jumping through hoops? The role of functional linguistics in an outcomes based curriculum'. *Interpretations* 28(3), 62–77.

Veel, R. (to appear) *Exploring Literacy in School Science*. Sydney: Disadvantaged Schools Component, New South Wales Department of School Education.

Veel, R. and Coffin, C. (1996) 'Learning to think like an historian: the language of secondary school history'. In R. Hasan and G. Williams (eds) *Literacy in Society*. London: Longman, 191–231.

Wilkinson, J. (1985) *Senior General Science*. Melbourne: Macmillan.

## Appendix: examples of a procedural recount and an exposition in school science

**Procedural recount**

**Seed experiment**

| | |
|---|---|
| **Aim** | On the 23rd September Stuart and Sean did an experiment to see if seeds needed soil to germinate. |
| **Record of events** | We collected 2 petri dishes and 40 seeds. We placed a thin layer of soil on one petri dish and some cotton wool on the other. We put an equal number of seeds in each petri dish and lightly sprayed them with water. We labelled them 'Soil' and 'No soil'. |
| | The next day we took the lid off both petri dishes. No seeds had germinated in the 'Soil' dish, but 1 seed had germinated in the 'No soil' dish. |
| | The following day 16 seeds in the 'Soil' dish had germinated. In the other dish 13 seeds had germinated. |
| **Conclusion** | In conclusion, we found that seeds do not need soil to germinate. |

(written by Year 8 student)

**Exposition**

**Cadmium**

| | |
|---|---|
| **Thesis** | Cadmium is a soft, silvery white metal that often occurs with zinc. It is used in metal plating, alloys, control rods in nuclear reactors, batteries, and plastics manufacture. Excessive amounts of cadmium in the body cause permanent bone damage even to the extent that the whole skeleton collapses. |
| **Arguments** | In Japan, workers using cadmium-based paints suffered from diseased bones. The disease begins with pains in the bone joints. Cadmium also causes high blood pressure and can damage male reproductive organs. Cadmium is ingested in water and food. However it is absorbed slowly and most of it is excreted before it can be absorbed. Cadmium can also be absorbed from the air: cigarette smoke contains some cadmium. As people get older the amount of cadmium in their bodies builds up. |
| **Reinforcement of thesis** | Cadmium levels in the environment therefore need to be kept low. The maximum permitted level of cadmium in a 1 kilogram fish is 1.4 milligrams (1.4 ppm). |

(from Wilkinson 1985: 75)

# 7 Constructing and giving value to the past: an investigation into secondary school history

*Caroline Coffin*

## 1 Introduction

This chapter explores the nature and function of written text in school history. The data it draws on derive from a major literacy research project conducted in Australian classrooms between 1992 and 1994 by the Disadvantaged Schools Program (Coffin in press). This project used the tools of systemic functional linguistics (SFL) to examine the grammatical patterning and structure of texts which were found to be central to the construction of historical knowledge within the secondary school context.

Throughout the chapter a trajectory is traced to show the relationship between history students' expanding linguistic repertoire and their movement from constructing the past as story (with a focus on particular, concrete events unfolding through time) to constructing it as argument (with a focus on abstract theses organized in text time). It is argued that as students move along this 'pathway' and learn how to reconstitute the past in increasingly abstract ways they are serving a type of apprenticeship. They are learning how to mean like a historian.

The chapter is divided into six sections. The main aim of the introductory first section (1.1–1.3) is to contextualize school history within the broader discipline of history. The focus of the section is, therefore, a discussion of the two modes of representation – the narrative and argument – which are central to the construal of historical experience both within and beyond the school classroom. The section examines the ideological motivations and consequences of these different ways of representing the past and in so doing considers how the privileging of certain kinds of meanings constructs a certain kind of pedagogic subject. The role that language plays in the 'making' of these pedagogic subjects will be the central focus of the discussion in the remaining sections. Section 1 also considers the contested nature of history – both the wider discipline of history and its recontextualization at the level of secondary schooling.

In section 2 a pathway that apprentices students into the written text types or genres of school history is mapped. At one end of the pathway lie the genres that comprise the domain of narrative and at the other end the genres that comprise the domain of argument. It is four key genres from this pathway which then become the focus of sections 3–5. In section 3 two key genres for recording the past are examined, in section 4 the main genre for explaining the past, and in section 5 a genre central to the task of arguing about the past. Across all three sections (3–5) the realization of each genre's social purpose is examined through an SFL analysis of text structure and lexico-grammatical patterning. Through the analyses the changing set of resources for constructing and giving value to the past is revealed. The chapter argues that it is the control and strategic deployment of these resources that enable a writer to, in different ways, background the subjective, ideological nature of his or her historical interpretation.

Throughout the chapter it is demonstrated how learning to mean like a historian is a process of socialization whereby a particular subject position is constructed. The chapter concludes by proposing that this process is, in turn, part of a more extensive pattern of socialization critical to students' participation in the wider community and culture.

## 1.1 Writing history as social process

Learning to make choices in genre and language resources that are valued in school history is to engage in a social practice in which socially significant meanings are constructed. It is through this practice that students learn to construct social experience that is historical in nature. In learning to construct 'historical reality' students are themselves constructed as discursive selves. In order to understand the complex of ideologies, values and beliefs that determine, and are determined by, the discursive practices in which historians and apprentice historians engage, we need to consider the two fundamental modes of representation which serve to build and give shape to historical knowledge – the humanities-based narrative and the logico-scientific argument.

The tension between narrative and argument as ways of recording as well as acting on and forming new knowledge is a source of ongoing debate at the level of both theory and practice and both within and beyond the context of history. In the late twentieth century, Lyotard has argued that there is a 'relative retreat of the claims of narrative or story-telling knowledge in the face of those of the abstract, denotative, or logical and cognitive procedures generally associated with science or positivism' (Jameson in Lyotard 1987). At the same time, however, despite arguing the demise of the master or meta narratives which once served as legitimators of scientific truth (and by implication of other 'truths' including those of history), Lyotard affirms 'the vitality of small narrative units at work everywhere locally in the present social system' (Jameson in Lyotard 1987). These observations concerning the role of small narrative units within an overall framework of enquiry are exemplified within the textual practices of school history. That is, our findings from the literacy research project showed that 'logical argument' is currently the favoured way of making meaning in secondary school history. At the same time, however, our research showed that while, on the one hand, history has witnessed the demise of the '**grand**' narrative there has been, on the other hand, a resurgence of alternative, once marginalized narratives claiming validity as a means of construing historical reality. Each of these paradigms – argument and narrative – will be examined in turn.

### 1.2 History as argument

Within schools, argument is a privileged resource for making historical meaning. The result of Mitchell and Andrews' research into the British curriculum shows that

> At sixteen the transition to academic status brings with it an increased expectation of the student's ability to argue . . . for history there is a move away from the teaching and learning of historical narrative and facts . . . History becomes in the final two years the subject of historical analysis and, because analyses differ, of historical debate. (Mitchell and Andrews 1994: 86)

Likewise, Coffin's research into Australian history curriculum (in press) confirms the privileged place of argument in upper secondary school. Evaluation practices at the level of high school matriculation are further evidence of its dominant (and gatekeeping) role.

By written argument we refer to texts where the overall purpose is to advocate a particular interpretation of the past. This is achieved through a process of analysis and debate in which a range of positions and arguments are considered. The ideology which constructs and gives value to such forms is complex. According to Jenkins (1991: 38), the process of 'seeing both sides', 'weighing things up' and 'adjudicating' can be viewed as a realization of liberal humanist values. Such values construct the writer as a disinterested arbitrator of knowledge whose position on the past is fluid and open and who can, therefore, offer an objectively derived 'true' account of the past. This mode of constructing knowledge is, according to Jenkins, the dominant mode in our social formation. It enables the role of interpretation to be backgrounded and the notion of 'the true account' to be foregrounded. Jenkins emphasizes, however, that 'the true account' is always ideologically shaped and points to the complex of ideologies derived from the historian's assumptions, view of knowledge, historical method and system of values and beliefs. From the outset this ideological complex constructs the historian as far from ideologically neutral (Jenkins, 1991: ch. 1).

Kress's account of argument proposes that it provides 'in culture specific textual forms the means for bringing difference into existence'. Its 'fundamental characteristic is to produce difference and hence openness' (Kress 1989: 12). Mitchell points out, however, that in the British educational tradition, whereas argument in the spoken mode 'may be valued as an open and transformative process, writing is the site of closure' (Mitchell 1995: 133). Certainly data from the literacy research project found that most written argument within the context of school history advocates and argues for a particular interpretation of the past even though alternative interpretations may be referred to and considered as part of the process of debate. In other words, despite recent curriculum innovations encouraging written texts which display an interplay of conflicting perspectives' in line with contemporary history's shift from 'the ideal of the Voice of History to that of heteroglossia' (Burke 1993: 6), these perspectives are necessarily accorded different degrees of meaning and significance by the writer. That is, in order that the text be valued by a teacher or examiner, alternative interpretations and arguments must be evaluated and judged in relation to each other. As a consequence the reader is persuaded to accept one perspective as having greater explanatory power or 'truth' than another. Thus rather than achieve openness we can argue that *written* argument is under pressure to reach closure.

In this chapter, section 5 will examine in detail the ideological nature of the arguing genres. It will show that although arguing about the past appears to be an activity whereby the historian pursues truth from a neutral, value-free position, the interpretations reached are inevitably subjective and ideologically motivated. Linguistic analysis will be used to argue that constructions of the past which appear to be the result of objective and disinterested logical enquiry are instead the outcome of linguistic and rhetorical strategies. The section will argue that the deployment of these strategies is made possible by the students' expanding repertoire of lexico-grammatical resources and their increasing potential for working with abstract meaning. Further, it will be proposed that this expanding potential equips students with socially powerful discursive resources. The claim will be made that by learning to construct argument students are learning to mean in a way that is valued by the dominant culture and that control of discursive resources will enable them to take up positions of power within the workplace.

### 1.3 History as story

Although argument, as stated above, holds a privileged place within the history curriculum (at least across the English-speaking countries), there are historians who see narrative as a mode of thinking and representation as legitimate as that of abstract logic (see White 1989: 31 for a discussion of the different ideologies which support this position). Despite criticism that the form privileges a single 'story' line and 'passes over important aspects of the past which it is simply unable to accommodate, from the economic and social framework to the experience and modes of thought of ordinary people' (Burke 1993: 235), there is, as indicated in Lyotard's theorizing (1987), a role for narrative in contemporary discursive practice. As mentioned earlier in this section, the emergence of alternative, once marginal, stories ('history from below') is revitalizing its role within the discipline (Burke 1993: 239–44). This new style of narrative stands in contrast to the traditional, totalizing approach where, to a large extent, the focus was on the political events and stories of great men, statesmen and generals. In the context of current pedagogical practice, the writing and reading of alternative narratives with new viewpoints is increasingly encouraged.

Written narratives in school history have the overall purpose of recording a series of historical events as they unfolded in real time. In historical narratives, therefore, the organizing principle is external time (In 1865 ... Fifty years later ... etc.) rather than internal or text time (**Firstly** ... The **final** argument ...). This temporal ordering of experience brings history into relationship with a widespread cultural practice of story-making whereby social experience is given a beginning, middle and end structure. Such a structure is the basis of the traditional literary narrative.

It is partly the association with fictional forms of writing and partly the reductionist nature of the narrative which has led to debate over its appropriateness as a form for representing the past as well as an interest in its ideological significance. In particular, questions of truth, subjectivity and objectivity have been explored. For some, the narrative form captures or imitates the natural order and structure of experience (narrative as mimesis). Counter to this is the view that narrative *gives* form and structure to a past which is naturally chaotic and fluid. In other words, rather than there being 'a true but "untold story" in the past waiting to be told ... there can be only past facts not yet described in a context of narrative form' (Mink reported in Carr 1991: 10). According to Mink, narrative imposes on the events of the past a form that in themselves they do not have: 'This form is a "product of individual imagination" which arises from the historian's act of telling and has no part in the events narrated' (in Carr 1991: 10).

The view that the narrative 'far from being a neutral medium for the representation of historical events and processes, is the very stuff of a mythical view of reality' (White 1989: ix) challenges its role as a value-free discursive form and questions the role of the historian as an objective recorder of an indisputable past. Indeed, it will be argued in this chapter that since the events of a historical narrative are selected, ordered and attributed with historical significance (either implicitly or explicitly), the narrative genres are clearly more than an objective record of the past. Just as in the case of the arguing genres, they serve to construct rather than merely reflect historical reality. As White comments 'narrativity is ... intimately related to, if not a function of, the impulse to moralize reality' (White 1989: 14). In narrative genres, however, the moralizing or interpretive apparatus is largely submerged whereas in the argument genres it is, to some extent, laid bare.

In section 3 narrative genres are examined as ideological instruments for presenting 'objective' recordings of past events. It will be argued that their objectivity is merely a rhetorical effect, a result of the linguistic realization and patterning of ideational, textual and interpersonal meaning, and that they serve to construct interpretations of the past which are invisibly but inevitably skewed. By erasing from view the interpretative process I will agree with Kress that narrative, as a textual form, can be 'a means of resolution of difference, of reproducing, in an uncontentious mode, the forms and meanings of a culture' (Kress 1989: 12).

The discussion in sections 1.1 and 1.2 above shows that the discipline of history is a contested site in which different paradigms and consequently different types of discourse compete for power. At stake, then, is a disciplinary politics of truth.

> Truth isn't outside power . . . it is produced only by virtue of multiple forms of constraint . . . Each society has its 'general politics' of truth: that is, the types of discourse which it accepts and makes function as true: the mechanisms and instances which enable one to distinguish true and false statements. (Foucault 1980: 131)

In history, and school history in particular, the question is: 'What are the types of discourse and written genres that are made to function as true and how do these change as students move through secondary school to the final matriculation year?'

It is the mapping and linguistic analyses of the changing patterns of written discourse made to function as true that will form the focus of sections 2–6. These sections will examine a selection of history texts taken from the category of narrative and argument as well as the category of explanation – a category which forms a linguistic bridge between narrative forms and those of argument. The role of these specific genres in rehearsing certain kinds of discursive resources and in privileging certain kinds of meaning will form part of a discussion on history's role in the formation of values and ideologies and hence, its role in the construction of a particular pedagogic subject position. In this way SFL will serve to illustrate and extend many of the points raised above. The case will be put that school history acts as a primary site in which discursive practices are rehearsed and students' meaning potential expanded. It will be argued that the discursive practice central to history is the interpretation and construction of social experience using the textual forms and linguistic resources of narrative, explanation or argument as a means of positioning and persuading a reader to accept interpretation as 'fact' or 'truth'. In this way it is in and through the study of history that social subjects capable of symbolic control are produced.

## 2 Apprenticing students into the genres of secondary school history

In the previous section we have noted that narrative texts which construct the past by recording and responding to a temporal succession of events are, at advanced levels of schooling, no longer privileged as meaning-making resources. In short, the time line as organizing principle is dispensed with and instead texts are rhetorically organized around a set of arguments. How, then, do students learn to move from iconic forms of representation to symbolic modes of organizing information? What types of texts or genres exist to create a literacy 'pathway' to assist students in this movement? How do they learn to reconstrue time and cause in order to bring past events into new meaning relations so that new interpretations can be formed?

Figure 7.1 shows the range of text types or genres that enact the process of moving from recording the past (the narrative genres) to arguing about the past (the argument genres). The figure also serves to chart similarity and dissimilarity (agnation) among the history genres with reference to one key feature – the use of either external or internal time as a resource for organizing the past (shown in the overlapping ellipses). (For further discussion of this topological perspective see Martin and Matthiessen 1991: 345–83.)

In order that students make the shift from constructing texts which are sequentially organized along a time line (the autobiographical, biographical and historical recount and the historical account) to constructing texts which are rhetorically organized (the consequential and factorial explanation and the exposition, challenge and discussion), they need to gain control of language which is highly abstract. It is this movement from more common-sense to more abstract modes of meaning-making and the linguistic resources that construct this movement which are the focus of discussion in sections 3, 4 and 5. The genres selected for analysis will be the historical recount (section 3), the historical account (section 3), the consequential explanation (section 4) and the challenge (section 5). (For a detailed analysis and discussion of the remaining genres refer to Coffin in press.)

## 3 Chronicling the past: naturalizing interpretations and perspectives

There are four key genres whose overall purpose is to record or chronicle the past: autobiographical, biographical and historical recount, and historical account. These genres comprise the chronicling genres. Within the set there is a movement from more congruent and personal constructions of the past (autobiographical recounts) towards more incongruent and impersonal constructions (historical accounts). Although the autobiographical recount will not be examined in detail here, it is important to note that its overall social purpose is to both entertain and inform. Its use of the personal 'I' voice combined with the writer's affectual response to the events recounted act to engage and involve the reader and thus to create solidarity. It is, then, a text which is openly 'subjective'. In contrast the following analyses of two other chronicling genres (historical recount and historical account) will show how a writer's voice can be impersonalized and his or her particular response to, or perspective on, events 'objectified' or 'naturalized'. In this way a seemingly 'neutral' record of

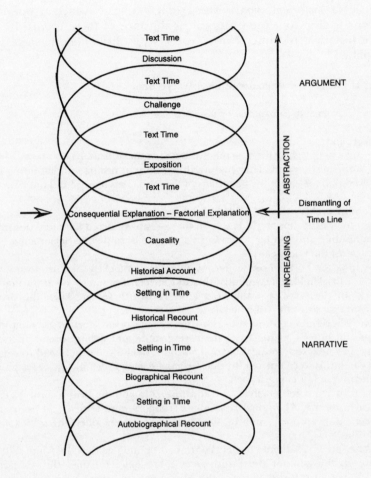

**Figure 7.1** Key genres in school history: a topological perspective

the past is presented. Choices at the level of genre and at the level of lexicogrammar will be examined.

### 3.1 Structuring a historical recount

The historical recount, a genre traditionally used in schools for presenting and constructing mainstream versions of the past and more recently for constructing alternative perspectives, moves through three main stages in order to achieve its purpose of recording past events. The function of the initiating Background stage is to summarize previous historical events which will make more meaningful the events focused on in the body of the text. The Record of Events stage records and elaborates a sequence of historical events. The Deduction stage, which is optional, functions to draw out the historical significance of these events. In the sample historical recount below (Text 1)[2] the three generic stages are exemplified.

**Text 1: The generic structure of historical recount**

**Eora Resistance to Europeans 1790–1816**

**Background**
The Eora people had lived in the Sydney area for at least 40,000 years before the Europeans arrived. They had lived by hunting, fishing and gathering and believed that they were the guardians of the land. This lifestyle did not last.

**Record of events**
When the Europeans arrived in 1788 they occupied sacred land and destroyed Eora hunting and fishing grounds. In 1790 the Eora people began a guerrilla war against the Europeans.

In 1794 the Eora, whose leader was Pemulwuy, attacked the European settlement of Brickfield. Thirty-six British and fourteen Eora were killed during this attack. In the same year the Eora killed a British settler. Then the British ordered that six of the tribe be killed.

The Aborigines continued to resist the European invaders by burning their crops and houses, taking food, destroying cattle and killing some settlers. In 1797 they attacked Toongabbie and within a week the farmers had to retreat and the farms were burned. In that year their leader, Pemulwuy, was captured by the British but later escaped.

By 1801 many settlers lived in fear of the Eora and the British started a campaign to destroy Aboriginal resistance. Troopers were sent to kill Aboriginal fighters and capture Pemulwuy. One year later settlers killed the leader in an ambush.

Other great Aboriginal leaders continued fighting against the white settlers. However, the guns of the British were more powerful than the Aboriginal spears. The British shot many of the Aboriginals and many others died of the diseases that the British brought.

**Deduction**
This period of black resistance in Sydney finally ended in 1816. It is a significant period in Australian history as it showed the determination of the Aboriginal people to resist the invasion. It also demonstrated how unjustly the Aboriginal people were treated by the White invaders.

*3.2 Constructing historical significance*

Although the Deduction stage of the historical recount is optional, I would argue that its absence leads to a less valued text. Its presence, in contrast, signals that the writer has begun her apprenticeship into power-ful historical discourse. That is, by taking up the meaning-making poten-tial of the Deduction, a writer learns to give significance to events and hence acquires the language resources that constitute 'significance' within the discipline of history. As O'Connor, drawing on Ricoeur (1981) and Mink (1974), puts it, the writer moves beyond the chronological or 'episodic' dimension of narrative – the dimension that describes 'what happened' – and learns the vertical, non-chronological operation which gives 'point' to a narrative. In other words, the writer learns to give the reasons for the narrative to be told (O'Connor 1991: 5–6).

In order to give significance or 'point' to a record of events there are two key sets of resources that a writer needs to have control of – those of the system of JUDGEMENT (a subsystem of the APPRAISAL system) and those of ATTRIBUTION (part of the system of ENGAGEMENT within the wider APPRAISAL system).

In SFL APPRAISAL is a set of systems (see Figure 7.2 below) which give language users choice in terms of how they appraise, grade and give value to social experience. The systems belong, therefore, to the category of interpersonal meaning (see Martin in press, 1996; Iedema et al. 1994, for a fuller discussion of APPRAISAL). In history, choice of APPRAISAL together with its linguistic realization and deployment across the staging of a text is critical to the construction of historical significance. Control of the system contributes significantly both to the construction of an interpretation of the past and to the positioning of a reader to accept the interpretation.

APPRAISAL may be realized directly. For example, the word 'unjustly' in the following extract from Text 1 realizes directly or 'inscribes' an explicit judgement – that the behaviour of the white invaders lacked integrity.

It also demonstrated how **unjustly** the Aboriginal people were treated by the White invaders.

The system of notation used to code such an analysis would use the short-hand – to stand for negative:

It also demonstrated how **unjustly** the Aboriginal people were treated by the White invaders. ( – integrity)

APPRAISAL may also be realized indirectly. That is, a word or set of words may be used to trigger or 'evoke' a particular judgement on the part of the reader. In this way ideational meaning is exploited for its inter-personal effect. When interpersonal meaning is triggered through the selection and construction of ideational meanings they are referred to as Tokens of APPRAISAL. The following sentence (also an extract from Text 1), for example, would prompt many readers to judge the Euro-peans' behaviour as negative and lacking integrity:

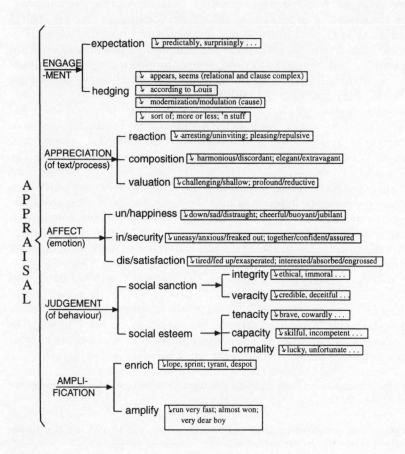

**Figure 7.2** The APPRAISAL system

When the Europeans arrived in 1788 they occupied sacred land and destroyed Eora hunting and fishing grounds.

The sentence would, therefore, be analysed as a Token of negative integrity. The notation used to code this analysis would be as follows:

When the Europeans arrived in 1788 they occupied sacred land and destroyed Eora hunting and fishing grounds. (t, – integrity)

Such a system of notation where t stands for Token and + for positive and – for negative will be followed in all subsequent APPRAISAL analyses.

The subcategories of JUDGEMENT will be written in full: NORMALITY (concerned with how unusual someone is), CAPACITY (how capable they are), TENACITY (how resolute they are), VERACITY (how truthful someone is) and INTEGRITY (how ethical someone is).

In history APPRAISAL choices are largely drawn from the systems of ENGAGEMENT, AMPLIFICATION, JUDGEMENT and VALUATION. In the chronicling genres, the main system at stake is the JUDGEMENT system. Choices from the JUDGEMENT system are largely realized indirectly. The JUDGEMENT analysis of Text 1 (see below) shows the typical patterning of JUDGEMENT resources in a historical recount.

### Text 1: Analysis of JUDGEMENT

#### Eora Resistance to Europeans 1790–1816

**Background**
The Eora people had lived in the Sydney area for at least 40,000 years before the Europeans arrived. **They had lived by hunting, fishing and gathering** (t, + capacity) and believed that **they were the guardians of the land**. (t, + integrity) This lifestyle did not last.

**Record of events**
When the Europeans arrived in 1788 **they occupied sacred land and destroyed Eora hunting and fishing grounds**. (t, – integrity) In 1790 the Eora people began a guerrilla war against the Europeans.

In 1794 the Eora, whose leader was Pemulwuy, attacked the European settlement of Brickfield. Thirty-six British and fourteen Eora were killed during this attack. In the same year the Eora killed a British settler. Then the British ordered that six of the tribe be killed.

**The Aborigines continued to resist the European invaders** (t, + tenacity) by burning their crops and houses, taking food, destroying cattle and killing some settlers. In 1797 they attacked Toongabbie and within a week the farmers had to retreat and the farms were burned. In that year their leader, Pemulwuy, was captured by the British but later escaped.

By 1801 many settlers lived in fear of the Eora and the British started a campaign to destroy Aboriginal resistance. Troopers were sent to kill Aboriginal fighters and capture Pemulwuy. One year later settlers killed the leader in an ambush.

**Other great Aboriginal leaders continued fighting against the white settlers.** (t, + tenacity) However, **the guns of the British were more powerful than the Aboriginal spears**. (t of British + capacity) The British shot many of the Aboriginals and many others died of the diseases that the British brought. (t, British – integrity)

**Deduction**
This period of black resistance in Sydney finally ended in 1816. It is a significant period in Australian history as it showed **the determination of the Aboriginal people to resist the invasion**. (+ tenacity) It also demonstrated **how unjustly the Aboriginal people were treated by the White invaders**. (– integrity)

### 3.3 Appraisal and ideology

The analysis of Text 1 shows that in the Record of Events stage there are no direct codings of JUDGEMENT. Instead the events selected act as ideationalized Tokens of JUDGEMENT influencing the reader to interpret the behaviour of the Europeans and Aboriginals in a particular light. Thus the Eora are constructed as having positive TENACITY but negative CAPACITY (in terms of military technology) whilst the Europeans are constructed as having positive CAPACITY but negative INTEGRITY. These judgements accumulate across the Record of Events stage so that their explicit rendering in the Deduction stage can be read as a logical, inevitable outcome of, or conclusion to, the previous text. It is in this way that the text overturns traditional notions of European 'discovery' and passive native submission and replaces them with a more contemporary interpretation of European colonization as brutal invasion versus determined resistance.

The construction of explicit JUDGEMENT in the Deduction stage which is linked to tokens of JUDGEMENT within the body of the text is a typical rhetorical pattern in the chronicling genres. It is this delicate interplay of interpersonal and ideational meaning at the level of discourse semantics which serves to construct a record of the past which appears objective, factual and logical but which, in fact, constructs a particular and therefore subjective perspective or interpretation. The writer appears to be letting events 'speak for themselves' but at the same time colours them with a significance that is ideological.

### 3.4 Attribution and naturalizing perspective

The JUDGEMENT analysis above has laid bare aspects of the discursive practice of history in which tokens of appraisal serve to obscure the subjectivity of a text and where JUDGEMENTS which are directly made are rendered 'objective' and 'logical' because of their rhetorical positioning. In the chronicling genres the resource of ATTRIBUTION (part of the system of ENGAGEMENT) also plays an important role in building an interpretation whilst simultaneously maintaining a 'neutral' voice. ATTRIBUTION is a system for reporting what other people think, say and feel, and the signalling in the text that those words or ideas belong to others rather than the writer of the text. In recounts, inscribed JUDGEMENT is often attributed to sources outside the text. For example, in the sentence 'Some argue that the Aboriginal people were treated unjustly by the White invaders', the negative judgement cannot be directly linked back to the writer. In addition the use of projection makes the proposition less negotiable: it is the 'some' that must be taken up and debated rather than the locution (the reported proposition):

Some argue that the Aboriginal people were treated unjustly by the White invaders.
(No, they don't)

In the sample recount (Text 1) it is events rather than people which are modally responsible for the judgements made. The reconfiguration of events as a segment of time allows time itself to play an agentive role. Through relational identifying process, 'time' takes on the agentive role of 'showing' or 'demonstrating' JUDGEMENT, which is dressed up as a nominalization (Halliday 1994: 171–2).

it [referring to the period and therefore events of resistance – my words] showed **the determination of the Aboriginal people to resist the invasion**. ( + resolve)

It also demonstrated **how unjustly the Aboriginal people were treated by the White invaders**. ( – ethics)

Realized as nominalization, JUDGEMENT becomes more presumed, more unassailable than realized as Locution. Realized as Locution, JUDGEMENT becomes less negotiable if attributed to sources external to the text. By eliding the role of the historian in interpreting events the combination of these resources plays a critical part in the naturalization of the past as 'objective fact'. We can say, then, that APPRAISAL systems form an essential part of the historian's (or apprentice historian's) discursive repertoire.

### 3.5 Ideology and the role of abstraction

In historical recounts, unlike in autobiographical and biographical recounts, there is a focus on groups of people and things, realized grammatically in the movement from specific and mainly human participants to participants which are generic and both human and non-human. This movement from specific to general is accompanied by a shift from more concrete to more abstract. As part of the concept of abstract we refer to things which are either 'abstract' or 'metaphoric'. Abstract things can be technical (e.g. investment, inflation, depression), institutional (e.g. policy, trade), semiotic (e.g. evidence, argument) or dimensional (e.g. period, era). Metaphoric things can be either processual (e.g. invasion) or quality (e.g. determination, strength).

The main contextual pressure which contributes to an increase in abstraction is the interplay between field (in terms of the expansion of time lines) and tenor (in terms of the developing status of the student as apprentice historian). In terms of time, the time span in a historical recount typically exceeds a person's lifetime. This results in considerable selection, editing and linearizing of events in the Record of Events stage. In the construction of unfolding time, therefore, the grammar tends to use circumstances (e.g. 'for at least 40,000 years', 'in 1794') rather than the conjunction system. In addition, sets of events which would be normally (or congruently) realized as temporal sequences of processes are compressed into nominal groups. For example, in the sample historical recount (Text 1), the nominal group – *a guerrilla war* – is the realization of a set of processes that took place over time. The more congruent realization would be:

> *The Eora people began to fight against the Europeans. First they attacked people, then they burned crops and houses. They used other guerrilla tactics as well.*

The process of reconstruing processes as nouns (nominalization) is in Halliday's terms one type of 'grammatical metaphor' whereby meanings typically realized by one type of linguistic choice are realized by other less typical choices (Halliday 1994: ch. 10).

It is by means of nominalization that the processes of fighting, attacking and burning can be repackaged as 'chunks' of time, for example, *this period of black resistance*. 'Periods', 'eras' and 'stages' are important dimensional resources for field building in history: they are the means by which one set of events can be brought into further relation with other sets of events on new timelines (thus facilitating intertextuality). Packaged as nouns their meaning potential can be expanded by describers and classifiers which can select from the APPRAISAL system. For example, *this period of black resistance* constructs Aboriginal behaviour to have positive RESOLVE whereas 'this period of early conflict' would foreground a different criterion for binding events together and therefore a different ideological bias. Selecting from the APPRAISAL system becomes increasingly expected as the student historian is apprenticed further into the discipline – as does the maintenance of 'objectivity'. Hence, in neither of the two examples does the writer explicitly intrude. In this way the classification of time, and therefore events, can encode an ideological perspective whilst maintaining 'objectivity'.

The seemingly natural division of time into parts (phases, periods, eras) plays a significant role in the historical process. As Whorf observed, it is this objectified view of time that is 'favourable to historicity ... [it] puts before imagination something like a ribbon or scroll marked off into equal blank spaces, suggesting that each be filled with an entry' (Whorf 1956: 153).

### 3.6 From recording to explaining: the role of the historical account

Following Figure 7.1, the genre that serves to apprentice students into further abstraction is the historical account. The historical account shares many of the features of the historical recount: it chronicles past events as they unfolded in real time and its structure is identical in terms of its initial and final stages, Background and Deduction. The main distinguishing feature, then, is the addition of causal links within the main temporal sequence – the Account Sequence stage (see Text 2 below for a generic stage analysis of a sample historical account). Thus, instead of presenting one event simply following on from another, events are given an agentive role and are construed as producing or causing subsequent events.

### Text 2: Historical account: analysis of generic staging

**What has happened to the Aborigines since the time of white settlement?**

**Background**

In the late 18th century, when the English colonized Australia, there were small tribes, or colonies of Aboriginal natives who had lived harmoniously and in tune with their surroundings for 40,000 years. However, there were no signs of agriculture or the Aborigines depending on the land. According to English law, this meant that they need not be recognized as rightful residents. The English immediately assumed that Australia was 'terra nullius', or uninhabited; to them it was an unsettled land which they did not have to conquer to gain power.

**Account sequence**

As a result of their belief in 'terra nullius', from 1788 onwards, the English began to occupy sacred land and use Aboriginal hunting and fishing grounds.

This abuse by the new British government soon led to Aborigines becoming involved in a physical struggle for power. The first main period of Aboriginal resistance in the Sydney area was from 1794 to 1816 when the Eora people, under the leadership of Pemulwuy, resisted the Europeans through guerrilla warfare.

This resistance resulted in the colonizers using different methods of control. In the 19th century Protection stations were set up where Aborigines were encouraged to replace their traditional lifestyles with European ones. Many Aborigines resisted, however, and as a result were shot or poisoned.

In 1909, the continuation of Aboriginal resistance led to the NSW Aborigines Protection Act which gave the Aborigines Protection Board the power to remove Aboriginal children from their own families and place them into white families, often as cheap labour.

In response to these injustices, the Aboriginal community began to fight for their rights. In 1967, they won the right to vote and in 1983 their struggle resulted in the creation of the NSW Aboriginal Land Rights Act. Their fight for land rights continues today. The Mabo case is a recent example of their success.

**Deduction**

The events of European settlement show the extent of Aboriginal losses. They also show the resistance of the Aboriginal people and some of the gains that they have made. This is an indication that their struggle will continue and more gains will be made. In this way the enormous losses that Aboriginal people have undergone, as a result of European colonization, might, to some extent, be compensated for.

At this point in the discussion it is important to note that, although from a typological perspective the historical account is distinct from the historical recount (in that its purpose is to account for why things happened in a particular sequence rather than simply retell the events in the sequence), examined from a topological perspective the boundaries between historical account and recount are fuzzy. At issue is the number of causal links a recount must have in order to be classified as account. We would argue that the two genres are best examined from a topological perspective and decisions of classification be based on the extent of causality. That is, if a text realizes most links between events as causal as well as temporal then the text would be regarded as account, whereas if most links between events are purely temporal then the text would be regarded as recount.

The introduction of causal elements into a retelling of the past marks an important ideological shift from viewing the past as a natural and arbitrary unfolding of events to viewing a sequence of events as underpinned and determined by causal patterns. By superimposing a causal paradigm on to a temporal one we would argue that the historical account plays a pivotal apprenticing role. Without losing the iconic form of a time line as a scaffold for text construction the genre serves to induct students into the role of history in *explaining* rather than simply recording the past.

The explanatory power of the historical account genre can, however, be critiqued in that it is limited to the mapping of causal relationships on to a temporal scaffold in which events unfold sequentially. Due to its oversimplified and reductive representation of the past it is a genre that has been challenged by theorists such as Lyotard and Foucault. Foucault's theories of history, for example, are built around the metaphors of archaeology (Foucault 1972) in which the role of chronology as an explanatory tool is greatly diminished. The *Annales* school also pointed out the limitations of the historical account as a model 'for the presentation of the large, synchronous, and anonymous forces' that, according to the *Annales*, 'truly govern history' (in Streuver 1985: 265).

Despite these critiques of the form, linguistic analyses show the importance of the historical account in extending a writer's lexicogrammatical choices for constructing causality. In the extracts from the sample historical account (Text 2) we can see how events are nominalized and construed as forms of beliefs or behaviour which are brought into causal relationship with new events. These events are in turn reconstrued as things (nominalized beliefs or behaviour) and, following a theme–rheme pattern, are constructed as producing new events. This pattern can be seen in Figure 7.3.

Learning to reconstrue processes as things and ascribe them with agentive roles provides students with the linguistic resources to elide the human agency that lies behind events. The potential to mask human agency is, as Iedema (1996) points out, central to administrative and bureaucratic practices where the institutional control of human resources

| As a result of their belief in 'terra nullius', | from 1788 onwards the English |
|---|---|
| Circumstance of cause – nominalized process as belief | |
| Theme | Rheme |

| began to occupy sacred land and use Aboriginal hunting and fishing grounds. |
|---|
| Rheme continued |

| This abuse by the new British government | soon led to | Aborigines becoming involved in a |
|---|---|---|
| Nominalized process as behaviour | causal process | |
| Previous Rheme picked up as Theme | Rheme | |

| physical struggle for power. |
|---|
| Rheme cont. |

| The first main period of Aboriginal resistance in the Sydney area | was from 1794 to 1816 when the |
|---|---|
| Nominalized events as behaviour and time | |
| Previous Rheme picked up as Theme | Rheme |

| Eora people, under the leadership of Pemulwuy, resisted the Europeans through guerrilla warfare. |
|---|
| Rheme cont. |

| This resistance | resulted in | the colonizers using different methods of control. |
|---|---|---|
| Nominalized process as behaviour | causal process | |
| Previous Rheme picked up as Theme | Rheme | |

**Figure 7.3** Theme analysis

is often linguistically obscured through the use of grammatical metaphor. Therefore, as a site for the rehearsal of both agency and grammatical metaphor, the historical account can be seen to play an important role in the formation of a discursive social subject.

### 3.7 Appraisal and the formation of a discursive social subject

The rehearsal of APPRAISAL resources plays an equally powerful part in the formation of a discursive social subject. The APPRAISAL analysis in Text 2 below shows the skilful interplay of inscribed and evoked JUDGE-MENT following a rhetorical pattern similar to that of the sample historical recount in Text 1. In Text 2 in the Account sequence stage the Europeans are constructed largely through Tokens of negative INTEGRITY whereas Tokens of positive TENACITY and CAPACITY are used in the construction of the Aborigines. These judgements are then reinforced in the Deduction stage where further grading occurs:

> In this way the **enormous** losses that Aboriginal people have undergone, as a result of European colonization, (t, European − integrity) might, to **some** extent, be compensated for.

Resources for measuring, such as 'enormous' and 'some', form part of the system of AMPLIFICATION.

In Text 2, then, the judgement of the Europeans' behaviour is intensified by measuring the extent of its negative INTEGRITY. In this sense it contrasts with Text 1 where the Tokens of JUDGEMENT are made explicit. The overall rhetorical pattern of the two texts is, however, similar: there is a gradual accumulation of JUDGEMENT until the desired 'volume', or level of APPRAISAL is reached, at which point these accumulated meanings are capitalized on (in the Deduction stage) either through inscriptions of JUDGEMENT or through AMPLIFICATION.

### Text 2: Analysis of APPRAISAL

**What has happened to the Aborigines since the time of white settlement?**

**Background**

In the late 18th century, when the English colonized Australia, there were small tribes, or colonies of Aboriginal natives who had lived **harmoniously and in tune with their surroundings for 40,000 years**. (t, + capacity) However, there were no signs of agriculture or the Aborigines depending on the land. According to English law, this meant that they need not be recognized as rightful residents. The English immediately assumed that Australia was 'terra nullius', or uninhabited; to them it was an unsettled land which they did not have to conquer to gain power.

**Account sequence**

As a result of their belief in 'terra nullius', from 1788 onwards, **the English began to occupy sacred land and use Aboriginal hunting and fishing grounds**. (t, − integrity)

**This abuse** ( − integrity) by the new British government soon led to **Aborigines becoming involved in a physical struggle for power**. (t, + tenacity) The first main period of Aboriginal resistance in the Sydney area was from 1794 to 1816 when the Eora people, under the leadership of Pemulwuy, resisted the Europeans through guerrilla warfare.

**This resistance** (t, + tenacity) resulted in the colonizers using different methods of control. In the 19th century Protection stations were set up where Aborigines were encouraged to replace their traditional lifestyles with European ones. **Many Aborigines resisted**, (t, + tenacity) however, and as a result **were shot or poisoned**. (t, European − integrity)

In 1909, **the continuation of Aboriginal resistance** (t, + tenacity) led to the NSW Aborigines Protection Act which gave **the Aborigines Protection Board the power to remove Aboriginal children from their own families and place them into white families, often as cheap labour**. (t, European − integrity)

In response to **these injustices**, (European − integrity) **the Aboriginal community began to fight for their rights**. (t, + tenacity) In 1967, **they won**

the right to vote (t, + capacity) and in 1983 **their struggle resulted in the creation of the NSW Aboriginal Land Rights Act.** (t, + capacity) **Their fight for
land rights continues today.** (t, + tenacity) The Mabo case is a recent example
of **their success.** ( + capacity)

**Deduction**
The events of European settlement show **the extent of Aboriginal losses.**
(t, European − integrity) They also show **the resistance of the Aboriginal people**
and some of **the gains that they have made.** ( + capacity) This is an indication
that their struggle will continue and more gains will be made. In this way **the
enormous** (amplification) **losses that Aboriginal people have undergone, as a
result of European colonization,** (t, European − integrity) might, to **some**
(amplification) extent, be compensated for.

### 3.8 The chronicling genres and the construction of a pedagogic subject position

In section 3 we have seen how APPRAISAL permeates the discourse
patterns of the Chronicling genres. We have also seen how the additional
layer of causal relations in historical accounts leads to the reconstrual of cause as abstract thing. Sample analyses have shown that
control of these resources enables writers to build a record of the past
where events appear to 'speak for themselves' and the writer does
not intrude. By learning how to construct chronicling genres students
are, therefore, learning how to present perspective as 'truth'. They
are learning how to appraise people's behaviour and the events
they engage in but without drawing attention to the role of writer as
judge.

Students are also learning how to resolve difference by construing the
past as a single line of narrativity. They are learning that a single, focused,
unproblematized story is a compelling tool for giving shape to the past. In
this way, they are acquiring the discourse strategies to construct a simpli-
fied yet plausible picture of social experience.

Critically, contemporary narrative practices (in school history) tend
not to teach students to render visible the part played by gender, class,
age and ethnicity in their reconstructions of the past. For some students
narrative patterns will be absorbed osmotically. Texts will be written and
read without a conscious understanding of the writer's role in ascribing
significance and how that significance is ideological rather than logical.
As a social practice, then, the narrative has the potential to produce
compliant social subjects. On the other hand, it also has the potential to
produce subjects with the discursive means to challenge 'naturalized'
world views. This, however, will depend on whether the constructed
nature of the historical narrative is revealed. It will also depend on
whether students are provided with a set of tools for recognizing, and if so
desired, resisting and challenging a particular ideological encoding of the
past.

## 4 Explaining the past

### 4.1 Structuring a consequential explanation

The two genres that serve to take students further along the pathway of constructing the past as story to constructing the past as argument are the factorial and consequential explanation (see Figure 7.1). The overall social purpose of explanations is to explain past events by examining causes and consequences. In contrast to historical accounts, in which causal connections are constrained by temporal sequence, explanation genres are able to integrate long-term, structural causes (or effects) with short-term precipitating events. The increase in the complexity of the explanation puts pressure on the method of text development. In the explanation genres, causes and consequences are no longer organized along a single external temporal thread. Instead the explanation is built up in text time by means of a logical scaffold from which an elaboration of causes or consequences unfolds. This section will examine in detail the textual shape of the consequential explanation as well as demonstrate its role in apprenticing students into increasingly abstract ways of thinking and writing about the past.

The generic shape of a consequential explanation is illustrated in Text 3. This sample consequential explanation shows that there are three generic stages that the genre moves through in order to achieve its purpose. These comprise the Input stage, the Consequences stage and the Reinforcement of Consequences stage. The main function of the Input is to identify a historical cause or input. The Consequences stage of the genre is concerned with presenting and elaborating the main effects of the input. These effects are then re-emphasized and appraised in the Reinforcement of Consequences.

**Text 3: Consequential explanation: analysis of generic structure and cause as macro and hyper-Theme.**

**What was the effect of World War II on Australian society?**

**Input**
World War II affected Australian society both during and after the war. The focus of this essay is its impact on Australia after it ended in 1945 and an explanation of how six years of involvement in warfare led to major economic, political and social changes.

**Consequence 1**
One major effect of World War II was a restructuring of the Australian economy: the unavailability of goods meant that Australia had to begin to produce its own. In addition, because better equipment, such as aeroplanes, machinery and ammunition, was needed during the war, industries such as the iron and steel ones, as well as ship building, were greatly boosted. In fact between 1937 and 1945 the value of industrial production almost doubled. This increase was faster than would otherwise have occurred and the momentum was maintained in the post-war years. This was partly the result of the post-war influx of immi-

grants which led to an increase in the demand for goods and services and therefore a growth in industry. The increase in human resources also made it possible for the government to begin a number of major development tasks. These projects required a great deal of material and created many new jobs. The overall result of this boom – full employment – greatly contributed to Australia's prosperity. By 1954–55 the value of manufacturing output was three times that of 1944–45.

**Consequence 2**
Another effect of the war was in the political arena. One of the main political developments that came out of the war was the establishment of closer relationships with America. This happened because, after Japan's defeat in World War II, Australia and New Zealand were both anxious to join the United States of America in an alliance for their joint protection in any further conflict in the Pacific. The resulting treaty was called ANZUS and was signed in 1951. Such a treaty has led to Australia being fairly closely tied to American policies which to some extent has restricted the country's freedom of action in international affairs.

**Consequence 3** ·
A third consequence of the war was in relation to Australian society. In this area the impact of World War II was considerable. The main reason for this was the Australian government's decision to develop an immigration programme that responded to the situation in Europe where thousands of families had been displaced. As a result many young immigrants came to Australia and began their own families. This wave of immigration greatly increased the country's population as well as contributing to the broadening of the average Australian's outlook.

**Reinforcement of consequences**
In conclusion it is clear that World War II benefited Australia by creating industrial and economic change. Other important changes that occurred as a result of the war were social, particularly the size and nature of the population, and political, namely Australia's relations with America.

## 4.2 Constructing causality

Text 3's purpose is to analyse and explain the effects of World War II on Australian society. A key resource for analysing and explaining is grammatical metaphor. In explanations the tool of grammatical metaphor plays a critical role in the genre's success. In consequential explanations the reconstrual of causality is the means by which the writer foregrounds the analysis of the consequences under focus and builds a scaffold for their further elaboration. The use of grammatical metaphor also makes possible the appraisal of these consequences.

As we have seen in section 3.6, grammatical metaphor (more specifically ideational metaphor) is a process by which congruent forms of cause – logical conjunctions such as 'so'– can become incongruently realized as either process (such as 'led to', 'resulted in') or thing (such as 'influence', 'outcome', 'effect'). The reconstrual of cause as noun allows the writer to construct experience as abstract thing which can then be brought into relationship with other abstract things and, in this way, serve as a basis for further analysis and elaboration of the consequence being focused on. For example:

> **One major effect of World War II** was **a restructuring of the Australian economy.**
> Cause as nominalized thing                    nominalized thing

Once reconstrued as thing, cause can also act as a 'departure point' (as demonstrated in the example above). By becoming a 'departure point' causality becomes foregrounded and attention drawn to the analytical nature of the text. In Text 3, for example, the Theme analysis in Figure 7.4 exemplifies how nominalized realizations of cause (the words underlined in Figure 7.4) consistently occupy prominent thematic position: both as macro-Theme (the opening generalization in a text which predicts its overall development) and hyper-Theme (the opening generalization in a paragraph which predicts the pattern of clause Themes and elaboration) (see Martin 1992: 437–9 for further discussion of macro and hyper-Theme).

The placement of causality in macro and hyper-Theme position also serves to build a scaffold for an explanation and hence is an important aspect of texture. Located in hyper-Theme and combined with internal cohesive devices causality becomes a staging and ordering device (e.g. **One** major effect, **another** effect, a **third** consequence). This creates a cohesive text with each main consequence presented in the hyper-Theme both relating anaphorically to the macro-Theme and cataphorically to the 'mini' account sequence used in its elaboration (see arrows in Figure 7.4).

Figure 7.4 serves to illustrate the rhythm created by the wave-like pattern of the text as it moves from a peak of abstraction and density in the macro-Theme through to a somewhat less dense hyper-Theme and then down to a relatively congruent and concrete condensed or 'mini' account sequence. This means that in the 'mini' account sequence cause tends to be realized through processes (such as 'led to') and logical connectors (such as 'because') rather than as nominalized thing. This is demonstrated in Figure 7.5 using paragraph 3 from Text 3.

Finally, the commodification or packaging of cause as thing allows consequences to be appraised. For example:

> One **major** effect of World War II was a restructuring of the Australian economy.

### 4.3 Giving value to consequences

Consequences are typically appraised and given value in terms of the extent of their influence. This type of APPRAISAL choice forms part of

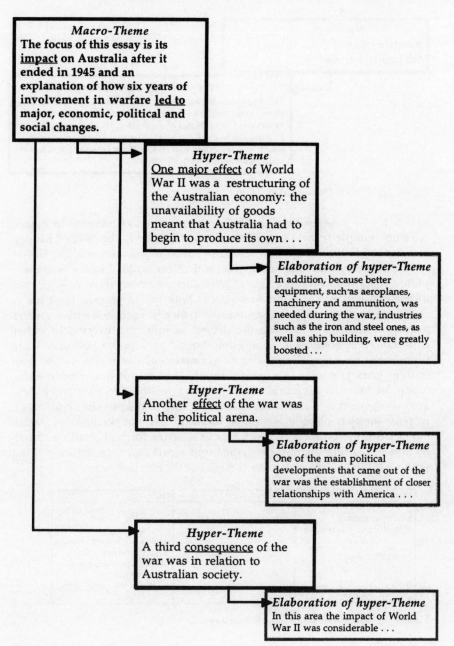

**Macro-Theme**
The focus of this essay is its <u>impact</u> on Australia after it ended in 1945 and an explanation of how six years of involvement in warfare <u>led to</u> major, economic, political and social changes.

**Hyper-Theme**
<u>One major effect</u> of World War II was a restructuring of the Australian economy: the unavailability of goods meant that Australia had to begin to produce its own . . .

**Elaboration of hyper-Theme**
In addition, because better equipment, such as aeroplanes, machinery and ammunition, was needed during the war, industries such as the iron and steel ones, as well as ship building, were greatly boosted . . .

**Hyper-Theme**
Another <u>effect</u> of the war was in the political arena.

**Elaboration of hyper-Theme**
One of the main political developments that came out of the war was the establishment of closer relationships with America . . .

**Hyper-Theme**
A third <u>consequence</u> of the war was in relation to Australian society.

**Elaboration of hyper-Theme**
In this area the impact of World War II was considerable . . .

Key
underlining = nominalized causality

**Figure 7.4** Macro-Theme, hyper-Theme, elaboration

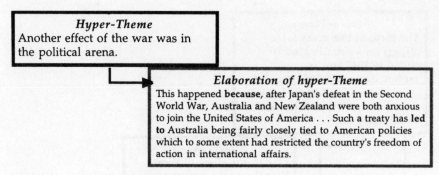

**Figure 7.5** Elaboration of hyper-Theme

VALUATION, a subclassification of the system of APPRECIATION. In Figure 7.6 some sample realizations of VALUATION, specific to the field of history, are displayed. Items such as these are critical to meaning-making in history. Their potential to grade cause and effect builds history as a discipline concerned with theorizing change and continuity. That is, whereas a minor consequence is often synonymous with minor change (and therefore continuity), a major consequence is typically associated with a greater degree of change. Measuring the degree of influence exerted by either causes or consequences is, in addition, bound up with the notion of significance. For example, the grading of a consequence as 'major' rather than 'minor' gives phenomena a greater significance or salience. The 'semioticizing' of salience is central to the practice of doing history: APPRAISAL analysis shows it is as much the historian's role to discern the significance of past phenomena as it is to pass moral judgement on past behaviour. VALUATION, therefore, serves as a set of resources for both grading causality and measuring degrees of change and significance. In Figure 7.6 the grading of the items along a low to high continuum is shown.

| Low | Median | High |
|---|---|---|
| minor, marginal, insignificant, unfounded | secondary | key, main, major, principal, important, crucial, significant, vital, largely, primary, critical, pivotal, complex, great, fundamental, far reaching, profound |

**Figure 7.6** Valuation: some sample realizations

Consequences may also be appraised in terms of their capacity to bring positive or negative change. For example:

In conclusion it is clear that World War II **benefited** Australia by creating industrial and economic change.

Typically, APPRAISAL is realized in the beginning and end stages of an explanation and thus frequently buried in highly metaphorical and abstract language. In the Input stage it is usually part of the macro-Theme and the valuation choice is often realized as classifier within a nominal group which may itself be part of an embedded clause. This choice of APPRAISAL realization makes its negotiation grammatically difficult. For example:

> The focus of this essay is its impact on Australia after it ended in 1945 and an explanation of how six years of involvement in warfare led to **major** economic, political and social changes.
> (Yes it is, no it isn't)

In the Reinforcement of Consequences stage APPRAISAL is often drawn attention to and reinforced through the use of interpersonal metaphor whereby assessments of probability normally realized as modal verbs may be realised as Attributes (e.g. 'it is evident', 'it is clear'). Through the shifting of modal responsibility, the proposition containing the APPRAISAL cannot be directly picked up and argued with:

> In conclusion **it is clear** that World War II **benefited** Australia by creating industrial and economic change.
> ('No it isn't', rather than 'no it didn't')

In the sample explanation, in the final proposition put forward, the appraisal of the changes as 'important' is realized through an epithet in the nominal group:

> Other **important** changes that occurred as a result of the war were social, particularly the size and nature of the population, and political, namely Australia's relations with America.

From the analyses above we can see that, in explanations, both the use of interpersonal metaphor and the 'burial' of appraisal in nominal groups, which in turn may be 'buried' in embedded clauses, function to obscure the subjective process of weighing up and measuring consequences or factors.

*4.4 The explanation genres and the construction of a pedagogic subject position*

In comparison to the chronicle genres, explanations are more explicitly concerned with explaining and therefore analysing the past. However, the process of interpretation underlying the explanation and analysis is largely elided. As we have seen in the sections above, elision is achieved through the use of rhetorical and linguistic strategies. One strategy is the deployment of APPRAISAL and interpersonal metaphor in order to naturalize the process of measuring and weighing up the significance of the factors or consequences relative to each other. The other is the presentation of a particular set of factors or consequences as uncontroversial 'fact'.

It could be argued that by learning to privilege a single line of explanation the writer can achieve a focus and thus produce an account which is persuasive precisely because of its narrowness of vision. In other words, although causes are presented as multiplex, and therefore relatively complex, the genre, like the chronicle genres, can be seen as a tool functioning to simplify social experience (in much the same way that variables are controlled in a scientific experiment). By learning to construct explanations, therefore, a social subject is trained to exclude competing and alternative explanations of the past which would disturb and problematize their chosen perspective.

Because explanations model the past as a space for explicit analysis and explanation they draw on a range of resources for both realizing and internally organizing causal phenomena. These include the resources of grammatical metaphor and internal cohesion. We would argue, therefore, that explanations expand students' potential for construing historical experience in increasingly abstract terms. Explanations also draw on resources for appraising causes and consequences and therefore change. The interpretation of historical phenomena together with, in the first place, its selection, is quite clearly an ideological activity. However, the ideological nature of the activity is largely concealed through the linguistic obfuscation of the writer's role and ideological position. Learning how to construct a consequential explanation, therefore, constructs a subjectivity capable of deploying a set of discursive resources which function to naturalize a reading position.

## 5 Arguing about the past

The arguing genres represent the end-point in the apprenticeship process. As discussed in the introductory section of this chapter, argument is highly valued within secondary school history: at the level of high school matriculation it is the main method of assessment. Success in school history, therefore, is dependent on a student's control of the lexico-grammatical resources and text structures that realize the arguing genres. In some respects the framework for arguing about the past is similar to that of the explanation genre. For example, as displayed in Figure 7.1, an important shared feature in the structuring of the texts is the use of text time or internal temporal relations.

The critical distinction between the explanation genres and the three key arguing genres is the foregrounding of the interpretative nature of historical investigation. Unlike explanations, the arguing genres draw attention to the formation of history as a set of interpretations and 'doing history' as a process of negotiating with these different interpretations.

Reconstructions of the past are therefore presented as hypothesis rather than fact, as possibilities or probabilities that have to be argued for.

Thus we can say that although some of the resources deployed in the arguing genres comprise those deployed in the explanation genres, they expand to comprise a range of new resources and the function of these additional resources is largely a persuasive one. The following section will explore some of the resources for persuading within the context of the challenge genre.

### 5.1 Challenging history

The challenge genre is an analytical text type which argues against a commonly held interpretation of the past. Its aim is to persuade the reader to reject the interpretation that historians, textbook writers, examiners or others have put forward. To do this the text moves through the stages of Position Challenged (which outlines the interpretation that will be argued against), Rebuttal Arguments (which marshals arguments and evidence which oppose the arguments and evidence supporting the position challenged) and Antithesis (in which an alternative interpretation is put forward). These stages are exemplified in the sample challenge (Text 4) below (please note that this is an abridged version in which short summaries of edited parts of the text are provided in brackets).

#### Text 4: Challenge: analysis of generic staging

**In what ways has Australia developed a positive relationship with its regional neighbour, Indonesia? (Abridged version)**

**Position challenged**
The Australian government argues that it has developed a good relationship with Indonesia over the last twenty-five years. It argues that its policies have led to improved political, economic and military cooperation between the two countries, to the benefit of both. However the critical issue is which sections of Australian society have cultivated these relations and with which sections of Indonesian society and who has actually benefited.

**Rebuttal arguments**
The main argument that is used to support the position that the relationship between Indonesia and Australia is a positive one is the increased political cooperation between the Australian and Indonesian government . . .
(evidence of relationship between political cooperation and development in trade)
This argument, however, does not take into account who benefits from the investments in Indonesia . . .
(evidence of lack of control over investment by majority of Indonesians)
In addition, the Australian people do not necessarily gain major benefits from these investments . . .
(evidence of this provided)
It is not only investment and trade that benefits some sections of society and not others. The interrelationship between Australian economic and political

policies needs to be considered in terms of their overall costs rather than just their benefits, particularly the issue of human rights.

The issue of East Timor and the Australian political response is a good example of the relationship between economic and political policy . . .
(evidence of Australian disregard for human rights for sake of Timor oil)

Loss of freedom for East Timor meant Australian complicity in allowing its invasion. As James Dunn states, 'Australian intelligence agencies were able to monitor the progress of Indonesian military preparations to assault East Timor . . . and simply chose to let events take their course' (*New Internationalist*, No. 253, March 1994). Despite condemnation of the invasion by the United Nations, and Amnesty International's systematic documentation of the human rights abuses carried out by the Indonesian government against the East Timorese (including frequent summary executions, disappearances, torture, enforced sterilization and mass executions), the Australian government has continued to extend *de jure* recognition of Indonesia's right to rule. Only recently Keating praised Indonesia as a 'nation of great tolerance'. Clearly such praise is not based on the current daily reality that exists for many Indonesian people. As Dr Buyang Nasution, an Indonesian Human Rights lawyer, argued in response to Keating's comment, 'if you were in our position, people who were oppressed, harassed, some of us were arrested unlawfully, even tortured . . . at least we would expect that foreign governments would not praise oppressive measures' (statement made on National Speaking tour to Australia, September 1994). Instead the Australian government's response has been to appease the Indonesian government. Such evidence of a policy of appeasement clearly demonstrates that the cost of the Australian government's economically influenced political policies has been the widespread abuse of large sections of people in order for a few to benefit economically.

Finally, another argument that is often raised in order to support the claim that Australia and Indonesia have developed a good relationship over the last twenty-five years is the degree of defence cooperation that exists between the two countries. Both the Indonesian and Australian governments claim that this cooperation helps to preserve both countries' national security. In Indonesia, however, an analysis of the Indonesian army shows that its role is largely one of internal policing. There has been military involvement in suppression of labour activists, including the killing of Marsinah, a 25-year-old factory worker, in 1993, and four people peacefully protesting over the building of a dam in 1994. Kopassus, in particular, is a military unit that is sent to regions of unrest and is able to override domestic laws. It has been associated with extra-judicial executions, disappearances and torture. Despite this, since July 1993, Australia has run an official programme of cooperation and training with Kopassus units. Senator Robert Ray claims that this will provide Australia with the opportunity to influence Indonesia in matters of human rights (letter to Amnesty International, 1993). However, there are no data to prove this assertion. Evidence shows that throughout Indonesia there has been no change in the pattern of political violence. Clearly, from the viewpoint of many of the people ruled by the Indonesian government, such a programme of defence cooperation does more harm than good and does not indicate improved or positive relations.

**Anti-thesis**

In conclusion, it can be seen that, from the perspective of many sections of both the Australian and Indonesian populations, the last twenty-five years can be characterized as a period in which relationships between Australia and Indonesia have changed but in a negative rather than positive way. A critical analysis of the economic and military arguments that are generally put forward to affirm the position that the relationship between Australia and Indonesia is a positive one proves this.

In the sample challenge 'In what ways has Australia developed a positive relationship with its regional neighbour, Indonesia?' we can see how internal temporal relations allow widely separated parts of the text to be connected logically and for rhetorical sequences to be built up. In this way a more complex web of interrelations between events is constructed. We can also see the critical role of linguistic and rhetorical strategies in persuading a reader to reject the assumption that Australia has developed a positive relationship with its regional neighbour, Indonesia. Two of the key resources used to position the reader to accept the rebuttal arguments – modality and hyper and macro-New – will be examined in section 5.2.

## 5.2 *Resources for persuasion*

In the sample challenge attention is drawn to the fact that events can be interpreted in different ways and that these different interpretations can vary in their truth status. The resources used to do this are drawn from the APPRAISAL system of ENGAGEMENT. This section will focus on modality, just one of the subsystems of ENGAGEMENT.

In the sample challenge it is through the resource of modality that claims by historians and other members of the public are presented as possibilities rather than indisputable facts. This, of course, makes them open to challenge and alternative interpretations can then be put forward. Here are two examples:

> In addition, the Australian people do not **necessarily** gain major benefits from these investments.

> Finally, another argument that is **often** raised in order to support the claim that Australia and Indonesia have developed a good relationship over the last twenty-five years is the degree of defence cooperation that exists between the two countries. Both the Indonesian and Australian governments claim that this cooperation helps to preserve both countries' national security. In Indonesia, however . . .

In contrast to the construction of the arguments that are being challenged (as presented in the extracts above), Text 4's rebuttal arguments, as summarized at the ends of paragraphs 7 and 8, are presented as categorical rather than as a possibility.

> Such evidence of a policy of appeasement clearly **demonstrates** that the cost of

the Australian government's economically influenced political policies has been the widespread abuse of large sections of people in order for a few to benefit economically.

Clearly, from the viewpoint of many of the people ruled by the Indonesian government, such a programme of defence cooperation **does** more harm than good and **does not indicate** improved or positive relations.

As can be seen from the examples above the key points of the rebuttal arguments are typically placed in hyper-New position. According to Martin (1992: 453–6), hyper-New is the closing generalization which consolidates the paragraph's point. In the context of the challenge genre the closing generalization is a deduction drawing out the significance of the previous evidence. The positioning of unmodalized propositions in hyper-New position functions to strengthen the rebuttal arguments.

In a challenge genre the hyper-New also functions to guide and prepare readers for the final Anti-thesis. Figure 7.7 shows how the deductions reached in each of the hyper-News accumulate and prepare the ground for the final macro-New, which functions to summarize the argument as a whole in the Anti-thesis. In this way the Anti-thesis reads as a logical end-point to the text. Importantly, however, the macro-New is not simply a replay of the hyper-Theme in that the build-up of compelling counter-arguments throughout the text provides a strong case for the adoption of a new position. As in the case of hyper and macro-Theme, metaphoric and abstract things are critical in pulling together the meanings that have accumulated. The patterning of metaphoric and abstract things, often as part of dense nominal groups, in both hyper and macro-New position is illustrated in Figure 7.7 where nominal groups are bolded and metaphoric or abstract things underlined.

### 5.3 Arguing genres and the construction of a pedagogic subject position

Close analysis of Text 4 shows that closure in terms of reaching a position on how past events should best be interpreted is the main objective of the genre. Although alternative perspectives and arguments are considered, the linguistic resources chosen to construct them skew the text in favour of the rebuttal arguments and the Anti-thesis. In other words, as proposed in section 1, the interpretation of the past as realized through the challenge genre is the outcome of linguistic and rhetorical strategies as opposed to objective and disinterested logical enquiry.

Clearly, apprenticeship into the oppositional paradigm of the challenge genre in which one perspective is 'proven' to have greater explanatory power and therefore greater 'truth' than another perspective is preparatory ground for society's future bureaucrats, lawyers and politicians. The acquisition of lexicogrammatical resources for persuading and positioning constructs a social subject able to argue issues of power and control.

| Paragraph 5 – hyper-New | It is not only <u>investment</u> and <u>trade</u> that benefits some sections of society and not others. |
| --- | --- |
| Paragraph 7 – hyper-New | Such <u>evidence</u> of a policy of <u>appeasement</u> clearly demonstrates that the <u>cost</u> of the Australian government's economically influenced political policies has been the widespread <u>abuse</u> of large sections of people in order for a few to benefit economically. |
| Paragraph 8 – hyper-New | Clearly, from the <u>viewpoint</u> of many of the people ruled by the Indonesian government, such a programme of <u>defence cooperation</u> does more harm than good and does not indicate **improved or positive** <u>**relations**</u>. |
| Paragraph 9 – macro-New | In conclusion, it can be seen that, from **the** <u>**perspective**</u> **of many sections of both the Australian and Indonesian populations, the last twenty-five years** can be characterized as **a** <u>**period**</u> **in which** <u>**relationships**</u> **between Australia and Indonesia** have changed but in a negative rather than positive <u>way</u>. **A critical** <u>**analysis**</u> of the economic and military <u>**arguments**</u> that are generally put forward to affirm the <u>position</u> that the <u>**relationship**</u> **between Australia and Indonesia is a positive one** proves this. |

**Key**
bold = nominal groups
underlining = metaphoric or abstract thing

**Figure 7.7** The patterning of hyper and macro-New in the challenge genre

## 6 Conclusion: school history as induction into the wider culture

Sections 3, 4 and 5 have analysed and discussed the set of genres which enable students to expand their repertoire of meaning-making resources and to participate in the apprenticeship process of learning how to mean like a historian. In these sections we have seen how each genre 'family' (the chronicling, explaining and arguing 'families') constructs a particular ideology of history as a learning area – either as story telling, as discovering explanatory principles or as logical argument. We have seen that history is a discipline drawing on paradigms from both the humanities and social sciences and that 'truth' and 'fact' emerge both through the straightforward telling of a story and through a series of logical propositions and deductions. Viewed linguistically, however, 'facts' and 'truth' are simply a rhetorical effect. That is, as the above discussion has clearly illustrated, although the historical process of enquiry is represented as a search for truth, interpretations of the past serve to defend specific ideological positions. As Jenkins (1991: 26) points out, the products of historians 'generally correspond to a range of power bases that exist at any given moment and which structure and distribute the meanings of histories along a dominant–marginal spectrum'.

In our analysis of a challenge genre (Text 4) we have examined the ideology that shapes end of school practices: clearly, at this point in schooling, the past is to be reconstituted as argument, and therefore abstract, and to be written from an objective, impersonal viewpoint. We saw how both the chronicle and explanation genres are instrumental in apprenticing students into writing in such a way. It is argued here that by expanding students' repertoire of language resources so that the past can be reconstrued in increasingly abstract and powerful ways, the school context acts to provide an apprenticeship into ways of meaning that are socially valued by the wider culture. Learning history is learning to control discursive resources which, on the one hand, erase contention and conceal difference and, on the other hand, draw attention to opposing perspectives and versions. In both cases the student learns to position and persuade a target audience, skills vital to participation in the post-Fordist cultures of the late twentieth century.

It is by learning the discursive resources of positioning and persuading that students acquire the resources to deal with information about, and/or the administration of, people and resources in government and industry. By learning the grammatically metaphorical discourse of bureaucratic control they are also acquiring the resources to take up positions of power in the workplace. At the same time an explicit and conscious understanding of how they themselves can be positioned by the language of history provides them with the resources to reflect on, and critique, mainstream workplace practices, construct alternative positions and work effectively towards and with change.

A critical question to ask, therefore, is what are the social consequences of the widespread demise of history (in Australia at least) across the state secondary school system, whilst at the same time numbers at private schools are maintained? What are the social implications for citizens' membership in the restructured workplace and their active participation in the maintenance of a genuine democratic process?

## Notes

1  In the recent British Cambridge History project the middle level of argumentation is described as displaying 'greater recognition of multiple viewpoints and the relativity of each' (Mitchell and Andrews 1994: 90).
2  The four text samples used in this chapter originate from a three-year research project (the Write It Right Project) which investigated the literacy demands of a range of secondary school subjects. A central purpose of the research project was to describe and analyse (from an SFL perspective) the texts that history students need to read and write at this level of schooling. In order to do this, syllabus documents, history textbooks, examples of student writing and model texts written by history teachers were collected and analysed. The practical outcome of this process was to develop units of work for classroom use which integ-

rated learning history with learning the language of history. As a result, some model texts were co-written by teacher and researcher for use in a particular unit of work. They were designed to provide input in terms of both content (relevant to the overall topic of the unit) and target genre. Texts 1, 3 and 4 are examples of this cooperative process whereas Text 2 is an example of authentic student writing.

It is important to note that all four example texts were regarded by the history teachers cooperating in the project as prototypical examples of history writing, examples which are increasingly difficult to find in contemporary school history textbooks, where the emphasis is on primary sources and the responsibility for constructing secondary texts is placed on the student.

## References

Burke, P. (1993) *New Perspectives on Historical Writing*. Oxford: Polity Press in association with Blackwells.

Carr, D. (1991) *Time, Narrative and History*. Indianapolis: Indiana University Press.

Coffin, C. (in press, 1996) *Exploring Literacy in School History*. Sydney: Metropolitan East Disadvantaged Schools Program.

Foucault, M. (1972) *The Archaeology of Knowledge*. New York: Pantheon.

Foucault, M. (1980) *Power/Knowledge*. New York: Pantheon.

Halliday, M. A. K. (1994) *An Introduction to Functional Grammar*. 2nd edition. London: Edward Arnold.

Iedema, R. (1996) *The Language of Administration*. Write It Right Industry Research Report No. 3. Sydney: Metropolitan East Disadvantaged Schools Program.

Iedema, R., Feez, S. and White, P. (1994) *Media Literacy*. Write It Right Industry Research Report No. 2. Sydney: Metropolitan East Disadvantaged Schools Program.

Jenkins, K. (1991) *Rethinking History*. London: Routledge.

Kress, G. (1989) 'Texture and meaning'. In R. Andrews (ed.) *Narrative and Argument*. Milton Keynes: Open University Press.

Lyotard, J. (1987) *The Postmodern Condition: A Report on Knowledge Theory and History of Literature*, Vol. 10. Manchester: Manchester University Press.

Martin, J. R. (1992) *English Text: System and Structure*. Amsterdam: John Benjamins.

Martin, J. R. (1996) 'Evaluating disruption: symbolising theme in junior secondary narrative'. In R. Hasan and G. Williams (eds) *Literacy in Society*. London: Longman.

Martin, J. R. (in press) 'Inter-feeling: gender, class, appraisal in *Educating Rita*'. In S. Hunston and G. Thompson (eds) *Evaluation in Text*. Oxford: Oxford University Press.

Martin, J. R. and Matthiessen, C. M. I. M. (1991) 'Systemic typology and topology'. In F. Christie (ed.) *Literacy in Social Processes: Papers from the Inaugural Australian Systemic Linguistics Conference, Held at Deakin University, January 1990*. Darwin: Centre for Studies in Language in Education, Northern Territory University.

Mink, L. O. (1974) 'History and fictions as modes of comprehension'. In R. Cohen (ed.) *New Directions in Literary History*. Baltimore: Johns Hopkins University Press.

Mink, L. O. (1978) 'Narrative form as a cognitive instrument'. In R. Canary and

H. Kozicki (eds) *The Writing of History*. Madison: University of Wisconsin Press.

Mitchell, S. (1995) 'Conflict and conformity: the place of argument in learning a discourse'. In P. Costello and S. Mitchell, *Competing and Consensual Voices*. Bristol: Multilingual Matters Ltd.

Mitchell, S. and Andrews, R. (1994) 'Learning to operate successfully in Advanced Level History'. In A. Freedman and P. Medway (eds) *Learning and Teaching Genre*. Portsmouth: Heinemann/Boynton Cook.

O'Connor, K. (1991) 'Narrative form and historical representation: a study of American college students' historical narratives'. Paper presented at the Conference for Pedagogic Text Analysis and Content Analysis, Harnosand, Sweden.

Ricoeur, P. (1981) 'The narrative function'. In J. B. Thompson (ed.) *Paul Ricoeur: Hermeneutics and the Human Sciences*. Cambridge: Cambridge University Press.

Streuver, N. S. (1985) 'Historical discourse'. In T. A. van Dijk (ed.) *A Handbook of Discourse Analysis*, Vol. 1. London: Academic Press.

White, H. (1989) *The Content of the Form: Narrative Discourse and Historical Representation*. Baltimore: Johns Hopkins University Press.

Whorf, B. L. (1956) *Language, Thought and Reality: Selected Writings of Benjamin Lee Whorf*, edited by J. B. Carroll. Cambridge, MA: MIT Press.

# 8 Entertaining and instructing: exploring experience through story

*Joan Rothery and Maree Stenglin*

## Introduction

Explorations in English-speaking cultures of the various discourses of everyday life, schooling, popular culture and literature frequently foreground 'story' as a highly valued social process in the life of the culture. This chapter will explore 'story' from the perspective of generic structure, an exploration which aims to illuminate some important reasons for the significance 'story' is accorded in these cultures. The first point to make in the introduction to this study is that 'story' is not a homogeneous social process but rather a typology where a range of story genres can be distinguished (Martin and Rothery 1980, 1981, 1984; Martin 1984, in press; Plum 1988; Rothery 1990). This typology has remained largely hidden in the linguistic and literary discourses of English-speaking cultures, a situation which has important implications for educational practice where students are inducted into a range of genres for learning the school curriculum. (This point will be picked up and elaborated throughout the chapter.) The second point to make is that within this typology, narrative, in certain discourses, including those of the English curriculum, is the most highly valued of the story genres (Rothery 1990, 1995; Rothery and Macken 1991; Rothery and Veel 1993). In order to articulate some of the reasons for this valuing, the generic structure of narrative will be the main focus of the chapter.

## A typology of story

The principal basis for establishing story as a typology is that all the story genres have a common social purpose of entertainment. This is largely achieved by giving the events spoken or written about a significance within their respective fields through the deployment of interpersonal linguistic resources. It is the interpersonal meanings which tell us that events are exciting, funny, terrifying, etc. In the examples of story genres examined in this chapter, interpersonal meanings are highlighted in bold. Social purpose is achieved though the functional staging of the genres which will be examined in four texts which exemplify some of the 'story' genres commonly produced in English in the oral and written mode (see Figure 8.1). The examination of these genres will also reveal that entertainment is only 'one part of the story' as far as this group is concerned. As we shall see, entertainment is co-opted very successfully in order to achieve ideologically driven socio-cultural goals, particularly in the area of narrative.

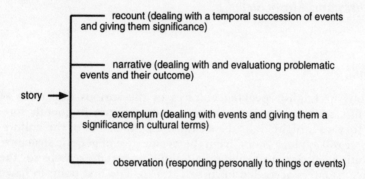

**Figure 8.1** A selective typology of story genres

The four genres – recount, narrative, exemplum and observation – are introduced through oral texts from Plum (1988). Oral examples have been deliberately included to demonstrate that story genres are firmly grounded in the everyday interaction of people in English-speaking cultures. Plum's texts have a common field, dog breeding, and were produced in response to questions which sought to elicit story genres (see Plum 1988 for a detailed account of his methodology for establishing an informal interview situation). Two written narratives are introduced later in the chapter. One, which was written in 1986 by an Australian secondary school student, won a short-story writing competition for secondary students conducted by a large daily newspaper in New South Wales. It can thus be seen to exemplify successful writing as judged by senior newspaper editors, literary critics and English teachers. The other was included in a public examination of secondary English in New South Wales. It should be noted that the texts dealt with in this chapter are short. No attempt is made to deal with the structure of longer texts such as novels, although there are similarities between them and the texts examined.

Recount

When reading Text 1 it needs to be kept in mind that it was produced orally in response to the question 'How did you get into breeding dogs?' The question led some respondents to shape an Orientation more in the nature of a mini-explanation as they recounted the sequence of events that made it possible for them to enter the world of dog breeding and showing. The Orientation of Text 1 thus exemplifies that the function of the stage is more abstract than introducing characters and settings. The function of the Orientation is to set up a context for the events that follow, to put them in a framework that leads the reader/listener into the following stage. Although the Orientation of Text 1 is a brief activity sequence, it is clearly distinguished from the following stage by the continuative 'Anyhow' which introduces the Record stage.

### Text 1: A Recount

**Orientation**
We're sitting here one day and eh – and the wife – I took a typewriter up and eh – the wife said she'd like a Miniature dachshund. And I said, 'Well, you sell this typewriter, you can have one.' See so I . . . I done the typewriter up so I said there is your dog.

**Record of events**
Anyhow, she placed some ads, and she sold it. She got a hundred and fifty dollars for it, exactly what the dog cost. So away we went and she bought the dog and brought it home. Anyhow, it died and we lost it.

So then we tried to buy another one. **Well, they are very hard to buy, you know, Miniature dachies, good ones are. Anyhow, we couldn't get one anywhere. I rang up – I must've spent a week on the phone, I rang just about anywhere in the country, you know, for the dog.** Eventually we run across Mrs Smith. Eventually we got on to Jenny K. She said, 'Yes well, sir, I'll sell you a dog.' She said, 'If I like you I'll sell you a dog.'

'Okay, fair enough.'

So, well, then we combed our hair, brushed our teeth, and away we went to Dapto, you know.

When we got down there **the dogs she showed us were absolute rubbish you know. Oh, they were terrible you know.** We kept knocking them back, we said we didn't want them. And then she said, 'Well', and she said, 'you obviously got an eye for dogs.' She said, 'Would you care to start to breed?'

And I said, 'Well, alright, we'll have a look at it.'

So she brought the brood bitch and we liked it. So we bought it.

**Reorientation**
You know, that's the basis of it, that's where we started.


## Narrative

Narratives deal with problems constructed in the Complication stage of the text. Typically the Complication is realized by an activity sequence which deals with some disruption of usuality so that the actions constitute a problem for one or more of the participants. In this oral narrative, the Complication is about the repetition of an action by one of the participants – hitting a dog with a hat and then putting it back on his head. The realization of this stage is marked in that the sense of repetition is constructed through the present continuous tense rather than the unmarked choice for the simple past. Again, these realizations are more commonly found in the oral mode.

### Text 2: A Narrative

**Abstract**
Oh one funny thing was . . .

**Orientation**
This friend of ours, who I might add is a nut, was playing with a fur hat on the floor.

**Complication**
And he had it in his hand and he was tormenting one of the dogs. And he's hitting the dog with this hat and putting it back on his head.

**Evaluation**
And I said, 'Don't do that Jim!' I said, 'You'll end up getting hurt.'
  'No – it's all right, no.'
  'Oh, okay.' So this person can't be told, so I thought, 'Bugger you,' walked out and left him to it.

**Resolution**
And he kept belting the dog with the hat, putting it back on his head. The dog jumped up, grabbed the hat and took the top of his ear off.

**Coda**
Well it's his own fault. I mean how stupid can you get? Putting a fur hat back on your head after you've been belting the dog with it and he's trying to get it.

(Plum 1988, Vol. 2: 202–3)

## Exemplum

Exemplums articulate moral judgements. The events written about in exemplums serve to illustrate that judgement. In the following text the moral judgement is specific to the field of animal breeding and showing, where the goal of physical perfection in animals is sought. The criteria for making a judgement of physical perfection are man-made. They lie in a realm beyond the general good health of the animal. The judgement about the value of the dog as an animal suited for showing is implicit in the text. The interviewer and the respondent both know the criteria for judging the quality of the dog. There is no need to articulate them in this context of shared knowledge.

### Text 3: An Exemplum

**Abstract**
I have a heartbreak story.

**Orientation**
This young dog here (pointing to a photo) he was my first, my first big-winning

dog. And he reigned supreme here for two and a half, nearly three years. And he did an incredible amount of winning. He's a multiple all-breeds best-in-show winner. He's taken two reserves at Royals, Sydney and Melbourne, two reserves at speciality shows, which draw massive entries, you know, between three–three-fifty, sometimes four hundred.

### Incident
He was running around in our exercise yard and just slipped. He was turning and slipped and dislocated his hip. And from that day on I have not been able to show the dog.

### Interpretation
**And he's in immaculate coat. He's even more coat than that (pointing to a photo). That's a twelve month old photo. And that broke our hearts because this dog could've done wonders.**

### Coda
As a stud dog he's proved to be more than successful. He's produced some beautiful progeny. You know, that's going to be his forte now. He'll be a stud dog now and not a show dog.

(Plum 1988, Vol. 2: 224)

## Observation

Observation is unique amongst the story genres in that there is no temporal sequence in the middle stage, Event description. Nevertheless the genre deals with particular events and the specific participants involved in them. As is the case with the other story genres, the events are given significance through the foregrounding of interpersonal meanings. In the observation this occurs in the Comment stage. In the four questions asked by Plum which sought to elicit story, observations were given in response to all of them. Instances of the genre were more common than narrative in response to two of the questions and they were given as frequently as exemplum for one (Plum 1988, Vol. 1: 226). In each instance the genre reads as an appropriate story response to the questions.

### Text 4: An Observation

#### Orientation
I don't know if you know of the big Spring Fair show that's held out at St Ives. Well, the biggest show of the year probably is the Royal but one that is rapidly overtaking it is what they call the RAS Spring Fair. It's held out at St Ives showground. It's an enormous thing, interstaters and even overseas people compete in it. And they have what they, what is called – their competition called the breed stall. Now this is open to all the specialist breed clubs and you put on a display for the whole three days of the . . . It's on the long weekend in October.

#### Event description
The Borzoi club won this for the last two years in a row. We're rather a crazy lot and this time we put on a follies type pageant, Flo Ziegfield, that type of thing. And we were all dressed up in the W. C. Fields and the Jean Harlow type thing

and the dogs, for God's sake, there were big dogs there, thirty-six inches at the shoulders, big massive dogs that were dressed up in fancy dress.

**Comment**
**Well it was a sight that'd stagger you, really, some of these dogs dressed up in frilly things and all this and the other. Big hunting dogs, you know, dressed up in follies type costumes. It sticks in my mind and will for quite some time. We have photos which I can't lay my hands on at the moment. But eh . . . well it was funny, it was fun and it was funny. And it drew enormous crowds, it was real spectacular. Yeah, that was a lot of fun.**

(Plum 1988, Vol. 2: 57)

### Explaining the staging of the story genres

Let us now examine the texts more closely in respect of how their ideational and interpersonal meanings are organized functionally in stages in order to achieve social purpose/s. The functional labels for each stage have a semantic orientation which aims to capture both the function of the stage in achieving the semantic unity of the text and its role in achieving the genre's social purpose. Some of the labels were introduced by Labov and Waletzky (1967) in their seminal work on narrative. They did not, however, account for their choice of labels through a linguistic analysis of their texts, nor did they describe the function of each stage in constructing the semantic unity of the texts they analysed. The focus in this analysis is on the function of stages and key aspects of their linguistic realization. Optional stages are noted, as are choices for interspersing stages.

Each story has an Orientation whose function is to 'orient' the listener/reader to what is to follow. This stage is common to all the story genres. The meaning of 'orient' is more abstract and complex than introducing main characters and establishing a physical setting, although this is what the Orientation often does. It means creating a context for understanding what is to follow in the subsequent stages of the genre. In Text 4, an observation, although the physical setting for the dog show is established, there is a strong focus on the importance of the show which serves to highlight in the following stages the somewhat incongruent behaviour of *the breed stall* for a leading show. Similarly, in Text 1, a recount, the Orientation gives the sequence of events that made it possible for a married couple to buy their first dog. In Text 3, an exemplum, the Orientation gives a history of the dog's success in the world of dog showing so the listener will appreciate the seriousness of the events that follow. The Orientation in Text 2, a narrative, is brief. It introduces the activity crucial to the events of the Complication.

There are other optional opening stages for the story genres which occur frequently in oral texts but infrequently in written ones. Abstract is one such stage which occurs in Texts 2 and 3. It gives a prospective evaluation of what is to come, for example, in Text 2: *I have a heartbreak story* and in Text 3: *Oh, one funny thing was* ... The Abstract establishes an interpersonal context for what is to follow. The other optional opening stage is Synopsis (Plum 1988), which gives a summary of the events of the story genre, for example: *This story is about a plane crash and how the two survivors were rescued.* The focus of Synopsis is experiential. None of the texts in this sample includes a Synopsis. A possible explanation for the more frequent occurrence of Abstract and Synopsis in oral story genres is that there is a need to 'tune' the listener in to what is to follow as effectively as possible. The spoken text unfolds in time as an ephemeral, transient product, unlike the written text, which can be revisited on the page as frequently as the reader wishes and thus can be developed differently. Linguistically the opening stages of the story genres are often characterized by an absence of conjunctive relations, except for additive ones. The exception to this is the mini-recount which can realize the Orientation, as in Text 1. In this case temporal successive conjunctions occur.

The concluding stages of the story genres 'round off the events' in various ways. The observation is the exception in this respect as it invariably lacks such a stage. As we will see when we examine the middle stages of this genre, it gives us a snapshot of events, frozen in time so to speak, so there is not the need to bring events to a conclusion. The recount ends with the Reorientation stage which brings the events full circle, with some reference to the starting point of the text. In oral texts, as in Text 1, the Reorientation often has an interpersonal focus in that it makes reference to the interaction which initiated the text. Plum had asked his interviewees how they got started in dog breeding and the speaker/narrator of Text 1 concludes the text with: *You know, that's the basis of it, that's where we started.* In written recounts, the Reorientation usually brings the reader back to the experiential starting point, for example: *We arrived home late in the afternoon after a wonderful day's outing at the beach.*

Coda is an optional and additional concluding stage for all the story genres. It is similar to the Abstract in that it gives an overall evaluation of the events of the text, but does so retrospectively. The Coda in Text 3 is very positive, indicating that unfortunate events can still lead to a successful outcome. In this respect, the Coda points implicitly to the 'moral' of the story: *As a stud dog, he's proved to be more than successful. He's produced some beautiful progeny. You know that's going to be his forte now, he'll be a stud dog now and not a show dog.* In other words, despite the dog's failure to meet the criteria for being a successful show dog, he is now valued as a suitable animal for breeding potential show dogs. So unfortunate events may have positive outcomes. The Coda in Text 2 evaluates the friend's behaviour negatively, thus justifying the dog's behaviour: *Well, it's his own fault, I mean how stupid can you get? Putting a fur hat on your head after you've been hitting the dog with it and he's trying to get it.* Again, written texts often 'bury' the moral of the story in the events of the text – to be extrapolated by the reader as part of their reading and understanding of the story. In a later section we will examine such a narrative closely.

## Distinguishing stories: the function of middle stages

The middle stage of recount is Record of events. As the name suggests, it deals with a sequence of events. In this respect, recount is similar to narrative and exemplum. Record of events is characterized linguistically by temporal successive conjunctions. Just as the observation presents us with 'a snapshot frozen in time', so the recount gives us a 'journey of how participants move from Point A to Point B'. The metaphor of a journey aptly describes the numerous recounts Plum received in response to a question which asked how the respondents became involved in breeding and showing dogs. Text 1 exemplifies what typifies recounts, clearly defined events which constitute the starting and end-point in the activity sequence of the field of the journey, while the transitivity patterns may be predominantly Actor^material Process^Goal as in Text 1, for example: *So away we went and she bought the dog and brought it home* (see Figure 8.2). The pattern of Actor^material Process is as common. Recounts which are literally about journeys frequently employ the latter, for example: *We travelled several hundred kilometres every day* (see Figure 8.3). In both types of transitivity pattern there is usually one participant who is principally Actor throughout the text. There is no changing pattern of participant roles for the main character as is often the case in narrative.

Contrary to what is often assumed about recounts, they are not necessarily about predictable or smoothly flowing activity sequences in the field. Text 1 provides a good example of this: *So away we went and she bought the dog and brought it home. Anyhow, it died and we lost it. So then we tried to buy another one.* In the sequence of events about buying a dog, the

| away | we | went |
|---|---|---|
| Location: place | Actor | material Process |

| she | bought | the dog |
|---|---|---|
| Actor | material Process | Goal |

| (she) | brought | it | home |
|---|---|---|---|
| Actor | material Process | Goal | Location: place |

**Figure 8.2** Transitivity structures from Text 1 (recount)

| We | travelled | several hundred kilometres | every day |
|---|---|---|---|
| Actor | material Process | Extent: distance | Location: time |

**Figure 8.3** Typical transitivity structure (recount)

death of the first dog that was purchased is not foregrounded as significant. Nothing is made of it through an interpersonal focus. It is simply one event in 'the journey' of buying a dog. In other words, the same experience can be constructed in various patterns according to the social purpose of the text. It is not the field knowledge that determines generic construction but the social purpose the field knowledge will serve. The construction of text is, above all, a socio-cultural event.

Again as might be expected with a text that is 'a journey', interpersonal meanings occur at different points, although there is a tendency for them to cluster around key events in recounts. Trying to find a good dog to buy was one such pivotal event in Text 1 and was foregrounded accordingly: *Well they are very hard to buy, you know, Miniature dachies, good ones are. Anyhow we couldn't get one anywhere. I rang up – I must've spent a week on the phone. I rang just about everywhere in the country, you know, for the dog.* There is a pattern of repetition that intensifies the difficulty: *I rang up – I must've spent a week on the phone, I rang just about everywhere in the country, you know, for the dog.* The difficulty is not insurmountable, but it is the kind of setback we all encounter in the journeys we make in the activity sequences of the many fields we engage in in everyday life.

The recount, like the observation, is reassuring. It confirms our own experience of journeys, regardless of the field, where once we engage in an initiating event to pursue a particular path, there is an end-point in view, despite some 'ups and downs' that we may encounter on the way. The recount thus serves to create a sense of solidarity among the members of a culture or subculture. It brings people together on the common ground of the multitude of journeys we take through our lives.

Text 2 is a narrative, the story genre most highly valued in many contexts of the culture. If a recount can be characterized as a journey, then narrative is an adventure. It deals with disruptions that constitute a crisis whose outcome is problematic for those involved in them. The challenge for participants is to confront the crisis and overcome the disruption. The Complication and Resolution stages deal respectively with the disruption of an activity sequence and its return to some kind of stability. The Evaluation foregrounds interpersonal meanings that give significance to the disruption dealt with in the Complication. In the Complication of Text 2 a man torments a dog rather than playing with it. The activity sequence is a disruptive one from the initiating event onwards. The man is the aggressor and the dog is the victim. The advice given to the tormentor in the

Evaluation about the likely outcome of the activity is ignored and the dog stops it by injuring his aggressor. Thus the *status quo* is resumed. Evaluation in narrative has the potential to function differently from similar stages in other story genres in that it can give significance retrospectively and prospectively as it does in this text. In the imperative clause, *Don't do that Jim!*, the identity of *that* is the activities depicted in the Complication. But in a projection, *you'll end up getting hurt*, a prediction is made about the likely outcome of Jim's behaviour, a prediction which is fulfilled in the Resolution.

Narratives are often adversarial in that participants are pitched against one another. This can be seen in the patterns of roles taken by participants in material Processes. One participant, or several, has the role of Actor in the Complication stage while another has the role of Goal. These roles are often reversed in the Resolution stage. This is the case in Text 2. In the Complication the man has the role of Actor in material Processes and the dog has the role of Goal. In the Resolution, the dog is the Actor and the man's hat and his ear are the Goal (see Figure 8.4).

The transitivity analysis enables us to see one aspect of how the stages of Complication and Resolution are constructed through the transitivity system. However, it would be wrong to see this pattern of changing participant roles as always indicating a protagonist/antagonist relationship. Narratives can deal with fields of disaster and rescue where the principal character(s) fights the elements often to save others. In this case the roles are more accurately characterized as 'heroic'. Nevertheless, regardless of the exact nature of the relationship between participants, narrative is about individuals struggling against adversity as represented by a disrupted activity sequence that leads to a crisis point. Dealing with the crisis is the crux of narrative so that 'usuality' is restored in the activity sequence of the field. It is a powerful genre for inducting members of the culture into valued ways of behaving, specifically facing up to problems, no matter how difficult or personally threatening, and attempting to overcome them, so that stability is restored and maintained in the activity sequences of the various fields that constitute the culture. In other words, narrative has an important role in constructing the value of individuation and in focusing on the necessity of conserving field activity sequences in order to maintain stability in the culture. The ideological significance of narrative outweighs that of other story genres.

In observation the stages Event description and Comment are both middle and concluding. The former is experientially focused, the latter interpersonally. As with most story genres, the experientially and interpersonally oriented middle stages can occur discretely, or as stages that are interspersed. The exception is recount where interpersonal meanings occur throughout the Record stage. In observation, the experientially oriented stage, Event description, is distinguished from comparable stages in other stories by its lack of temporal conjunctive relations. Conjunctive relations are additive. As a consequence there is no development of an

**Complication**

| he | was tormenting | one of the dogs |
|---|---|---|
| Actor | material Process | Goal |

| he | 's hitting | the dog | with this hat |
|---|---|---|---|
| Actor | material Process | Goal | Means |

**Resolution**

| The dog | jumped up |
|---|---|
| Actor | material Process |

| grabbed | the hat |
|---|---|
| material Process | Goal |

| and | took | the top of his ear | off |
|---|---|---|---|
| | material Process | Goal | material Process |

**Figure 8.4** Transitivity structures in the Complication and Resolution stages of Text 2

activity sequence as in recount and narrative. Hence the notion of 'a snapshot frozen in time' is deployed to characterize observation as a story genre. While the events depicted may be out of the ordinary, they do not foreground the disruption of an activity sequence, or a crisis point to be confronted. The events are thus constructed as 'locally' significant rather than having implications for 'ways of behaving' in a range of cultural contexts.

The relationship of the stage Comment, which foregrounds interpersonal meanings, to that of Event description can be demonstrated by identifying cohesive ties between items in each stage. These are typical of the ties found between items in corresponding stages in other story genres. They are ties that play a crucial role in giving the experiential meanings significance through the deployment of interpersonal resources. Anaphoric reference is one such cohesive resource. In the first clause of the Comment stage: *Well, it was a sight that'd stagger you*, the identity of *it* is retrieved from the text of the Event description. Similarly in the clause, *It sticks in my mind*, *it* refers to preceding text (see Figure 8.5).

Lexical items expressing reaction are another crucial resource for constructing significance. In that same clause, one such item is *stagger*. It could be glossed as 'amaze' and thus analysed as a choice for a mental reaction Process. Within the transitivity structure of the first clause, *it* is Carrier and the Attribute is *a sight that would stagger you*. But as we have noted, *it* refers to the situation depicted in Event description. Thus the interpersonal meaning, *a sight that would stagger you*, is attributed to the situation depicted in the Event description stage (see Figure 8.6). Through such relationships the significance of the Event description stage is constructed. Another resource for constructing significance is repetition, or near repetition, of lexis, and clauses, both within and between stages. The repetition serves to intensify meaning. In the Event description, *there were big dogs there, thirty-six inches at the shoulders, big massive dogs that were dressed up in fancy dress* is picked up in the Comment stage, *some of these dogs dressed up in frilly things and all this and the other. Big hunting dogs, you know, dressed up in follies type costumes . . . well it was fun and it was funny . . . Yeah, that was a lot of fun.* The repetition of *fun* both sums up and emphasizes the entertainment value of the events depicted. The Comment stage confirms that observation focuses on the significance and interest of local events for their own sake. Indeed the entertainment derived from depicting the unusual in the observation is often reassuring. We can experience variety and diversity in the fields of the culture without their stability or predictability being seriously threatened in any way.

The last of the story types to be examined in this section is the exemplum, a story genre more closely related to narrative in that it deals with

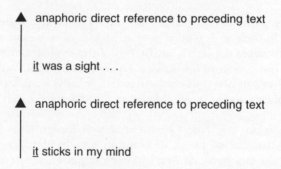

**Figure 8.5** Reference structures in Comment stage of Text 4

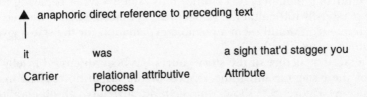

**Figure 8.6** Transitivity and reference structure in the Comment stage of Text 4

disruption. The Incident stage in Text 3 deals with a problem, the accident that results in a very successful show dog having his career cut short. The disrupted activity sequence, the dog slipping and dislocating his hip while undertaking an exercise run, is given a significance in the Interpretation stage that takes it beyond the disruption to the everyday life of the dog. In fact, nothing is made of the dog's or owner's distress about the injury. The significance is established in a field of the culture, that of dog showing. No longer is the dog a suitable candidate for showing because he does not fulfil the man-made requirements of the 'champion dog'. A judgement is made about the suitability for showing on the basis of 'man-made' values for showing dogs. For most dog owners, the significance of an accident to the animal is in the domain of recovery or near recovery to good health. The highly specific requirements for dog showing are unknown and irrelevant to them. Thus the field-specific significance of the events must be clearly articulated for the reader/listener. The moral of the exemplum is that positive outcomes are possible from negative events. It may well be summed up as 'making the best of things'. The exemplum is similar to the narrative in that it deals with disruption to usuality but, unlike narrative, the significance of the disruption may be more local or field-specific. Narrative, on the other hand, deals with values that are more constant across the fields of the culture.

Plum found that he elicited a range of story types in response to the same question. For example, when 34 respondents were asked to tell what happened in a surprising show success, 6 per cent responded with a recount, 15 per cent with a narrative, 35 per cent with an observation and 38 per cent with an exemplum and 6 per cent with non-story genres (Plum 1988: 226). It is clear from reading the texts that all are appropriate responses to the question in the context of everyday interaction. However, in the context of schooling in Australia, this is not the case. When students are asked to write a 'story', narrative is expected, although not explicitly asked for, and it is more highly valued in English than other story genres (Rothery 1990; Rothery and Macken 1991). Yet a similar situation prevails in the written mode to the spoken. When students are asked to write a 'story' in school they respond with a range of genres

(Martin 1984; Rothery 1990). It is interesting to speculate about the reasons for the value placed on narrative in the school context. Its powerful role in inducting members of a culture into valued ways of behaving that may be personally difficult, even dangerous, so that stability is restored to activity sequences, would seem a possible explanation for the status given to this story genre.

The generic structure of the story genres has been discussed briefly in terms of their staging and some aspects of the linguistic realization of these stages. Figure 8.7 shows the generic structure of observation, recount, narrative and exemplum. Optional stages are shown with round brackets. The sign ^ indicates that the stage to the left precedes that to the right. Choices for recursion of stages have not been shown nor for interspersing stages which foreground interpersonal meanings with those dealing with experiential meanings.

### Dealing with disruption: the generic structure of narrative

We have already noted that narrative has a different role from other 'stories' in the life of the culture. Through its generic structure, regardless of field, it advocates valued behaviours that serve to restore 'usuality' and hence maintain the existing order. Invariably, too, the focus is on the actions of one or several participants in confronting problems. In this respect, also, narrative has a powerful cultural influence. For young readers, in particular, it highlights the important role of the individual in the culture. The individual, or a few participants, must take responsibility for

recount        (Abstract) ^ (Synopsis) ^ Orientation ^ Record of events ^  Reorientation ^ (Coda)

narrative      (Abstract) ^ (Synopsis) ^ Orientation ^ Complication ^
               Evaluation ^  Resolution ^ (Coda)

exemplum       (Abstract) ^ (Synopsis) ^ Orientation ^ Incident ^
               Interpretation ^ (Coda)

observation    (Abstract) ^  (Synopsis) ^ Orientation ^ Event Description ^ Comment

**Figure 8.7** Generic structure of recount, narrative, exemplum and observation

making decisions and initiating actions that resolve problems. There is little doubt that in Western cultures this pattern of behaviour is encouraged and highly valued across the fields that constitute the culture. The analysis of the following narrative, 'If You Lose You're Dead', by Cathryn Cooper will demonstrate how the generic structure of narrative both entertains and implicitly instructs the reader about valued ways of behaving.

There is another perspective to narrative which needs to be mentioned. The genre can also be exploited to subvert cultural practices so that readers are made aware of a range of roles for participants in activity sequences that challenge the *status quo* in the culture. Feminist writers have taken advantage of this potential in writing narratives which subvert gender roles in certain activity fields (Cranny-Francis 1990). Narrative thus has the potential for changing the culture as well as maintaining it.

### Text 5: 'If You Lose, You're Dead'[1]

**Orientation**
This stage orients
the reader to
what is to follow

'We're gonna be late' Matt said, as we skidded down the main street, hearts pounding.

'I know, I know' I panted, between clenched teeth. 'Just shut up and run.' We turned the corner on the main street at two minutes to nine. I don't know why Matt and I always manage to be late for school. It just seems to happen. No matter what time we get up, we always turn up at about three minutes past nine, without fail. That morning was no different. We pounded past the computer place and I paused for a moment to look in the window.

'Benji, will you come on?' Matt said, tugging my arm. 'We haven't got time to look in the window!'

'Hang on' I said slowly lowering my back-pack to the ground. 'Hang on Matt! They've got "Shootout"'. Look, right there!'

'Benji!' Matt said in exasperation. 'We haven't got time! We . . .'

'Oh shut up, will you. I've gotta get that game. No-one else has it yet.' I shouldered my way into the dark little shop. 'Wonder how much it is?'

'Benji, what about school?'

'I've got a cough' I said absently, looking over the disk. 'It just developed. I think I'd better get home. I'll see you later, okay?'

'Benji . . .'

'Look would you shove off? I can look after myself.'

Matt turned away, sighing, picked up his bag and went down the steps.

**Orientation**
(continued)

'Hey, wait! Have you got any money on you? This costs $15 and I've only got $10.' I grabbed his arm. 'C'mon Matt. This is important.'

Sighing, Matt forked out the money.

'Thanks a million.'

He nodded and went back down the steps. 'I wish you wouldn't, Benji. All that money for a computer game!'

I ignored him, picked up the disk and dropped it on the counter. An old man watched me over a pair of horn rimmed glasses. I laid out the money, and he took it greedily.

**Foreshadowing**
**of unusual events**

['You'd best watch out for that game. 'Tis bad.'

I stared at him for a second. 'Are you kidding? What do you mean "bad"?'

He shook his head slowly and shoved the disk towards me. 'Take it. Take it, please.' In the dim light I saw him shudder. Puzzled, I picked up the disk, put it in my pocket and moved toward the door.

'I'll be seeing you.' I said as I walked out. He looked long and hard at me and then ducked beneath the bench.

'Weird' I muttered, picking up my bags. 'Really weird.']

I turned back along the main street, keeping close to the sides of the buildings. Not that anyone would worry if they saw me heading in the wrong direction – people mind their own business where we live.

**Complication/Evaluation**
A usual sequence of events
is disrupted thus causing a
problem for one or more
of the characters. The Evaluation gives significance to
the events in the Complication through expressions
of attitude, reaction,
incredulity, impossibility,
improbability.
(The Evaluation in this
narrative is interspersed
with Complication. It is
printed in bold.)

I let myself into the house with the spare key Mum keeps hidden under the African violet and went upstairs to my room. The only clear place was my desk where my computer sat. I pulled myself into the chair and inserted the disk, turned it on and waited. A few seconds later the title appeared on the screen. 'Shootout', the program said, and then reeled off a whole list of instructions which I read quickly.

A cowboy appeared on the screen and the words, *'Are you ready pardner? Yes or no'* came up. I typed in 'Yes'.

*'O.K, you have three cartridges. On the count of three, shoot. If you win, you score 20 points. If you lose you are dead.'*

The cowboy on the screen moved his hands to his guns.

*'One . . .'*

I tightened my grip on the joystick and leaned over the keyboard.

'*Two.*'

I crouched, ready . . .

'*Three!*'

Before I could move, the cowboy on the screen had whipped out his guns and there were two short explosions. I felt a burning sensation in my left arm.

'*You lose, pardner*' the screen printed up. I read the words in disbelief. '*You're lucky, that other one went wide. There is a hole in your wall.*'

**I spun round horrified, clutching my arm. Just as the computer had said, there was a hole straight through my 100 m sprint pennant. I turned back to the computer. 'Hey, wait a minute. What is this? This can't be.'** I punched reset into the computer but it ignored my command. Instead it printed '*What's the matter, pardner? Want another shootout?*'

**I looked at the tiny bullet-hole in my arm, in disbelief. 'What the heck is going on here? I don't believe it!'**

'*On the count of three, shoot. If you win, you score 20 points. If you lose, you're dead*' the computer said. '*You have two cartridges left.*'

'Stop!' I yelled, typing every terminate command I knew.

'*One*', the computer said. I continued to type.

'*Two.*'

**'This computer is going to shoot me!' I screamed without making a sound.**

'*Three!*'

| | |
|---|---|
| **Resolution (temporary)** A stay in events due to action taken which averts disaster but does not resolve the problem | I ducked, hoping for the best and felt something whistle over my head. I was safe! |
| **Complication/Evaluation** Events move to a crisis point. The **Evaluation** predicts possible outcomes for events. | Cautiously, I peered over the top of the desk at the computer. The screen said: '*Too bad, pardner. Why aren't you shooting at me?*' Slowly I climbed back onto my chair. '*You have one cartridge left. You had better shoot, pardner, or you are dead. If you miss, I get a free shot at you. If you hit me, you score 20 points. On the count of three.*' It looked as if the only way I was going to get rid of this mad cowboy was to shoot him. I grabbed at the joystick, my hand shaking. |

'*One . . .*' I moved my finger to the fire button.

'*Two.*'

'*Three!*'

I fired at him with my shotgun, using my last cartridge, and missed. I saw the cowboy smile.

'*Too bad, pardner. My free shot. You're dead.*'

**This can't be happening, I told myself. I can't be shot dead by a cowboy on a computer screen. It's not possible. It's . . .**

'*One.*'

**I imagined the headlines in The Sydney Morning Herald. 'Benjamin Trundall, aged 12 years and 9 months, was found dead in his home this afternoon. It appeared that he had been shot through the heart by two tiny bullets that were fired from close range. The only evidence we have so far is a computer game by the name of "Shootout" that was found by the boy's body. Further details tomorrow . . .'**

'*Two.*' The cowboy on the screen was moving towards his guns.

**I stood there, sick with fear and unable to move. I struggled for clear thought. 'Hey, grab a hold on yourself, Benji. This is not a bad dream – it's for real. You've gotta do something!' Yeah, but what? 'Pull the plug!' I suddenly thought. 'Cut off the electricity! PULL THE PLUG!'**

'*Thr . . .!*'

**Resolution**
The problem is resolved or an attempt is made to resolve it.

I dived for the cord full length, wrapped my fingers round it and yanked. There was a huge explosion and a shower of sparks. I scrambled under the bed, not really knowing whether I was dead or alive.

I must have lain under that bed, with three dirty football socks under my nose and the bed springs sticking into my back, for a full ten minutes before I peeped out. The room was silent. I slid out from beneath the bed and cautiously crawled over to the desk and, dreading what I would find, peered over the top of it.

The computer screen was blank. I let out my breath in a long gust, so relieved I felt I would burst. I ejected the disk cautiously, put it back into its cover and turned for the door when something caught my eye. Lying on the desk was a tiny shotgun. I pocketed it and went down the stairs out of the house and down to the dam. There I flung the disk as far as I could. I gazed down at my arm where a tiny hole oozed a thin trickle of blood, and tried to grasp what had just happened to me. Mind numb, I went inside and made myself a Vegemite sandwich.

'If You Lose You're Dead' has the generic structure of: Orientation ^ Complication/Evaluation/Temporary Resolution ^ Resolution. The '/' line between Complication and Evaluation and Temporary Resolution denotes that these do not occur as discrete stages in this text but are interspersed. This choice for constructing Complication and Evaluation is unmarked in written texts as it enables suspense to be built up incrementally and maintained so that the reader's interest is engaged and heightened throughout the narrative. 'If You Lose, You're Dead' has an optional stage, Temporary Resolution, which has not been discussed previously. Again the choice of this stage is linked to mode. The Temporary Resolution is a feature of the written narrative. It plays a role in building up suspense. It is less frequent in oral narratives which tend to be shorter perhaps because there is a strong pressure in this mode 'to get on with the action'. It takes a very skilful story-teller to keep the listener engaged with an oral narrative where the Resolution is withheld while a Temporary Resolution is developed.

The Orientation stage in this narrative is quite long for a short story. An Orientation of this length is only successful if it signals to the reader the generic location of the text. As we shall see, this Orientation achieves that task successfully. It begins by introducing two of the main characters, Matt, and Benji, the narrator, through the activity sequence of 'going to school'. The context for the events of the Complication is introduced when Benji is distracted by a computer game in a shop window. The characterization of the boys is largely achieved through the dialogue they engage in. Benji's use of imperatives in his interaction with Matt establishes him early in the piece as a forceful character who dismisses Matt's questions as irrelevant to his concerns. Benji's distraction becomes a serious intention to buy the computer game and he misses school so he can play it.

Already a minor disruption to the field activity sequence has been introduced through the narrator's decision to miss school but the potential significance of this is established in the bracketed section of the Orientation which can be identified as having the function of foreshadowing a major disruption in an activity sequence. When the narrator purchases the game the shopkeeper warns him to *watch out for that game*, it is *bad*. An astute reader would also realize that *bad*, in the sense of 'evil', is used attributively mainly in relation to living creatures and thus gives a clue to likely developments in the narrative. At this point the reader is able to locate him/herself as being engaged with a narrative text. This assertion can be tested by removing or changing the section bracketed in the Orientation. If the text is changed so that the purchase of the game follows a usual course of events, the Orientation leads the reader to wonder 'where the text is going'. This is not a journey of significance as in a recount or narrative but a sequence of events going nowhere.

A key strategy for introducing disruption in the Complication is first to establish the usual sequence of events in a field. In the Complication/

Evaluation of 'If You Lose You're Dead' this is done through the narrator going through the routine actions for entering his home, seating himself at his desk, inserting the disk into the computer and going through the instructions for playing the game 'Shootout'.

> I let myself into the house with the spare key Mum keeps hidden under the African violet and went upstairs to my room. The only clear place was my desk where my computer sat. I pulled myself into the chair and inserted the disk, turned it on and waited. A few seconds later the title appeared on the screen. 'Shootout', the program said, and then reeled off a whole lot of instructions which I read quickly.

The conjunctive relations in this section of the text are temporal successive marking the usuality of the sequence of events. In Figure 8.8 the text has been divided into units that can be related conjunctively. The inserted *then* indicates the temporal successive relation between the material Processes underlined.

Although it is the narrator's turn in the game, at this point the computer cowboy takes over. This counter-expectation is marked by the fact that it is possible to insert the concessive conjunction *but* at the beginning of the clause *Before I could move*. The concessive conjunctive relation marks another change in respect of the text's field. No longer is it a vicarious field of playing on a computer game but an actual duel, with one participant using live ammunition.

> [But] Before I could move the cowboy on the screen had whipped out his guns and there were two short explosions. I felt a burning sensation in my left arm.

1. I let myself into the house

2. and (then) went upstairs.

3. The only clear place was my desk where my computer sat.

4. (Then) I pulled myself into the chair

5. and (then) inserted the disk

6. (then) turned it on

7. and (then) waited.

8. (Then) the title appeared on the screen.

**Figure 8.8** Conjunctive relations in the Complication stage of Text 5

Predictably the Evaluation begins shortly after this. The interpersonal meanings make the preceding events significant by foregrounding the narrator's reactions of fear and incredulity: *I spun round horrified . . . What is this? This can't be.* As the disruption continues so does the Evaluation: *I looked at the tiny bullet hole in my arm in disbelief. What the heck is going on here? I don't believe it.* The linguistic strategies are typical of this stage: attitudinal lexis such as *disbelief*, choice for the interrogative, exclamation, mental Processes such as *believe* and negation. It is important to examine the role of these choices more closely. The nominalization *disbelief* and the mental Process *believe* construct Benji's inner reaction to the extraordinary field of disruption. This is a crucial aspect of Evaluation, to show the mental/emotional reaction of the participant confronting disruption. The interrogative, another typical choice in stages foregrounding interpersonal meanings, is not addressed to another participant but is another strategy for highlighting the participant's confusion and inability to comprehend the events. It thus highlights their unusuality. The choices of negative polarity in Text 5 are: *This can't be, I don't believe it, This can't be happening.* The choice for negative polarity acts similarly to the choice for interrogative. It draws attention to the unusual or unexpected events and thus contrasts them with what might have been some of the instances expected to occur. The choice for the exclamative, *I don't believe it!*, is to be expected when meanings about surprise and incredulity are part of the meaning of exclamation. This choice in the mood system carries these meanings quite apart from the lexis and transitivity structure of the message. There is some repetition, *Just as the computer had said, there was a hole straight through my 100m sprint pennant.* The anaphoric text reference clearly establishes cohesive ties between the structures in the Complication and Evaluation stages, for example: *What is this? This can't be. I don't believe it!* The identity of the reference items *this* and *it* is retrieved from the previous sections of the Complication stage. Having first signalled how extraordinary the events are, the Evaluation then articulates the likely outcome of the events: *'This computer is going to shoot me!' I screamed without making a sound.* The choice of future tense clearly indicates that this is a prediction. The reader is forced to contemplate a negative outcome for the narrator.

This brief discussion about of the first part of the Evaluation in 'If You Lose You're Dead' indicates how the stage builds up tension and suspense about the outcome of events and highlights their danger for the narrator through interpersonal linguistic resources. The less obvious effect is that the interpersonal meanings serve to create a sense of responsibility for the narrator to counteract the disruption and overcome it. As with the foreshadowing in the Orientation stage this claim can be tested by removing the Evaluation so that the disruption is maintained but not commented on. The Complication is printed below without Evaluation. When this is done the events depicted become difficult to follow and almost 'pointless' in substance. The text below makes it apparent that it is the interpersonal meanings that drive the text forward and give it momentum as well as significance.

### Complication stage in Text 5

I let myself into the house with the spare key Mum keeps hidden under the African violet and went upstairs to my room. The only clear place was my desk where my computer sat. I pulled myself into the chair and inserted the disk, turned it on and waited. A few seconds later the title appeared on the screen. 'Shootout', the program said, and then reeled off a whole list of instructions which I read quickly.

A cowboy appeared on the screen and the words, '*Are you ready pardner? Yes or no*' came up. I typed in 'Yes'.

'*O.K, you have three cartridges. On the count of three, shoot. If you win, you score 20 points. If you lose you are dead.*'

The cowboy on the screen moved his hands to his guns.

'*One . . .*'

I tightened my grip on the joystick and leaned over the keyboard.

'*Two.*'

I crouched, ready . . .

'*Three!*'

Before I could move, the cowboy on the screen had whipped out his guns and there were two short explosions. I felt a burning sensation in my left arm.

'*You lose, pardner*' the screen printed up. I read the words in disbelief. '*You're lucky, that other one went wide. There is a hole in your wall.*'

I punched reset into the computer but it ignored my command. Instead it printed '*What's the matter, pardner? Want another shootout?*'

'*On the count of three, shoot. If you win, you score 20 points. If you lose, you're dead*', the computer said. '*You have two cartridges left.*'

'Stop!' I yelled, typing every terminate command I knew.

'*One*', the computer said. I continued to type.

'*Two.*'

'*Three!*'

I ducked, hoping for the best and felt something whistle over my head.

Cautiously, I peered over the top of the desk at the computer. The screen said: '*Too bad, pardner. Why aren't you shooting at me?*'

Slowly I climbed back onto my chair.

'*You have one cartridge left. You had better shoot, pardner, or you are dead. If you miss, I get a free shot at you. If you hit me, you score 20 points. On the count of three.*'

It looked as if the only way I was going to get rid of this mad cowboy was to shoot him. I grabbed at the joystick, my hand shaking.

'*One . . .*' I moved my finger to the fire button.

'*Two.*'

'*Three!*'

I fired at him with my shotgun, using my last cartridge, and missed. I saw the cowboy smile.

'*Too bad, pardner. My free shot. You're dead.*'

'*One.*'

'*Two.*' The cowboy on the screen was moving towards his guns.

'*Thr . . . !*'

The Temporary Resolution is a device for highlighting that the problem still has to be resolved, thus heightening both suspense and awareness of the need for a permanent resolution. In this narrative the narrator has a temporary reprieve but young readers will tell you this is not the end as the computer cowboy is still active. The continuing interspersion of field disruption and evaluative interpersonal meanings through the Complication and Evaluation culminate in crisis points of a different kind. The field disruption reaches a high point when the narrator's one last shot gives him the opportunity to 'shoot' the cowboy, thus scoring 20 points and putting the cowboy out of the game. If he misses, however, the cowboy's 'free' shot may kill him. The Evaluation ultimately reaches a point where the narrator accepts the reality of the situation, thus making it possible for him to acknowledge he must take action to resolve it. Before he reaches this point, however, there is a contrast set up between a negative outcome to the events and a positive one, a strategy which highlights the need for strong resolve on the part of the main character. First, the negative scenario is played. It takes the form of a genre embedded within the narrative – a news story of the kind likely to appear in a television newscast:

> I imagined the headlines in The Sydney Morning Herald. 'Benjamin Trundall, aged 12 years and 9 months, was found dead in his home this afternoon. It appeared that he had been shot through the heart by two tiny bullets that were fired from close range. The only evidence we have so far is a computer game by the name of "Shootout" that was found by the boy's body. Further details tomorrow . . .'

Finally, a positive orientation to action emerges although the difficulty of achieving this is emphasized: *I stood there sick with fear and unable to move. I struggled for clear thought.* Then comes the breakthrough: 'It's for real.' The identity of *it* is retrieved from the Complication stage from the point of disruption to the usual activity sequence for playing a computer game. This is followed by imperatives which function as predictions about the course of action to be taken. *Pull the plug! I suddenly thought, Cut off the electricity! PULL THE PLUG!*

So effective is the writer's construction of suspense and tension through her use of interpersonal resources that we may overlook how simply the problem is resolved by the narrator disconnecting the computer from its source of power. Usuality is restored through this activity sequence although the writer keeps us waiting for a little longer before we are sure of this positive outcome. Nevertheless, the narrator has acted positively and successfully against a science fiction world 'made real'. How would readers have reacted if he had carefully crawled out of the room and left the computer to its own devices? Dissatisfied? Let down? Wondering what would become of this extraordinary game? Of course writers do create such texts but in doing so they exploit their knowledge of generic structure and the readers' expectations. The more familiar the writer is with generic structure the more numerous are her/his options for working with it. The particular strength of this writer is her exploitation of interpersonal resources to construct the danger and reality of the events of 'Shootout'. One gets the sense she could make us believe anything as the section displayed in Figure 8.9 shows.

We noted in the analysis of the oral narrative that the construction of Complication and Resolution often involved changing patterns of participant roles for the main characters in these stages. In the Complication stage of 'If You Lose You're Dead', both the computer cowboy and the narrator have the role of Actor. This is a significant strategy for building up the contest between them as Figure 8.9 shows. In the Resolution the narrator is Actor throughout the stage. The last paragraph reveals his supremacy (Figure 8.10).

Thus the narrative fulfils its function to confirm that disruption can and must be dealt with in order to restore equilibrium to the field. This message, regardless of the field, is conveyed through the generic structure of narrative. It is a powerful tool for learning an important part of the culture.

Articulating the generic structure of narrative has a significance beyond explicating how one part of mainstream Western culture works. It

| The cowboy on the screen | moved | his hands | to his guns |
|---|---|---|---|
| Actor | material Process | Goal | Location: place |

| I | tightened | my grip | on the joystick |
|---|---|---|---|
| Actor | material Process | Goal | Location: place |

| Before | I | | could move |
|---|---|---|---|
| | | Actor | material Process |

| the cowboy on the screen | had    whipped out | his guns |
|---|---|---|
| Actor | material Process | Goal |

**Figure 8.9** Transitivity structures in the Complication stage of Text 5

enables us to develop a critical orientation to the story genres, and narrative, in particular. Such an orientation comes from understanding that texts are socio-cultural constructs. While individuals produce them, they do so within a set of conventions that serve particular social goals.

The importance of this understanding can be better perceived if we

| I | ejected | the disk | cautiously |
|---|---------|----------|------------|
| Actor | material Process | Goal | Manner |

| put | it | back into its cover |
|-----|-----|---------------------|
| material Process | Goal | Location: place |

. . . Lying on the desk was a tiny shotgun.

| I | pocketed | it |
|---|----------|-----|
| Actor | material Process | Goal |

| (I) | went | down the stairs | out of the house |
|-----|------|-----------------|-------------------|
| Actor | material Process | Location: place | Location: place |

| and   down to the dam |
|-----------------------|
| Location: place |

| There | I | flung | the disk |
|-------|---|-------|----------|
| Location: place | Actor | material Process | Goal |

as far as I could.

**Figure 8.10** Transitivity structures in the Resolution stage of Text 5

consider how story genres have been regarded recently in British and Australian educational contexts. For almost two decades, 1970 to the late 1980s, story was constructed by many British and Australian educators (Dixon 1967; Britton 1970; Mallick 1973; Walshe 1981) as a means for personal growth. Such educators believed that young writers through the exploration of actual and vicarious experience developed a better understanding of it and hence 'grew' as human beings. In making such claims they cited the interpersonal meanings of stories to support them. It was their view that interpersonal meanings of the kind examined in this chapter were expressions of the actual reactions of the writer. They were creative and personal responses to experience. Of course in some instances such responses may be those of the writer but regardless of this, such meanings are socio-culturally grounded to give significance to events. They are there to position the reader to view the events in particular ways. They are not 'natural' – they are cultural in origin. Once a reader/writer has an explicit knowledge of the generic structure of 'stories' s/he can exploit the structure in ways that may be considered culturally reproductive or subversive. It is these choices that will be further examined in the following section.

## Naturalizing cultural values: embedding a message in narrative

Earlier in this chapter, when examining exemplum as a story type, we noted that a message or 'theme' can be embedded in a narrative. Such a narrative involves the participants in the activity sequences of fields of the culture. These are the vehicles for dealing with inner change on the part of the participants. Such changes are the consequences of the resolution of conflict between mainstream ethical values held in the culture. The message is the moral or the value at the heart of the narrative. It is in the deepest sense what the narrative is about. Of course a narrative may present more than one message to a reader, or different messages to different readers. But there is what we call 'a dominant reading of a message', which is not a haphazard affair. As we shall demonstrate, the generic structure of the text, and in particular the meanings of the Evaluation, construct this reading of the message. The Evaluation holds the key to unpacking the dominant message.

The following thematic narrative 'CLICK' was presented to secondary students in New South Wales in 1987 in a public examination at the end of Year 10 of their schooling. The students were given the following context for the question about the narrative:

This question tests your understanding of the story 'CLICK'. You are expected to write about 15 lines.
   'CLICK. The television switch sounded through the room like a padlock snapping open.'
   Why do you think the story ends this way?

To answer this question successfully, students must be able to give a mainstream reading of the message which, in a thematic narrative, is never stated explicitly.

**Text 6**

**Orientation**

CLICK. The television dial sounded through the room like snapped fingers. First there was soft static. Then loud voices swelled up.

'The Sheriff will get you for this, Kid.'

'You won't be around to find out, Slade.' BANG! BANG!

CLICK, CLICK, CLICK. Jenny turned the dial to Channel 4.

'Mr. and Mrs. Williams, if you answer this question correctly, the water bed will be yours!'

CLICK, CLICK.

'I'm Popeye the Sailor Man.'

'Jenny, what are you doing tonight?' Her mother's words floated into Jenny's mind. But she didn't answer.

'Jenny!' This time her mother's voice demanded an answer.

'Uh, I'm not sure, Mum.' Jenny leaned forward to turn the dial to Channel 8. CLICK, CLICK. The last part of *Secret Loves* was on.

'Jenny, don't watch television again all night. I hate to leave you here alone when your father is gone too. But find something else to do. Promise?'

'Sure, Mum.' Jenny stared at the television, trying to hear what the mother on *Secret Loves* would say when she heard that her daughter was pregnant.

In the back of her mind Jenny thought she heard her mother say something. Then she heard the hallway door close.

'See you later, Mum.' Jenny didn't say it very loudly. Her mother couldn't have heard it anyway.

On the screen the mother was holding her daughter in her arms and crying, 'What will the family think ? What will the family think?'

Jenny thought about her family. There wasn't much to it. Her father was on the road a lot, driving his truck. Her mother worked at night as a waitress. Jenny didn't have any brothers or sisters. It wasn't a real family. They never did much together.

*Secret Loves* ended and a commercial came on. It was for the sex appeal toothpaste. A beautiful girl with white teeth was sitting with her boyfriend in a sportscar. She smiled at the guy and ran her hand through his hair. The guy reminded Jenny of somebody in her class. Jenny daydreamed about being in a sportscar with him and looking like the girl in the commercial. She thought about it every time she brushed her teeth. She wouldn't brush with anything but that toothpaste.

**Complication/Evaluation**

The wail of a police siren came into the room. Jenny started to go to the window. But she didn't get up. Doctor Harding had started the girl's heart again. The beautiful nurse wiped his forehead. Someone told the girl's family that the operation had been a success. Doctor Harding took off his surgical mask and the camera zoomed in on his face.

A commercial came on. Jenny heard the sound of an ambulance coming down the street. She heard her neighbours' voices in the hallway. They were talking about an accident.

Jenny decided to check out the accident during the commercial. She could probably get back in time before the show started again. She went out into the hallway and walked down the stairs until she got to the top of the stairs outside the block of flats. From there, she saw the girl.

The white body and red blood were like fresh paint splotches against the black footpath. The image froze into Jenny's mind. **The girl's face was horrible and beautiful at the same time. It seemed more real than anything Jenny had ever seen. Looking at it, Jenny felt as though she was coming out of a long dream. It seemed to cut through the cloud in her mind like lightning.**

Suddenly Jenny was aware of everything around her. Police cars were pulling up. Ambulance lights were flashing around. People sobbed and covered their faces.

Jenny walked down the stairs to the street where the girl lay. She was already dead. **No handsome young doctor had come and saved her. No commercial interrupted the stillness of her death.**

**For a second, Jenny wanted to switch the channel to escape the girl's face. She wanted to turn off its realness. But the girl wasn't part of her television world. She was part of the real world of death and unhappy endings.**

Two ambulance men came from the ambulance and gently put the dead girl on a stretcher. The crowd of people broke into small groups and whispered to each other as they drifted away. Jenny stayed until the ambulance drove away. She watched its flashing lights and listened to its wailing siren fade into the night air.

**Resolution**

Finally, Jenny walked back upstairs to the flat. As she opened the door, she heard the sound of the television. The last part of *Doctor's Diary* was still on.

Jenny eased down into her chair in front of the television. It was the chair she always watched television in. But now she felt uncomfortable. The television seemed too close.

Jenny tried to get back into the show. But all the characters' lines sounded phony. And Doctor Harding's face wasn't the same. His smile seemed fake and he looked too handsome like a plastic doll.

Then the words started running through Jenny's mind. 'People never die on *Doctor's Diary*.' At first they were just words that Jenny couldn't stop saying in her head. 'People never die on *Doctor's Diary*.' The words made Jenny remember the dead girl's face. 'People never die on *Doctor's Diary*.' Then the words started meaning something.

CLICK. The television switch sounded through the room like a padlock snapping open.

The Orientation of 'CLICK' is long. Its role is crucial in establishing a context for the events to follow and the dominant message of the narrative. Jenny is constructed as a teenager engrossed in watching television, soaps, ads, whatever is showing. She is often alone at night as her father is away from home and frequently her mother works. The Orientation focuses very strongly on Jenny's absorption in television viewing.

The Complication introduces the events that disrupt Jenny's usual pattern of television viewing. She is drawn outside by the sound of an ambulance siren to see a young girl dead on the street after a traffic accident. The girl's death constitutes a serious disruption to the activity sequences of driving a car and crossing the road as a pedestrian. The crisis point is the sight of the dead girl: *The image froze into Jenny's mind.*

The focus of the interpersonal meanings in the Evaluation stage of a narrative indicate to a reader whether the text is a thematic narrative (Rothery 1995). In 'If You Lose You're Dead' the Evaluation focused on the narrator's reaction to the activity sequence disruption as depicted in the Complication and the problem of dealing directly with that. In

'CLICK' there is no problem to be resolved as far as the accident is concerned. The girl is dead. The focus from the beginning of the stage is on the girl's death as a token of reality: *It seemed more real than anything Jenny had ever seen.* It is this focus that locates the narrative as thematic. The Evaluation in thematic narrative foregrounds an inner conflict on the part of the main participant between moral/ethical values. The activity sequence of the Complication and, in this instance, the Orientation are tokens for the values. Television viewing in 'CLICK' represents illusion while the death of the girl is a token for reality. This is the struggle for Jenny, whether she will choose to reject the illusory world of television and embrace the world of reality as it exists in everyday life. The Evaluation thus plays a crucial role in 'delivering' the message of thematic narrative. It is a message about an ethical struggle. In this sense, thematic narratives could well be called psychological or psycho-drama (see Macken 1996).

In the Resolution Jenny returns to her home and television viewing. Usuality is restored within the field. But no longer can she lose herself in the world of television which now seems phony and unreal. Jenny's decision to reject this world and take a new direction is summed up in the last line of the text about which the Year 10 secondary students were asked to write: 'CLICK. The television switch sounded through the room like a padlock snapping open.'

The embedding of the message in a narrative text gives it a powerful naturalizing effect. This is the way the world is, without a doubt, is the legacy of the thematic narrative. Although the Evaluation is the crucial stage for 'reading' the message, the reader has already been positioned in the Orientation of the text to be receptive to its values. Here are two excerpts from the opening stage which serve this function. The first, spoken by Jenny's mother, constructs television viewing as undesirable, expresses guilt about leaving the daughter alone and suggests any other activity is preferable to watching television.

> Jenny, don't watch television again all night. I hate to leave you here alone when your father is gone too. But find something else to do. Promise?

The imperatives and negative polarity reveal the strength of the mother's attitude as does the negative affect of the appraisal item *hate*. The question *Promise?* is more a token for an imperative than a question requesting a response. Thus the reader is positioned 'to take on' the mother's viewpoint as authoritative and credible.

The second excerpt is about Jenny and her family:

> Jenny thought about family. There wasn't much to it. Her father was on the road a lot, driving his truck. Her mother worked at night as a waitress. Jenny didn't have any brothers or sisters. It wasn't a real family. They never did much together.

In the first clause Jenny is Senser in the mental cognition Process *thought*. Thus we read what follows from her viewpoint. The choice for negation is a recurrent grammatical pattern in this section. *There wasn't much to it, Jenny didn't have any brothers or sisters, It wasn't a real family, They never did much together*. We have already noted in the discussion of Evaluation in 'If You Lose You're Dead' that negative polarity sets up an explicit contrast with what might have been expressed in positive polarity – that there was a lot to her family; she had brother and sisters; it was a real family and they did things together. There is also an implicit causal conjunctive relation between *There wasn't much to it* and the following clauses so that a pattern of causality is established to justify Jenny's assertion about her family, which in turn is a rationalization for her absorption in television viewing.

> There wasn't much to it:
> [because] her father was on the road a lot
> [because] her mother worked at night
> [because] Jenny didn't have any brothers or sisters
> [so] it wasn't a real family.

In these and other parts of the Orientation, the reader is strongly positioned to regard television viewing in an unfavourable light and Jenny's family situation as an explanation for her identification with the 'world of television'. Such a positioning is essential if the reader is to accept television viewing as a token for a world of illusion *and* to see this world in a negative light.

In discussing the narrative 'If You Lose You're Dead' we noted that the generic structure analysis enabled the reader to develop a critical orientation to the text, that is to see it as a socio-cultural construct which is in no sense 'natural' in the way it renders experience, but rather ideologically motivated in its concern with individualism and the restoration of stability to activity sequences. Similarly such an analysis of 'CLICK' enables a critical orientation to be developed by the reader but now there are additional layers of meaning, also ideologically motivated, which are articulated in such an analysis. Firstly there is the message which we may or may not wish to endorse and, secondly, there is 'the packaging' of the message in the activity sequences chosen as tokens for its values. For example, in 'CLICK', television programmes and advertisements are tokens for illusion. Do readers agree with this representation? Do they agree with this message? Is living a life of illusion necessarily bad? There are members of the artistic community, makers of films and plays who have stated their preference for a world of illusion.

Let us explore further the packaging of this message. What if Jenny had been portrayed as an obsessive reader of literature? Would we accept this as readily as a token for the illusory-deficit lifestyle? Is Jenny's family as inadequate as she portrays it? Lurking behind her negative assertions is the notion of 'the ideal family' so frequently posited by some political groups and media representatives. Jenny's family life may well be a very usual one in Western cultures in the late twentieth century. In other words a critical orientation opens up possibilities for resistant and challenging readings which we will explore further in the following section regarding the story in the English curriculum.

## Story in the English curriculum

The analyses undertaken in the previous sections of this chapter have shown English to be a powerful site in the school curriculum for transmitting moral and ethical values that are sited in mainstream Western culture (Hunter 1994). While it may be said this is true for all areas of the school curriculum there are distinctive differences as far as English is concerned. English is not a clearly defined field of study as, for example, geography, mathematics and history are. The texts of English, whether they be novels, short stories, drama or film deal with a wide range of fields. What is common to the way they are treated is a concern with ethical issues. There is no clearly defined aesthetic approach to texts studied in English. Add to this the fact that the goals of English are left implicit, or even misrepresented, and that the students are given virtually no tools for achieving them, it is not surprising that success in English is achieved mainly by students from the middle class who bring with them a rich cultural capital of literacy, field experiences and mainstream ethical positions which they constantly draw on in the classroom. To introduce the perspectives opened by generic structure analysis into the English curriculum would be to radically change the nature of the school subject English.

## Note

1  Cathryn Cooper, 'If You Lose, You're Dead' from the anthology *If You Lose You're Dead*. Alexandria, NSW: Millenium Books. We have been unable to trace the copyright owner of this story, originally published in the *Sydney Morning Herald* as part of a story-writing competition in New South Wales.

## References

Britton, J. (1970) *Language and Learning.* Harmondsworth: Penguin.

Cranny-Francis, A. (1990) *Feminist Fiction: Feminist Uses of Creative Fiction.* Cambridge: Polity Press.

Dixon, J. (1967) *Growth through English.* London: National Association for the Teaching of English and Oxford University Press.

Halliday, M. A. K. (1985) *An Introduction to Functional Grammar.* London and Melbourne: Edward Arnold. (2nd edn 1994.)

Hunter, I. (1994) 'Four anxieties about English'. *Interpretations* 27(3), December, 1–19.

Labov, W. and Waletzky, J. (1967), 'Narrative analysis: oral versions of personal experience'. In J. Helm (ed.) *Essays in the Verbal and Visual Arts.* American Ethnological Society, Proceedings of Spring Meeting. Washington, DC: University of Washington Press, 12–44.

Macken, M. (1996) 'Specialised literacy practices in junior secondary English'. PhD thesis, University of Sydney.

Mallick, D. (1973) 'A small but disturbing experiment'. *English in Australia* 25, 47–53.

Martin, J. R. (1984) 'Types of reading and writing in primary school'. In L. Unsworth (ed.) *Reading, Writing and Spelling: Proceedings of the Fifth Macarthur Language Symposium.* Sydney: Macarthur Institute of Higher Education, 34–55.

Martin, J. R. (1985) *Factual Writing: Exploring and Challenging Social Reality.* Geelong, Vic.: Deakin University Press. ECS806 Sociocultural Aspects of Language and Education (republished by Oxford University Press 1989).

Martin, J. R. (in press) 'A context for genre: modelling social processes in functional linguistics'. In R. Stainton and J. Devilliers (eds) *Communication in Linguistics.* Toronto: GREF (Collection Theoria).

Martin, J. R. and Rothery, J. (1980) *Writing Project Report No. 1.* Working Papers in Linguistics, Department of Linguistics, University of Sydney.

Martin, J. R. and Rothery, J. (1981) *Writing Project Report No. 2.* Working Papers in Linguistics, Department of Linguistics, University of Sydney.

Martin, J. R. and Rothery, J. (1984) 'Choice of genre in a suburban primary school'. Paper presented at the Annual Conference of the Applied Linguistics Association of Australia, Alice Springs, August 1984.

Plum, G. (1988) 'Textual and contextual conditioning in spoken English: a genre based approach'. Unpublished PhD thesis, University of Sydney.

Rothery, J. (1990) '"Story" writing in the primary school: assessing narrative type genres'. Unpublished PhD thesis, University of Sydney.

Rothery, J. (1995) *Exploring Literacy in School English.* Write It Right: Resources for Literacy and Learning. Sydney: Disadvantaged Schools Program Metropolitan East Region, NSW Department of School Education.

Rothery, J. and Macken, M. (1991) *Developing Critical Literacy: An Analysis of the Writing Task in a Year 10 Reference Test.* Issues in Education for the Socially and Economically Disadvantaged: Monograph 1. Sydney: Metropolitan East Disadvantaged Schools Program.

Rothery, J. and Veel, R. (1993) 'Exposing the ideology of literature: the power of deconstruction'. *English in Australia* 105, 16–29.

Walshe, R. D. (1981) *Every Child Can Write.* Rozelle, NSW: Primary English Teaching Association.

# Index